Proceedings: Irish MSS. series. Vol. 1, pt. 1

Royal Irish Academy

BIBLIOLIFE

PROCEEDINGS

OF THE

ROYAL IRISH ACADEMY.

IRISH MSS. SERIES.

VOLUME I.—PART I.

DUBLIN:

PRINTED BY M. H. GILL,

PRINTER TO THE ACADEMY.

1870.

Price Five Shillings.

LEABHAR NA H-UIDHRE.

~~~~~~~~~~~~~~~~

LEABHAR NA H-UIDHRE, in the library of the Royal
Irish Academy, is the oldest volume now known, entirely in the
Irish language, and is regarded as the chief native literary monu-
ment—not ecclesiastical—of ancient Ireland. The historical and
philological value of the contents of this manuscript is well
known; and to meet the desire for its publication in its integrity,
the Royal Irish Academy has had an exact copy of it executed in
lithograph, elaborately collated with the original. The volume will
be accompanied by Professor O'Curry's hitherto unpublished descriptive catalogue of its contents, compiled for the Academy. The
entire edition is limited to two hundred copies, printed on thick,
toned paper, and which can be obtained only by subscribers.

————————

Subscription, £3 3s. per Copy.

Applications from Subscribers are to be addressed to the Treasurer
of the Royal Irish Academy, 19, Dawson-street, Dublin; *or*
to the Academy's Publishers, Hodges, Foster, & Co., Dublin;
and Williams and Norgate, Henrietta-street, Covent Garden,
London; 20, South Frederick-street, Edinburgh.

PROCEEDINGS

OF

THE ROYAL IRISH ACADEMY.

IRISH MSS. SERIES.

I.—Descriptive Catalogue of the Contents of the Irish Manuscript, commonly called "The Book of Fermoy." By James Henthorn Todd, D. D., F. S. A. L. & E.

INTRODUCTORY REMARKS.

IN presenting to the Academy a Catalogue of the contents of the ancient Irish MS. commonly called the "Book of Fermoy," it was my wish to have accompanied it by some account of the history of the MS.; but I regret to say that I have found but little to record. I am not sure that the title "Book of Fermoy" is ancient, or that it was the original name of the volume, neither can I ascertain when the MS. was first so called. It is not mentioned under that name by Keating, or, so far as I know, by any ancient authority.* It is not mentioned by Ware, Harris, Archbishop Nicolson, or O'Reilly, in any of their published writings. It has been said that it was once in the possession of the Chevalier O'Gorman; but this has not been established by any satisfactory evidence. There is in the box which now contains the MS. a paper giving a short and very imperfect account of its contents,

---

* A collection of papers relating to the Book of Fermoy was deposited in the Library of Trinity College, Dublin, by the late Dr. John O'Donovan, in 1845. These papers (now preserved in the box H. 5, 7), consist chiefly of extracts from, or references to the Book of Fermoy, made for philological or grammatical purposes.

written about the beginning of the present century, in which it is said to have been then in the possession of William Monck Mason, Esq. This paper is apparently in the handwriting of Edward O'Reilly, author of the Irish Dictionary; but, if written by him, it must have been written at an early period of his life, when his skill in ancient manuscript lore was very inferior to what it afterwards became. Unfortunately the paper is not dated. The Book of Fermoy was sold in London, at the sale by auction of Mr. Mason's books, by the well-known auctioneers, Sotheby and Wilkinson, in 1858. There I purchased it, together with the autograph MS. of O'Clery's "Life of Red Hugh O'Donnell," with a view to have both MSS. deposited in the Library of the Academy. For the Book of Fermoy I gave £70, and for the Life of Red Hugh £21, in all £91, which sum was advanced in equal shares by Lord Talbot de Malahide, Gen. Sir Thomas A. Larcom, the late Charles Haliday, and myself; and it may be worth mentioning, to show the rapid increase in the market value of Irish MSS., that the Life of Red Hugh O'Donnell, which in 1858 brought the sum of £21 in a London auction, had been sold in Dublin, in 1830, at Edward O'Reilly's sale, for £3 7s.

The Book of Fermoy might, with equal propriety, be called the Book of Roche. It is a loose collection of miscellaneous documents, written at different times, and in very different hands; a great part of it relates to the family history of the Roche family of Fermoy; but it contains also a number of bardic poems and prose tracts on the general history of Ireland, and a very curious collection of legendary, mythological, and Fenian tales.

It begins with a copy of the *Leabhar Gabhala*, or "Book of Invasions," written in the fourteenth or beginning of the fifteenth century, very much damaged, and imperfect at the end.

Then follows that portion of the book which contains the legendary and mythological tales, written in the fifteenth century. This is in many respects the most interesting and valuable part of the volume; it contains also some historical bardic poems on the O'Connors, or O'Conors of Connaught, the O'Keeffes of

Fermoy, the Mac Carthy, Roche, and other families of the south of Ireland.

The volume concludes with some fragments of medical trea-tises in the usual exquisitely neat handwriting peculiar to Irish medical MSS. These fragments were certainly no part of the ori-ginal Book of Fermoy ; they probably belonged to the family of O'Hickey, who were hereditary physicians, and whose name occurs more than once inscribed in the margins and blank places of this portion of the MS.

J. H. T.

Trin. Coll., Dublin.

CATALOGUE.

I. A Stave of eight leaves (10½ inches by 8), written in double columns, containing a fragment of the *Leabhar Gabhala*, or "Book of Invasions." The leaves are numbered in the upper margin, 1 to 8, in red pencil, by a modern hand.

Fol. 1. *a.* This page is very much rubbed and defaced, so as to be quite illegible. It begins with the letters Cio . . . . In the upper margin, in black ink, in a modern hand, is the letter B.

Fol. 1. *b. col.* 1. begins with the words Sem bna ro ʒab an Crria, Cam ir an Cbrraic, Iaret arancoraiρ, "Shem settled in Asia; Ham in Africa; Japhet in Europe." This is a short prose account of the establishment of the descendants of Japhet in the principal countries of Europe.

Ibid. col. 2. A short poem, beginning Maʒot mac an iaret ata cinti a clann, " Magoth [read Magog,*] son of Japhet, well known are his descendants."

Ibid. A prose tract, beginning baat mac ʒoimer mc iaret ir uab ʒaebil, "Baath, son of Gomer, son of Japheth, from him are the Gaedil." This short tract contains an account of the building of the Tower of Babel, and the Confusion of tongues, with a tabular list of the

---

* *Magog.* In the Book of Lecan there is a copy of this poem beginning, fol. 25. b. col. 2. It is there attributed to "Fintan," i. e. Fintan Mac Bochra, the person who is fabled to have survived the Deluge in Ireland.

seventy or seventy-two languages into which the speech of man was divided.

Fol. 2. a. col. 2. A short poem beginning beпла ιn ботαιn beċαιb lιb, "Régard ye the languages of the world." This is in the Book of Lecan, fol. 26. a. col. 1.

Ibid. Then the history is continued in a prose tract, beginning Sпu mαc Єппu mαc zαebιl ιпе coιппαċ bo zαebιlιb, "Sru, son of Esru, son of Gaedil, was the leader of the Gadelians." See Book of Lecan, fol. 26. a. col. 2.

Fol. 3. a. col. 2. A poem by Gilla Caemhain (ob. 1072), beginning Zαebιl zlαιп ocαιc zαebιl, "Gaedhil Glas, from whom are the Gaedhil." This poem occurs in the Book of Lecan, fol. 26. b. col. 2. & Leabhar Gabhala (O'Clery), p. 60. The poem ends fol. 4. a. col. 2.

Fol. 4. a. col. 2. A short prose paragraph, enumerating the several conquests of Ireland, beginning Scuιпιm bo пcelαιb nα nzαebιl, "I have done with the Stories of the Gaedhil." *Book of Lecan,* fol. 27. a. col. 2.

Ibid. A poem attributed to Fintan (sixth century), beginning Єпι ce ιαппαιzcαпbιm, "Erin, if it be asked of me." See Yellow Book of Lecan, col. 741.

Fol. 4. b. col. 1. The narrative is continued in prose to the Deluge. Then follows an anonymous poem,* beginning Cαпα ιп lαιznι ιп luαпαb zпιnb.

Ibid. col. 2. The prose narrative continues to the coming of Ceassair (*pron.* Kassar), grand-daughter of Noah. Then follows a poem (anonymous) beginning Ceαппαιп cαnαп cdιnιc пι, "Ceassair, whence came she?"

Fol. 5. a. col. 1. The prose narrative continues to the death of Ceassar at "Carn Cuili Cessrach in Conacht." Then follows an anonymous poem, beginning

Cecпαċα cпαċ bon cuп cιnb

ро ппιc eпenn пe nbιlιnb.

This poem, with a gloss, is preserved in O'Clery's Book of Invasions, p. 3.

Ibid. col. 2. A poem attributed to Fintan, beginning Cαιn пαιnb bo пιnbпαmαιп. See Leabhar Gabhala (O'Clery, p. 2).

---

* This poem is quoted by Keating.

Fol. 5. b. The history is then continued to the arrival of Partholan, and his death.

Fol. 5. b., lower margin. There is a line of Ogham, in a modern hand, blotted, and with the exception of one or two letters, quite illegible.

Fol. 6. *a. col.* 1. A poem (anonymous), beginning ᚐ ᚉᚐᚓᚋᚐᚔᚅ ; ᚉᚂᚐᚔᚏ ᚉᚒᚔᚅᚇ ᚉᚐᚓᚋᚚᚔᚅᚇ, "Ye nobles of the fair-sided plains of Conn." This is attributed to Eochaid Ua Floinn (ob. 984), in the L. Gabhala of the O'Clerys (p. 15), and by O'Reilly (*Writers,* p. lxv).

Fol. 6. *b. col.* 1. The prose history is continued.

Ibid. col. 2. A poem which O'Reilly, p. lxv. (*loc cit.*), attributes to Eochaidh Ua Floinn, or O'Flynn, beginning Ro bo ᚋᚐᚔᚈ ᚔᚅ ᚋᚒᚔᚅᚈᚔᚏ ᚋᚖᚏ, "Good were the great people." Eochaidh O'Flynn flourished in the second half of the tenth century.

Fol. 7. *a. col.* 1. A poem headed ᚇᚒ ᚈᚔᚅᚏᚐᚁ ᚚᚐᚏᚉᚆᚑᚂᚐᚅ ᚔᚅ ᚏᚑᚓᚁᚒᚏ, and beginning ᚚᚐᚏᚈᚐᚂᚐᚅ ᚉᚐᚅᚐᚏ ᚈᚐᚔᚅᚔᚉ. This poem contains an account of the principal adventures of Partholan, and ends with a notice of the battle of Magh Itha, fought by Partholan against the Fomorians, which is said to have been the first battle fought in Ireland. O'Reilly (*loc. cit.*) attributes this poem to Eochaidh Ua Floinn. It is given in O'Clery's L. Gabhala, p. 9, with a gloss. At the end are the words, ᚔᚏ ᚔᚐᚁ ᚏᚔᚅ ᚈᚏᚔᚐ ᚏᚉᚓᚂᚐ ᚅᚐ .ᚉ. ᚌᚐᚁᚐᚂᚐ ᚓᚏᚓᚅᚅ ᚔᚐᚏ ᚅᚁᚔᚂᚔᚅᚁ, "These are the history [or traditions] of the first conquest of Ireland after the Deluge."

Fol. 7. *b.* The history is then continued in prose to the coming of Nemed, thirty years after the destruction of Partholan's people ; with the taking of Conaing's tower in Tor-inis, now Tory island.

Fol. 8. *a. col.* 2. A poem beginning ᚓᚏᚔᚒ ᚑᚂᚂ ᚑᚔᚏᚅᚔᚁ ᚌᚐᚓᚁᚔᚂ, "Noble Erin, which the Gaedhil adorn." This is preserved in the L. Gabhala of the O'Clerys, with a copious gloss, (p. 25), and is there attributed to Eochaidh Ua Floinn. See also O'Reilly, *Writers,* p. lxvi. The poem ends imperfectly, fol. 8. b. col. 2.

II. Next follow sixteen staves, which constitute most probably what remains of the true Book of Fermoy. They are in a very different hand (or rather hands) from the fragment of the Book of Invasions already described, which had probably no connexion with the Fermoy collection of Legendary Tales and Poems.

These sixteen staves are in good hands, probably of the 15th century, and are numbered in the upper margin in Arabic numerals, in a hand of the 17th, and in black ink. The pages are in double columns; size of column, 10.2 inches by 8. A full column contains thirty-six lines.

(1.) The first stave consists of six leaves, and is numbered fol. 23–28, from which it appears that twenty-two leaves have been lost since the folios were numbered, unless the eight leaves of the former part of the volume have been included. The following are the contents of this stave :—

Fol. 23. *a.* The legend of Mór Mumhan (Mór or Moria of Munster), daughter of Aedh Bennain, king of West Luachair (i. e. of West Kerry), and wife of Cathal Mac Finguine,* king of Munster. This tract begins Aeᴅ bennaın pı ıploċpu, ba meıc bec laıp, ⁊ ceopa ınƷena ("Aedh Bennain, king of West Luachair, had twelve sons, and three daughters"). A space has been left for an ornamental capital A, which, however, was never inserted.

Mór was, and is to this day, proverbial for her great beauty. As she approached to womanhood, she was suddenly struck with an irresistible desire to travel, and stole away from her father's house. For some years she continued to wander alone, shunning the haunts of men, and traversing on foot the wilds and forests. At length she arrived at Cashel, in torn and ragged garments, foot-sore, and miserable; but, notwithstanding, her transcendent beauty shone forth, so as to attract the attention of Cathal mac Finguine, king of Munster, who, after some inquiries as to her parentage, finally married her. After this her taste for wandering left her, and she became as celebrated for her wisdom and domestic virtues as for her beauty.

---

* *Cathal Mac Finguine.* Aedh Bennain was the lineal descendant of Cairbre Pict, surnamed Luachra, from Sliabh Luachra, where he was brought up. He died, according to Tighernach, in 619, Ann. Ult. 618, Four Mast., 614. If so, it is difficult to understand how his daughter could have been the wife of Cathal Mac Finguine, who died 737 (Four Mast.). Aedh Bennain is called king of Munster by Tighernach, and king of Iar Mumha, or West Munster, by the Four Masters. But he was really king of Iar Luachair (West Luachair). The district was divided into East and West, and had its name from Cairbre Luachra; it is now Ciarraighe Luachra, or Kerry. See *Wars of the Danes*, p. li, n. ³; lxv. n. ³.

Besides the adventures of Queen Mór, this tract contains also the story of the abduction of her sister Ruithchern, the battles fought by their brothers on her account, and the death of Cuana, son of Calchin, King of Fermoy, with whom Ruithchern had eloped. He flourished in the seventh century, and was celebrated for his liberality and hospitality.*

This tale, under the title of Citeb Ruitceapna pe Cuana mac Cailcin ["Elopement of Ruithcearna with Cuana mac Cailcin"], is mentioned by Mr. O'Curry in the curious list of ancient tales which he has printed from the "Book of Leinster," *Lectures*, p. 590. A copy of it is preserved in that ancient book (H. 2. 18, Trin. Coll. Dublin); the only other copy (if I mistake not) which is known to exist.

Fol. 24. *a.* A curious Legend, giving an account of the fifty wonders which occurred in Ireland on the night when Conn of the hundred Battles, King of Ireland in the third century, was born.†

It begins, bai pinɜen mac lucta aibci pamna in bpuim pinɜin, "On Samhain's night (i. e. All Hallow Eve), Fingen Mac Luchta was at Drum-Fingin;" a space being left for an ornamented initial b, which was never inserted. The fifty wonders were related to Fingen Mac Luchta, King of Munster, by a lady named Bacht, who sometimes visited him from the fairy mound called Sith-Cliath, which Mr. O'Curry thought was originally a Tuatha De Danaan mound, now Cnoc Aine in the county of Limerick.

This is a very rare tract, if indeed another copy exists; it contains various topographical, historical, and legendary notices, which throw much light on several superstitious practices not yet entirely forgotten; it records the origin of several roads; explains the ancient names of some rivers, and describes a few of the formerly existing monuments of Tara.

Fol. 25. *a. col.* 2. A poem of 35 stanzas, beginning, Cia po aɜpap coip um cpuachain, "who is it that asserts a right to Cruachan," i. e. a right to the sovereignty of Connaught; Cruachan was the fort or palace of the Kings of Connaught. It is now Rathcroghan,‡ county of Roscommon. The ornamented initial C which ought to have decorated the beginning of this poem was never inserted.

---

* See O'Flaherty, *Ogyg.*, p. 336.
† *Ibid.* p. 318.

‡ See O'Donovan, (Four Masters, 1223, n. '.)

The author of the poem is not mentioned. His object was to arouse Muircheartach, son of John O'Neill, lord of Tir-Eoghain [Tyrone], to assert his claim to the throne of Connaught, in right of his mother Una, daughter of Aedh, King of Connaught, who died in 1274 (Four Masters); which year was therefore the date of this poem, for it must have been written before the successor had been inaugurated; or at least before the confusions consequent on the death of Aedh had come to an end. No less than three Kings of Connaught were set up within that year, 1274, as we learn from the Four Masters, viz.: 1. Aedh (son of Rudraighe, son of Aedh, son of Cathal Croibhdearg), who was murdered in the abbey of Roscommon, after a reign of three months, by his kinsman Rudraighe, son of Toirrdealbach, or Turlogh, son of Aedh, son of Cathal Croibhdearg. 2. Another Aedh, son of Cathal Dall, son of Aedh, son of Cathal Croibhdearg: he was elected by the people of Connaught, but was murdered a fortnight after. 3. Tadg, son of Toirrdealbach, son of Aedh, son of Cathal Croibhdearg, who was permitted to reign for four years, but was slain, in 1278, by the Mac Dermots. It is evident, therefore, that Muircheartach O'Neill (who must have been young at the time), did not yield to the exhortations of the poet to risk his life and fortunes in this troubled sea of factions. The following genealogy, gathered from the present poem, and from the Annals of the Four Masters, will assist the reader in understanding what has been said :—

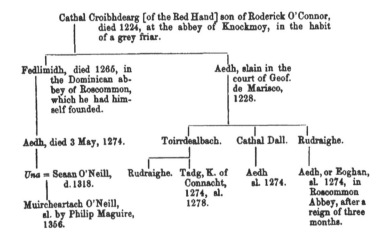

Cathal Croibhdearg [of the Red Hand] son of Roderick O'Connor, died 1224, at the abbey of Knockmoy, in the habit of a grey friar.

Fedlimidh, died 1265, in the Dominican abbey of Roscommon, which he had himself founded.

Aedh, slain in the court of Geof. de Marisco, 1228.

Aedh, died 3 May, 1274.   Toirrdealbach.   Cathal Dall.   Rudraighe.

Una = Seaan O'Neill, d. 1318.   Rudraighe. Tadg, K. of Connacht, 1274, sl. 1278.   Aedh sl. 1274.   Aedh, or Eoghan, sl. 1274, in Roscommon Abbey, after a reign of three months.

Muircheartach O'Neill, sl. by Philip Maguire, 1356.

The present poem is very rare, if not unique; no other copy of it was known to Mr. O'Curry. It belongs to a class of bardic poems which are extremely valuable for local and family history.

Fol. 26. *a. col.* 1. A poem of fifty-eight stanzas, beginning, Moꞃ loꞁceꞃ luchꞇ an ꞁnꞇꞁuꞁ᷎, "Much do slandering people destroy." The initial M has been written by a modern hand, in the space left vacant for an ornamented letter. The author of the poem, which is addressed to David, son of Thomas O'Keeffe, of Fermoy, was Domhnall Cnuic an Bhile Mac Carthy. It seems that David O'Keeffe had taken offence at some reflections said to have been cast upon him by the poet, who accordingly addressed to him the present poem as a reparation. In it the usual amount of flattery and conciliatory remarks is applied to the wound, the poet denying also the heavy charge brought against him, and putting the blame of it on slandering and backbiting tongues.

This is another of that class of bardic poems throwing light upon local family history. Mr. O'Curry knew of but one other copy of it.

One stanza of the poem (fol. 26. b. col. 1) seems to have been an after insertion, in a space originally left blank for it.

Fol. 27. *a. col.* 1. (six lines from bottom) begins a poem of forty-nine stanzas, the author's name not mentioned. It is in a good hand, by a well practised scholar, but not the same scribe by whom the foregoing poem was written. It begins ꞁaꞁle ꞃuchaꞁn ꞃꞁꞇ Єmna, "A mansion of peace is Sith Emna [the fairy hill of Emain.]" The initial letter ꞁ is as usual omitted. Five lines at the beginning of col. 2. are obliterated, and nearly illegible, by damp. The poem, which is otherwise quite perfect, is a panegyric on Randal, son of Godfrey, King of the Hebrides, whose royal residence was Emhain Abhla [Emania of the Apples], in the isle of Múilé (*pron.* Moolé), now Mull.

Randal was descended from Godfrey, or Geoffrey, King of Dublin and of the Hebrides, who is surnamed *Mearanach* in the Annals of Ulster, and who died of the plague in Dublin in 1095. Hence, this poem must have been written before that year, for in it the poet exhorts his hero to lay claim to the throne of Ireland, and tells him that the stone which is on the side of Tara would proclaim him as the lawful sovereign. The allusion here is to the celebrated Lia Fail, or stone of destiny, which was said to utter a sound when the true heir of the crown was inaugurated upon it, but to remain silent at the inauguration of an usurper. It is remarkable that the poet speaks of this stone as being still in his own time at Tara. But notwithstanding his assertion of Randal's legitimate right to the Irish throne, the prudent poet advises him to remain in the enjoyment of the ease and happiness which surrounded him in his beautiful island.

The language of the poem is a very ancient and pure style of Irish, containing, however, a few words peculiar to the Scottish dialect. For this reason the philological interest of the poem is very great, and that interest is increased by the historical facts of which it is the only record. The fairy palace of Eamhain Abhla, or Sith-Eamhna, for instance, is celebrated in the romantic legends and tales of the Tuatha De Danaan, but its exact situation was never before known. The present poem identifies it with the residence of the Kings of the Hebrides, in Mull, in the twelfth century. "This poem alone," wrote Mr. Curry to me, soon after I had purchased the Book of Fermoy, "is worth the price you gave for the whole book, and I know of no other copy of it." Mr. Hennessy has a remarkably fine copy of this poem.

Fol. 28. a. col. 1. On the upper margin, in an old hand, is written, Taḋg Mᶜ Domnuill oḃ. c. c., *i. e.* "Tadg Mac Domhnuill Og cecinit." In other words, Tadg was the author of the poem, if his name be rightly decyphered (for the writing is injured and very obscure). The poem begins, Ḃepp ó ḃaḃ ingill mna muṁan, "It is a short time since the women of Munster were pledged," i. e. since they were deemed worth having pledges given for them. The initial Ḃ is inserted, with a rude attempt at ornamentation, by a modern hand.

This poem is a kind of elegy on the death of Siubhan [or Johanna] daughter of Cormac Mac Carthy; but it gives little information as to her history, or the time when she lived.

(2). The second stave consists of eight leaves, numbered foll. 29-36. Its contents are as follows :—

Fol. 29. *a. col.* 1. In the upper margin is the title of the first tract, Incipit caṫ Cpinna, "Here beginneth the battle of Crinna." This is a remarkably fine copy of this old historical Tale. It is in prose, and begins ḃai pi ampa pop hEpenn, i. copmac mac aipt mac con ceḋ chataiḃ.* Crinna was a place on the borders of Meath and Louth,

---

* " There was a noble king over Erinn,   the Hundred Combats."
viz., Cormac, son of Art, son of Conn of

in the ancient Bregia, not far from Douth on the Boyne, near Drogheda.
There the battle was fought between three Ulster princes, brothers,
all named Fergus,* and Cormac mac Art, grandson of Con of the
Hundred Fights. Fergus Dubhdedach had usurped the throne, and had,
moreover, with his brothers, insulted Cormac at a feast given by him in
Bregia. Cormac succeeded in making alliance with Tadg, son of Cian,
son of Oilliol Olum, King of Munster, and also with the famous champion Lugaidh Laga. This latter hero had slain Art, Cormac's father,
at the battle of Magh Mucruimhe [near Athenry, Co. of Galway], and
Cormac demanded of him as an Eric, in reparation, that he should join
him on the present occasion, and cut off the heads of the three Ferguses.
To this Lugaidh Laga agreed, and in the battle that followed at Crinna,
with their united forces, utterly defeated the Ulster princes, and
brought their heads to Cormac. By this victory, gained A. D. 254,
Cormac became firmly fixed on the throne of Ireland, which he held
for twenty-three years.

Another very good copy of this Tale will be found in the Book of
Lismore. Keating, in his history of Ireland, has given a summary of
it, including most of the legendary and marvellous incidents, which I
have not thought it necessary to dwell upon.

Other copies of the Tale are also preserved; but they are very inferior to the copies in the vellum books, the "Book of Fermoy," and
the "Book of Lismore." The other copies are on paper, transcribed, no
doubt, from ancient copies, but with many mistakes and inaccuracies.

Fol. 32. *a. col.* 1. (line 16). Here begins an ancient prose tale, entitled
bꞃuꞙen mc̄ ꝺaꞃeꝺ aꞟꞃo ꞃꞀoꞃana ("The Court of the son of Daire
down here") beginning, buꞽ ꝶoꝺoꞃb moꞃ ꞽc aꞇeꞇ-ꞇuaꞇaꞽb Eꞃenn an
aꞽmꞃꞽꞃ ꞇꞃꞽ ꞃꞽᵹ Eꞃenn ["There was a great conspiracy among the
Athech-tuatha of Erinn in the time of three kings of Erinn"], the three
kings mentioned being "Fiacho Findolaigh (or Fiacha Finnolaidh),
King of Ireland; Fiac mac Fidheic-Caich, or Fiac-Caech, King of
Munster; and Bres mac Firb, King of Ulster."

This is an account of the insurrection of the people called Athech-
tuatha against the Milesian chieftains and nobles in the first century of

---

* But distinguished by the surnames
Fergus Dubhdedach [black toothed], Fergus Foltleabar [of the flowing hair], and
Fergus Cas-fiaclach [crooked toothed],
who was also called Tene fo Breagha, or
"Fire through Breagh," in allusion to his
frequent irruptions into Bregia.

the Christian era. It relates to a most difficult and obscure incident in the history of Ireland—an incident which has been most probably greatly disfigured by the partizanship of historians, and of which we have only the account of the ultimately successful party. All revolutions which have failed in their object are not unnaturally liable to similar misrepresentations. The very name Athech-tuatha is variously interpreted. Some have sought to identify the people so called with the Attacotti mentioned by Ammianus Marcellinus, and by St. Jerome, as a tribe of marauders, who, with the Picts and Scots, caused great disturbance to the Britons, and are said to have appeared also on the continent of Europe. But no mention is made of them until the middle of the fourth century; and in true Celtic pronunciation the name *Athech-tuatha* bears no similarity to Attacotti. The word *Tuatha* signifies *people, tribes,* or the territories they inhabited; but *athech* is the word whose etymology and meaning make the difficulty. Keating seems to translate the compound word by Oaop clanna, the clanns who were not free, that is to say, the clanns who were under an obligation to contribute by a rent of cattle and food to their chieftains; in opposition to the Saop clanna, or free clanns who were not under any such rent or tribute. This is also Mr. O'Curry's interpretation, who tells us that the word *athech* signifies nothing more than Rent-Payers, Rent-paying Tribes or People.* If this be the true signification, it will follow that in the word Athech-tuatha we are not to look for an indication of their genealogical descent, but only a description of their civil condition; they were not *free;* in other words, they were compelled by an external force or moral obligation to pay tribute to their chieftains.

This, however, is not the place for a dissertation on this subject, which very much needs a patient and dispassionate investigation by competent Irish scholars. It must be enough to say here, that there seems no reason to suppose these Rent-paying tribes to have been of

* *People.* O'Curry's Lectures, p. 363. (O'Donovan's *B. of Rights*, p. 174, n. ™). It is to be regretted that Mr. O'Curry did not give us his opinion on the etymology and origin of the word *Athech* or *Aitheach;* his interpretation of it must therefore rest on his own authority. Lynch [*Camb. Evers.* p. 65], explains it "plebeiorum hominum genus." O'Reilly (Dict. in voc.) supposes it to be quasi pacac cuac, which he interprets "a plebeian." But pacao or acao, signifies *a giant,* and, therefore, Dr. O'Conor explains the words "gigantea gens." *Rer. Hib. Scriptt.* vol. i., Proleg. i. p. 74. n. Let it be observed, however, that the word is not *fathach,* or *athach,* but *athech,* which is not necessarily the same thing. See O'Donovan, *Supplem. to O'Reilly's Irish Dict. sub vow.*

a different race from the dominant Milesian nobility of the time. They were dissatisfied with their condition ; they were unable to supply the extravagant demands of their rulers ; they regarded themselves as the victims of an intolerable oppression ; they therefore organized a secret conspiracy to murder the kings, and all the ραοη-clαnnα, "free clans," or nobles. Their plan was in accordance with the ancient customs of their race. For a year and a half the plot was kept secret, during which time they laid by cattle and other viands, mead, and such strong drinks as were then in use, for a great banquet, to which they invited the kings, above named and their nobles. Fiacha Findolaigh, King of Ireland, was also, it should be mentioned, King of Connaught, so that the three provincial kingdoms, as well as the supreme power, were represented on the occasion. The unsuspecting guests all arrived on the appointed day at the Court of Mac Dareo, in a plain in Breifne, the O'Rourke country, in the present county of Leitrim. For nine days the guests revelled in all the luxuries of the table ; on the ninth, especially, the excellence of the viands, the flavour and admirable quality of the drinks, surpassed every thing that had been till then experienced. All suspicion was lulled ; all was joyousness and noise, and goblets circulated, until at midnight, the royal party—kings, chieftains, nobles and their followers—all lay senseless in the utter helplessness of intoxication. This was the moment so long looked for by their treacherous entertainers. The Athech-tuatha arose, and basely murdered their unconscious guests. Not a man was suffered to escape, and the plain in which the *Bruidhen mac Dareó* (or Court of Mac Dareo) stood, was thenceforth justly named *Magh Cro*, or the Plain of Blood.

The insurgents were completely successful; but their notions were not republican, and they at once placed upon the vacant throne one Cairpre-cind-chait, or Cairpre of the Cat's head, who had been their principal leader in the massacre.

All the "free tribes," it is said, had been entirely extirpated, with the exception of the queens of the three murdered kings, who by some means escaped. They were each pregnant, and having found refuge in Alba, or Scotland, soon after gave birth to three princes, by whom was afterwards restored the ancient race of the murdered sovereigns.

It is not possible of course to receive all this as authentic history; but that some such event did take place cannot be doubted. The bards, who were always in the interest of the chieftains and royal races, can-

not be supposed to have gratuitously invented a tale so dishonourable
to their race and sovereigns ; and the very inconsistencies of the history,
the different order in which the succession of kings, during and after the
revolution, is given by different bardic historians and annalists, clearly
show that attempts were made to tamper with the truth. Keating
gives the succession of supreme kings of Ireland thus :—[the dates are
the supposed years of the accession of these sovereigns to the throne]:—

B. C. 12.   Crimthann Nia Nair, killed by a fall from his horse.
A. D.   4.   Feradach Finn-Fectnach, son of Crimthann Nia Nair.*
A. D. 24.   Fiacha Finn, slain by his successor.
A. D. 28.   Fiacha Finnolaidh (son of Feradach Finn-Fechtnach), slain by
the Athech-Tuatha.
A. D. 54.   Cairbre Cinn Chait, the usurper, king of the Athech-Tuatha.
A. D. 59.   Elim, son of Connra.
A. D. 79.   Tuathal Techtmar, son of Fiaca Finnolaidh ; escaped in his
mother's womb from the slaughter of the nobles.

The "Four Masters" give the order of events and dates as follows :—

B. C.   8. [74].   Crimthann Nia Nair.
A. D. 10 [90].   Cairpre Cinn-Chait.
A. D. 15 [95].   Feradach Finn-fechtnach, son of Crimthann Nia Nair ;
died A. D. 36.
A. D. 37 [116].   Fiatach or Fiacha Finn, slain by his successor.
A. D. 40 [119].   Fiacha Finnfolaidh, slain by the Athech-Tuatha.
A. D. 57 [126].   Elim Mac Connra, slain by his successor.
A. D. 106 [130]. Tuathal Teachtmar.

O'Flaherty retains the same order of the events, but alters the dates
to the years which I have put in brackets.

The account given by Tighernach is as follows :—

A. D.   79.   Crimthann Nia Nair : died A. D. 85.
A. D.   85.· Feradach Finn-Fechtnach.
A. D. 110.   Fiacha Findolaidh, or Findfolaidh.
[A. D.·128.   Elim Mac Conrach, or Mac Connra, is mentioned as king of
Emania only.]
A. D. 130.   Tuathal Teachtmar.

It is curious that Tighernach makes no mention whatsoever of the
rebellion of the Athech-Tuatha, and their Cat-headed king. Fiacha Finn-

---

* *Nia-Nair*, or *Niadh-Nair*, "hero of Nar," his wife's name.

olaidh is said to have been slain in his palace of Tara, or as others
say, in Magh Bolg, by Elim Mac Conrach, king of Ulster, who was
himself killed in the battle that followed, by Tuathal Techtmar, in
vengeance for the death of his father.*

It will be seen that these accounts, each given by high authorities,
are not only widely discrepant, but also utterly inconsistent.

This tale of the slaughter of the nobles is enumerated among the
curious list† of ancient tales published by Mr. O'Curry from the "Book
of Leinster," under the title of Cpꝫain Caippꝛe Cinn Caiꞇ ꝼoꞃ
ꝛaeꞃ clannaib hEꝛenn, "Slaughter of the free clans of Erinn by
Cairpre Cinn-chait." There is a copy of it in the Trin. Coll. MS. H. 3.
17, and another which Mr. O'Curry calls "a detailed, but not very
copious account," in the MS. H. 3. 18. (*Lectures*, p. 264.)

Fol. 33. *a. col.* 1. (Five lines from bottom) is a tale with this title—
Cni ꝺiaꝛoibe in ceꞃ ꝼoꞃ ulꞇaib ꞃó ꞃiꞃ, "This was how the debility
came on the Ultonians," beginning Ciꝺ ꝺiaꝛaibe an ceꞃ ꝼoꞃ ulꞇaib?
.nin., "Whence [proceeded] the debility that was on the Ultonians? not
difficult *to tell.*"

The story is this : Crunnchu, son of Agnoman, was a rich farmer‡ of
Ulster, whose wife had died. Not long afterwards, as he was sitting in
his house alone, a strange woman, well clad, and of good appearance,
entered, and seated herself in a chair by the fire. She remained so
until the evening without uttering a word, when she arose, took down
a kneading trough, went to a chest, as if she was thoroughly at home,
took out some meal, kneaded it, baked an excellent cake, and laid it on
the table for the family. At night Crunnchu, perceiving her excellent qualities, proposed to her to become his wife ; to this she consented,

---

* *Father.* See Tighernach, *Rer. Hibern.
Scriptt.* tom. ii. p. 29. An instance of
the confusion which exists in the history
of these events is furnished by Mr. O'Curry.
In one place (*Lectures*, p. 263) he tells
us that Fiacha Finnolaidh was slain by the
insurgents at Magh Cro ; in the very next
page (p. 264) he says, that Fiacha succeeded to the throne after the death of
Cairpre Cinn Chait, but was afterwards
slain by a second body of rebels at Magh
Bolg. For both statements he could have

cited high authority ; but it is curious
that he does not seem to have perceived
their discrepancy.

† *List.* Another list of these tales is
given in the MS. H. 3. 17. in Trin. Coll.
Dublin. See O'Donovan's Catalogue.

‡ *Farmer.* The word so translated is
aiꞇeach in the original ; the very same
word which occurs in the disputed compound Ciꞇeach ꞇuaꞇa, "the farmer or
tribute-paying tribes," of which we have
already spoken.

and they lived together in great happiness and prosperity, until she became pregnant.

At this time the great annual fair of the Ultonians was proclaimed, and Crunnchu pressed his wife to accompany him thither. This, however, she refused on the ground of her approaching accouchement; so Crunnchu went alone. The sports consisted of sham fights, wrestling, spear-throwing, horse or chariot racing, and other athletic games. In the race, the horses or chariots of the King of Ulster (the celebrated Conchobhair Mac Nessa*), carried off the palm from all competitors. The bards and flatterers of the Court extolled the royal horses to the skies; they were the swiftest in the world—nothing could compete with them. In the excitement of the moment, Crunnchu publicly denied this statement, and declared that his own wife could excel in fleetness the royal steeds. He was immediately seized, and detained in custody until his words could be put to the proof. Messengers were sent for his wife; she urged her condition and the near approach of the pains of childbirth; but no excuse, no entreaty, was suffered to prevail; she was carried by the messengers to the race course, and forced to run against the king's fleet horses. To the surprise of all, she outran the horses, and reached the goal before them; but in the very moment of her triumph she fell in the pains of labour. Her agonies were increased by the cruel circumstances which had prematurely caused them; but she brought forth twins—a son and a daughter. In the irritation of the moment she cursed the Ultonians, and prayed that they might be periodically seized with pains and debility equal to that which they had compelled her to undergo. And this was the *Ces* [debility or suffering], or as it was also called, *Ces naoidhean* [infant or childbirth suffering†], of the Ultonians.

A tale called Cochmapc mna Cpuınn, "Courtship of the wife of Crunn,"or Crunnchu, is mentioned in the ancient list‡ of Tales, published by Mr. O'Curry, from the Book of Leinster (*Lectures*, p. 586). The

---

* *Conchobhair Mac Nessa.* O'Flaherty dates the beginning of his reign B. C. 13, and his death, A. D. 47.

† *Childbirth suffering.* It is added that this plague continued to afflict the Ultonians for nine generations. The Book of Lecan says during the reign of nine kings, to the reign of Mal Mac Rocraidhe, A. D. 130. But there were but seven reigns from Conchobhar Mac Nessa to Mal, inclusive. See the list given O'Conor, *Stowe Catalogue*, pp. 101, 102.

‡ *List.* It is also in the corresponding list in Trin. Coll. MS. H. 3. 17, under the title of *Tochmarc mna Cruinn m͞e Agnomain.* O'Donovan's Catalogue, p. 319.

story is also given in the *Dinnseanchus*, where Crunnchu's wife is named *Macha*, and she is mentioned as one of three ladies so called, from whom Ard-Macha, or Armagh, may have had its name.*

Mr. O'Curry states (*ibid.* note), that the whole of this tale is preserved in the Harleian MS. 5280, in the British Museum.

Fol. 33. *b. col.* 2. On the upper margin we have Cınaeɼ .h. apɼaȝaın .cc. "Cinaeth O'Hartigan cecinit." This poet, called by Tighernach the chief poet of Leth Chuinn (the northern half of Ireland), died A. D. 975. The poem here attributed to him begins Ꝺoluıꝺ aıllıll ıp ın caıllıꝺ ı oulꝺpeaꝺ, "Ailill went into the wood in Cul-breadh." The object of the poem is to describe the manner of death, and places of interment of the seven sons of Aedh Slaine, King of Ireland, A. D. 595 to 600.

Several good copies of this poem exist in the Academy's collection, and in that of Trinity College. The present copy is one of the best of them.

Fol. 33. *b. col.* 2. (eight lines from bottom). A poem headed Poɼhaꝺ na canoıne .cc., "Fothadh na Canoine [of the Canon] cecinit," beginning Cepɼ cech pıȝ co péıll, ꝺo clannaıꝺ neıll naıp, "The right of every king clearly, of the children of noble Niall;" the next lines add, "except three, who owe no submission so long as they are in power, the Abbat of great Armagh, the King of Caisil of the clerics, and the King of Tara."

This poem was addressed to Aedh Oirnighe, when he became king of Ireland in 793, by Fothad of the Canon, so called because he gave a decision, which was regarded as a law or Canon, exempting the clergy from military service. (See O'Curry, *Lect.*, pp. 363, 364; Four M. 799, and O'Donovan's note *, p. 408). Fothad was tutor, as well as poet, to King Aedh Oirnighe, and in the present poem gives that sovereign advice as to his conduct in the management of his kingdom.

There is a damaged copy of this poem in the Book of Leinster; and other copies, more or less perfect, in the Academy, and in Trinity College. The present is a very good copy, and quite perfect.

* *Name.* Book of Lecan, fol. 266. b. b. [pagination of lower margin]. The original, with a translation, and a curious poetical version of the story, are published by Dr. Reeves in his "Ancient Churches of Armagh," p. 41, sq. See also Dr. S. Ferguson's agreeable volume, "Lays of the Western Gael," pp. 23 and 233.

On the upper margin of fol. 34. b. col. 1. a modern reader of the volume has written his name thus:—" Uill. ua heaᵹᵖᵃ," "William O'hEagra, 1805." The O'hEagra are called by O'Dugan* "kings" of Luighne, the present barony of Leyny, in the county of Sligo. The name is now O'Hara.

Fol. 34. *b. col.* 2. A tract headed ınᴅaᴘᴃa Mochuᴅa aᴘ Raıᴄın, "Banishment of Mochuda out of Raithin." It begins Mochuᴄᴄa mac · ᴘınaıll ᴅo cıaᴘaıᴣı Luacᴘa a cenel, "Mochuda, son of Finall, of Ciariaghe Luachra [now Kerry] was his family."

This is a curious and valuable account of the banishment of St. Mochuda† from Raithin, now Rahan, near Tullamore, King's County, and his settlement at Lismore, where he founded a celebrated school and episcopal see in the seventh century. The banishment of this holy man from his original seat at Raithin seems to have been due to the jealousy of the neighbouring clergy, and is said to have been owing partly to his being a native of Munster. The names of all the clergy who took part in this proceeding are given (a singularly curious list),—and the conduct of the joint kings of Ireland, Diarmait and Blathmac, is severely censured.

This tract ends fol. 36. b. col. 2. imperfectly, the next leaf (fol. 37) of the MS. being lost.

———

(3). The third stave consists of six leaves; the first leaf is numbered 38, showing that the loss of fol. 37 has taken place since the numbering of the leaves in black ink, which has been already spoken of.

Fol. 38. *a.* begins imperfectly. This leaf has been greatly damaged and stained. It contains the life of St. George, of which the Academy possesses a very fine copy in the Leabhar breac.

The present copy ends fol. 42. b. col. 2.

Fol. 42 *b. col.* 2 (eight lines from bottom), is a short legend, entitled,

---

* *O'Dugan.* See Topogr. poems transl. by O'Donovan, p. 59.

† *St. Mochuda.* He is also called St. Carthach. A beautiful woodcut of the round window of the Church of Raithin (still nearly perfect) may be seen in Dr. Petrie's Essay on the Round Towers.

Dr. Reeves is of opinion that the expulsion from Raithin had some connexion with the Paschal controversy. Tighernach records it at 636 in these words: " Effugatio Cairthaigh a Raithin *in diebus Paschæ;*" and it is remarkable that St. Cummian's paschal letter was written in 634.

Scel ᵱalcᵱach na muice annᵱo ᵱıoᵱ, "The story of the pigs' Psalter down here;" it begins Єᵱᵱuc amᵱaı bo hı cluaın mc noıᵱ," "There was a noble bishop at Cluain-mic-nois." The name of this bishop was Coenchomrach; see Mart. of Donegal, July 21 (p. 199). He died 898 (Four M.) which was really 901. The present copy of the legend is damaged, but other copies exist in the Academy's collection. The original scribe seems to have written as far as line 9, col. 2. fol. 43. a., and to have left the tract unfinished, but it was afterwards taken up where he had left off, and completed by another hand, on the next page. This continuation begins line 10, fol. 43. a. col. 2., under which a line is drawn in modern ink. The portion of the column thus for a time left blank is now occupied by the following curious note by the Scribe of the life of St. George, already noticed :—

Aᵱaıᵭ laıᵱᵱ ın mbᶜᵵuıᵭ ᵱo ᵱaın ᵱeoıᵱᵱı o uıllıam oᶠlceaᵭa, ᵭo ᵭaıbıc mac muıᵱıᵱ mhıc ᵱᶜaın ᵭo ᵱoıᴄᵱı, ⁊ ᵭo bıaᵭ blıaᵭna ın cıᵹeᵱna an ᴄan ᵭo ᵱᴄᵱıbaᵭ anᵱo hı .ı. mıle blıaᵭan ⁊ ceıᴄᵱı .c. blıaᵭan ⁊ ᵱechᴄ mblıaᵭna ᵭeᵹ ⁊ ᵭa ᶠıᶜıc; ⁊ ın ᵭaᵱa la ᶠıᶜıᴄ ᵭo mı nouemᵭ. ᵭo cᵱıᵭnuıᵹeᵭ anᵱo hı, ⁊ a ᵱaıᵹıᴄaᵱıuᵱ ᵭo bı ᵹᵱıan ınᴄan ᵱın ⁊ a caınᵱeᵱ ᵭo bı ınᴄ eᵱᵹaı; .a. ᵭo bıᵭ leıᴄıᵱ ᵭomnach ın blıaᵭan ᵱın, ⁊ a 15 ᵭo bıᵭ nuaᶠmıᵱ oıᵱ, ⁊ ıᵱe aıᵱᵭ ᵱennaᵭ ᵭocıᵹeᵱnaᵭ ᵱanuaıᵱ ᵱın ᵭo lo .ı. mıᵱcuıᵱ, ⁊ 6 laeᴄa aᵱ ᵱon ın concuᵱ.

A prayer along with this life of S[t]. George, from William O'Hiceadha [O'Hickey], for David, son of Muiris, son of John Roitsi [Roche], and the year of the Lord when this was written here was a thousand years and four hundred years, and seventeen years, and two score [1457]; and it was finished here the twenty-second day of the month of November; and the Sun was in Sagittarius at that time, and the Moon was in Cancer; A was the Dominical Letter, and 15 was the Golden Number, and the planet that dominated at that hour of the day was Mercury, and 6 days on account of the concurrent.

The year here designated, whose Sunday letter was A, and golden number 15, was 1457-8; that is, from 1 January to 24 March, was called 1457, according to the old style reckoning; and from 25 March to the end of the year was 1458. It is not worth stopping to explain the astrological characteristics.

This note is followed by four lines of consonant and *Coll* Ogham, in which the two modes of writing are mixed up together in a way which renders it very difficult to read them; and the difficulty is greatly increased by the injury sustained by the lower corner of the MS., which renders one-third of each line illegible.

(IV.) The fourth stave contains but five leaves, numbered in the
same hand as before, 44–48. It is greatly damaged by damp
and dirt.

Fol. 44. *a.* Here commences a Tract on the Destruction of Jerusalem
under Vespasian and Titus, taken apparently from the account given
by Josephus; it is of considerable length, and ends fol. 48. a. col. 2.
It begins Oa bliaban ceachpachab babap na huibaibi, &c., "The
Jews were 42 years, &c."

Fol. 48. *b.* is occupied by a poem, but so obliterated by dirt and
damp that it cannot be easily decyphered, at least without giving more
time to the task than I have now at my disposal.

————

(V.) The fifth stave contains eight leaves, numbered as before,
from 49 to 56. The leaves are all injured in the outer
margin.

Fol. 49. *a. col.* 1. On the upper margin, in the handwriting of the
original scribe, now nearly obliterated, are the words in nomine pacpip
7 pilii 7 rpipicup pancci. amen; under which is written, in a later
hand, the title of the following tract: Cocmapc Cpeblainne, "The
Courtship of Treblainn." It begins Fpoech mc pibai pole puai
o pib pibai 7 o lob pibai, &c., "Froech, son of Fidach of the Red
Hair, of Sidh Fidaigh, and of Loch Fidaigh," &c.

The tale belongs to the time of Cairbre Niafar, called in many of
these tales erroneously King of Ireland; he was in fact only King of
Leinster; but because he dwelt at Tara, he is sometimes called King of
Tara, which led to the mistake. He was contemporary with Conchobhar Mac Nessa, and therefore flourished about the end of the first
century.* Treblainn was his foster daughter, although daughter of
a Tuatha De Danann chieftain. The story is as follows:—

At this time there dwelt in the west of Connaught a young chieftain, named Froech, son of Fidach, of the race of the Firbolgs. He
was as distinguished for his remarkable beauty as for his valour. His

————

* *Century.* See O'Flaherty, *Ogyg.* p.   Rer. Hib. Scriptt. vol. ii. p. 14).
273; and *Tighernach*, B. C. 2. (O'Conor,

fame having reached the ears of the lady Treblainn, she contrived to convey to him a hint, that it would not be displeasing to her, if he would ask her in marriage from her foster-father. In this there was nothing, perhaps, absolutely improper—at least for a young lady brought up at an Irish Court in the first century. But whether she exceeded the rules of decorum or not I do not pretend to say, when she went a step further, and gave her lover to understand that, if her foster-father refused his consent, she was quite prepared to take the law into her own hands, and elope with him. Froech, at least, saw no impropriety in this declaration of her independence. His vanity was flattered, and he at once communicated with King Cairbre on the subject. As the lady had foreseen, however, his suit was refused, and in accordance with her promise, she managed to elude the vigilance of her guardians, and eloped with her beloved, who soon after joyfully made her his wife.

Like all tales relating to the Tuatha De Danaann, this story is full of curious necromantic and magical narratives, some of which are perhaps worthy of preservation.

In the list of ancient tales published by Mr. O'Curry from the Book of Leinster is a legend, called *Tain bo Fraech*, "the Cowspoil of Fraech," which, notwithstanding the difference of title, Mr. O'Curry thought was the same as that now before us. *Lectures*, p. 585, n. (115). Mr. Hennessy thinks it a different tale, although the hero was the same.

Fol. 51. a. col. 1. A tale beginning buſ coıppɼe cɼom mac ꝼeɲaꝺaıᵹ mıc luᵹach mıc ꝺallaın mıc bɼeɼaıl mıc maıne ṁoıɼ, a quo .ı. maıne Connachꞇ. "Coirpre Crom* was the son of Feradach, son of Lugaidh, son of Dallan, son of Bresal, son of Maine mór, a quo Hy Maine in Connacht, &c."

This is a short legend giving an account of how the iniquitous Cairbre Crom, King of Hy Maine, in Connaught, was murdered and his head cut off; and how he was afterwards restored to life by the miracles of St. Ciaran of Clonmacnois, who replaced his head, but in such a manner that it remained from that time forward somewhat stooped, a circumstance from which Cairbre received the name of *Crom*, or *the Stooped*.

* *Cairpre Crom*. See the genealogical   Customs of Hy Maine."
table in Dr. O'Donovan's "Tribes and

This story is interesting in consequence of the topographical information it contains. Seventeen townlands are enumerated which the grateful king, on the restoration of his head, conferred upon St. Ciaran and his church for ever.* See Proceedings of the Kilkenny Archæological Society, New Ser. vol. i. p. 453.

The present is a very excellent copy of this legend.

Fol. 51. *b. col.* 1. (line 14), a tract beginning Riᵹ uapal oipmio-neaċ oipeċōa ōo ᵹaō plaiceṁnup pōōla pecc naill .i. conō.c. caċaċ mac peiōlimiᵹ peċcmaip, "Once upon a time a noble, venerable, famous king assumed the sovereignty of Fodla [i. e. Ireland], viz., Conn of the Hundred Fights, son of Fedhlimigh Rechtmar." This is a full account of the exploits, reign, and manner of death, of the celebrated Conn of the Hundred Battles, called by O'Flaherty,† Quintus Centimachus. He was treacherously slain by his kinsmen near Tara, on Tuesday, 20 October, A. D. 212, according to O'Flaherty's computation. The history is continued after the death of Conn, until the accession of his son Art-aonfir, or the solitary (so called because he had murdered all his brothers), who was slain at the battle of Magh-Mucruimhe, near Athenry,‡ in the county of Galway, A. D. 250, by his successor and nephew, Lugaidh. The revolutionary times§ that followed are passed over briefly until Cormac, son of Art, the commencement of whose reign is dated by O'Flaherty from the battle of Crinna, A. D. 254 ; his glories‖ and

---

* *For Ever.* O'Donovan, *ubi supra*, p. 15. 81.

† *O'Flaherty, Ogyg.* p. 144, 313.

‡ *Athenry.* O'Flaherty, *Ogyg.* p. 327.

§ *Times.* The chronology, as well as the succession of so called kings, is very confused in this part of Irish history. The following is O'Flaherty's arrangement of the events :—

Art Aonfir, King of Ireland, slain at the battle of Magh Mucruimhe by his successor, A. D. 220.

Lugaidh Laga or Mac Con. In 237, his followers appear to have given him the title of king, which he disputed with Art. After the battle of Cenn-febrath (dated by O'Flaherty, 237), he fled beyond sea. In 250 he

became undisputed king, having slain his rival and uncle, Art ; but in 253 he was expelled by Cormac, son of Art, and took refuge in Munster. Cormac, however, was himself also driven into Connaught, by Fergus Dubhdedach [of the Black Tooth], who seized the kingdom, but was soon after slain by Cormac at the battle of Crinna, A. D. 254. From this event O'Flaherty dates the beginning of Cormac's reign, although Lugaidh Laga was allowed to retain the name and pomp of king to 267 or 268, when he was murdered at the instigation of Cormac, by the Druid, Ferchis mac Comain, *Ogygia*, p. 151.

‖ *Glories.* See O'Flaherty's panegyric, *Ogyg.* p. 336.

successful government are then described, until the story comes to the following romantic event which lost him the crown :—At the south side of Tara dwelt the family of Fiacha Suighdhe, brother of Conn of the Hundred Battles, and consequently Cormac's grand-uncle. These people were called Deisi, i. e. Right-hand, or Southern people, from their position in reference to Tara ; and subsequently Deisi Temrach, or Deisi of Tara, to distinguish them from the Deisi of the county of Waterford. The barony of Deece, in the county of Meath, still preserves their name. Some time before, Cormac had sent out his son Cellach in command of a party of warriors to assert his right to the Boromean tribute, or annual tax of cows, which had been imposed upon the men of Leinster about 150 years before by the King Tuathal Teachtmar. Cellach returned with the cows; but, as an insult to the Leinster men, he had brutally carried off 150 maidens. Amongst these was one named *Forrach*, who did not belong to the Leinster families liable to the cow tribute, but was of the neighbouring race of the Deisi, the allied tribe descended from Fiacha Suighde. In fact, Cellach had carried off, and reduced to slavery, his own cousin.* When this became known to her uncle, or grand-uncle, Aengus Gaei-buaibhtech, he undertook to avenge her. He had announced himself as the general avenger of all insults offered to his tribe, and for the better discharge of this duty carried with him a cele-

* *Cousin.*—The following Table will help the reader to understand this relationship :—

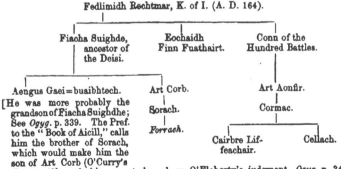

Fedlimidh Rechtmar, K. of I. (A. D. 164).

Fiacha Suighde, ancestor of the Deisi. — Eochaidh Finn Fuathairt. — Conn of the Hundred Battles.

Aengus Gaei=buaibhtech. — Art Corb. — Art Aonfir.

Sorach. — Cormac.

Forrach. — Cairbre Lif-feachair. — Cellach.

[He was more probably the grandson of Fiacha Suighdhe; See *Ogyg.* p. 339. The Pref. to the " Book of Aicill," calls him the brother of Sorach, which would make him the son of Art Corb (O'Curry's *Lect.* p. 48), and this seems to have been O'Flaherty's judgment. *Ogyg.* p. 340. The *Seanchas na relec*, first published by Dr. Petrie (*Round Towers*, p. 98), makes him the son of Eochaidh Finn Fuathairt. This must be wrong, for the whole story hangs on his being of the Deisi; but it shows how old the confusion about his genealogy was.]

brated javelin, called *Gaei-buaibhtech*, or poisonous dart. He immediately went to Tara, and found his kinswoman at a well called Nemnach, near Tara, engaged with the other captives in carrying water to the royal residence. Without delay he led her to his own house, and having put her in safety, returned to Tara; there he sought the presence of the king, behind whose chair stood the young prince Cellach. Aengus, after some words of angry altercation, struck Cellach with his formidable spear, and slew him in his father's presence. On withdrawing the spear, the blade touched King Cormac's eye, and blinded him for ever; the other end of the spear-handle at the same time struck Setna, the king's house steward, in the heart, and killed him on the spot. In the confusion Aengus escaped, and safely reached his home.

It was then the law that personal blemishes, such as the loss of a limb or an eye, incapacitated the sovereign from the active government of the kingdom; Cormac therefore left Tara, and retired to Aicill, or Acaill, now the hill of Skreen, where he had a residence. He resigned his crown to his son Cairbre Liffeacair, although for nearly a year Eochaidh Gonnat, grandson of Fergus Black Tooth, took advantage of the confusion, and usurped the throne; two years afterwards Cormac was accidentally choked by the bone of a salmon which stuck in his throat.

At Acaill, Cormac is said to have compiled the curious book of Brehon Laws, called the "Book of Acaill," of which two copies now exist in the Library of Trinity College, Dublin, and one,[*] a much more valuable and perfect MS., in the Stowe collection, now in the possession of the Earl of Ashburnham. In the Preface to this work is an account of the loss of Cormac's eye, and the deaths of his son and steward, essentially the same as that given in the tract before us, although differing in many of the details. Mr. O'Curry has published an extract from this Preface, from the Trinity College MS., E. 3. 5 (*Lectures*, p. 43; and Append. xxvii. p. 511).

The "Action" taken by King Cormac, to recover damages from the Deisi for the loss of his eye, and for the double murder of his son and steward, is extremely interesting, as illustrating ancient criminal proceedings under the Brehon Law; and these proceedings are much more clearly described in the tract before us than in the Preface to the Book of Aicill. Cormac first sent his Brehon, Fithal, to demand reparation from

---

[*] *One.* See Dr. O'Conor's Stowe Catalogue, vol. i. p. 262 (No. xxxvii.)

Aengus and his tribe, and to dictate the terms that would be accepted. These were referred to an assembly which, in due time, met on the hill of Uisnech ; the terms of reparation were insisted upon by Daire, Cormac's youngest son, who represented his father on the occasion, and were the following :—1. That the Deisi should no longer hold their territory in the neighbourhood of Tara of free patrimony, but by service. 2. That they should own themselves the vassals* and tributaries of Cormac and his descendants for ever.

These terms were indignantly rejected by the Deisi, whose an-cestor, Fiacha Suighde, was the elder brother of Cormac's grandfather Conn of the Hundred Battles : the result was a series of wars, and a lasting feud, which ended in the expulsion of the Deisi from Meath, and their wandering in different parts of Leinster and Munster for many years, until they settled at length, in the fifth century, in the present county of Waterford, in a territory where the two baronies of Decies without Drum, and Decies within Drum, still bear testimony to their emigration.

But these subsequent adventures of the Deisi† are not included in the present tract, which ends abruptly, and perhaps imperfectly, on fol. 55. b. col. 2.

There is no other copy known of this important historical tale, which is well worthy of publication.

This tract, although written in prose, contains, like all such bardic tales, some poems inserted into the narrative. The following are the initial lines of these poems :—

ὁρonan ϝola ϝeiρ cρο̄ɣaṁ (5 stanzas). Fol. 51. b. col. 2.

Ϝuιl ċuιnὁ ὁo ċuaιɟ ϝoċalmaιn (11 stanzas). Fol. 52. b. col. 2.

Cρι ρluὁιὁιɟ ɟaċ en bliaὁan (9 stanzas). Fol. 53. a. col. 1.

Cιɟιὁ aṁna ιmcolaιῆ ċuιnὁ (9 stanzas). Ibid. col. 2.

---

* Vassals. The legal steps by which the free tribes were to be reduced to the state of tributaries and vassals are minutely described, and are extremely important as illustrating the Brehon Laws, and the condition of civilization at the time when the Book of Aicill was compiled.

† Deisi. In the Trinity College MS. H. 2. 15. p. 67. a. col. 1. (ten lines from bottom), is a tract "On the blinding of Cormac mac Airt, and the expulsion of the Deisi from Meath." In H. 3. 17. col. 720. is also an account of the blinding of Cormac ; and col. 728, line 27 of the same MS., is an account of the Gaibuaibhtech, or poisonous dart with which Aengus inflicted the wound.

Rı mac ⲡeⲓⲟⲗⲓⲙⲓⳟ aⲙⲣa conn (2 stanzas). Fol. 53. b. col. 1.
Cⲣⲓ mⲓc a cunn ⲣoⲟuaⲗa (7 stanzas). *Ibid.* col. 2.

Fol. 56. *a.* This leaf contains a long poem of fifty-eight stanzas, written across the full page, and not in columns; it occupies the whole of this, and nearly the next page. The poem is anonymous, composed in praise of David Mac Muiris Roche, and begins, Ⲟleaⳟaⲛ cunⲟⲣaⲟ ⲟo ⲥoⲙaⳜ, "A covenant must be fulfilled." It gives a curious account of various border battles, forays, and plunderings by the Lord of Fermoy, whose hospitality and other virtues the poet celebrates. Mr. O'Curry told me that he had never seen another copy of this poem.

(VI.) The sixth stave contains six leaves numbered in continuation, and in the same hand as the foregoing, from fol. 57-62. The double columns are here continued.

Fol. 57. *a. col.* 1. A short legend, beginning, Ⲁⲣoⲓⳙe ⲟuⲓⲛe ⲧⲣuaⳟh ⲃoⲥⲥ, "A certain miserable poor man." This is a story of a miserably poor man who came one day to beg for alms from King David. David had nothing to give, and the poor man asked him to give him at least a blessing in his bosom; David did so, and the beggar wrapping his cloak closely round the place where David had pronounced the words of blessing, hastened home; there he cast his cloak into a well, which immediately became full of great fish. The poor man sold the fish, and soon became immensely rich, &c., &c.

Ibid. (line 19). A legend beginning, Ceⲓⲧⲣe haⲓⲣⲟⲓ an ⲃomaⲓⲛ .ⲓ. coⲓⲣ, ⲛ cⲓaⲣ, ⲧeⲣ, ⲛ ⲧuaⲓⳟh, "The four cardinal points of the world, viz., East and West, North and South." This is an account of the persons (*four*, in accordance with the points of the compass), whom God willed to live through and survive the Deluge, in order that the history of the world after that great destruction of all monuments might be preserved. The margin is injured by damp; but enough remains legible to see that one of these was Fintan, son of Lamech, to whom it was committed to preserve the history of the Western world, viz., Spain, Ireland, and the countries of the Gaedhil. He is fabled to have lived in the South West of Kerry, to the middle of the sixth century. Another was Firen, son of Sisten, son of Japhet, son of Noah, who was appointed to preserve the history of the North, from Mount Rifia to the

Mur Torrian, or Tyrrhene Sea. Fors, son of Electra, son of Seth, son of Adam, was to preserve the history of the East; and Annoid, son of Cato,* . . . . son of Noah, was responsible for the history of the South.

Fol. 57. *a. col.* 2. A tract beginning Da mac ampa la .bb., "Two celebrated sons had David." The margin is greatly injured, and not easily read. This seems to be some worthless legend of David and his son Solomon.

Ibid. (line 18). The Life and Martyrdom of St. Juliana, beginning Do bı apoıle uppaıġı. Her martyrdom is commemorated in the Irish Calendars of Aengus and Maelmuire O'Gormain, as well as in the Roman Martyrology, at Feb. 16.

The Life of St. Juliana ends fol. 58. a. col. 1. line 33.

Fol. 58. *a. col.* 1. (line 34). Begins a tract with the following title: Cuapupcbaıl luodıp pcaıpıoc, "The account of Judas Iscariot." This is one of the innumerable legends connected with the voyages of St. Brendan. The beginning of the tract is injured.

Fol. 58. *b. col.* 1. The beginning of this tract is injured. It is a legend of the wanderings of two of St. Columcille's priests or monks, who, on their return to Hy from Ireland, were driven by adverse winds into the northern seas, where they saw strange men, and great wonders. The details may not be altogether worthless, as it is possible that there may be a substratum of truth.† On the upper margin, a modern and bad hand has written, meapuġad clepeach coluımcılle, "Wanderings of Columcille's clerks." This tract begins O caımıc depeaġ pıże] plaıcemnup domnaıll m̄c aeda, m̄c aınmıpech. Ends fol. 59. b. col. 1.

Fol. 59. *b. col.* 1. This tract is headed beacha baıppe Copcaıde añpo pıp, "The Life of Barre of Cork, down here." It begins Mo-baıppe dā. do chonnaccaıb do ıapcıneol, &c., "Mobairre was of the Connachtmen by family." Ends fol. 60. col. 1. There appears now a considerable defect between fol. 59 and 60, which had taken place before the folios were numbered, and is not noticed in the count; four pages at least must be missing. Some paper copies of this life are extant.

---

* Some words in the MS. are here illegible.

† *Truth.* In the Trinity College MS. H. 2. 16 [col. 707 al. 711, line 29] is a tract entitled Eadcpa Clepech Coluımcılle, "The Adventures of Columcille's clerks."

Fol. 60. *a. col.* 1. The title is written in a bad modern hand, beaca molaᵹa, "Life of St. Molaga." The tract begins Molaᵹa bi. bᵖeᵖa�643 muiᵹi ᵖene a cenel, .i. be uib cuᵖcᵖaib, &c., "Now Molaga, his race was of the men of Magh Fene, i. e. of the Hy Cusgraighe." St. Molaga was the founder of the Church and Monastery of Tech Molaga, now Timoleague,* county of Cork, and of many other churches in Ireland. The present tract is extremely valuable for its topography and local allusions. The tract ends abruptly, as if the scribe had never quite finished it; but there is nothing lost. Ends fol. 61. b. col. 1.

Fol. 61. *b. col.* 1. This tract is headed Θacᵜᵖa Coᵖmaic m͞c Ɑiᵖc, "Adventures of Cormac Mac Airt." It is one of the many fairy tales and romantic stories of which that celebrated hero has been made the subject. It begins Peccuᵖ bo bi Coᵖmac hui Cuinn a Liacᵖuim, &c, "Once upon a time Cormac, grandson of Conn, was at Liatruim, i. e. Tara." This story has been published, with a translation, by the Ossianic Society,† along with the tract called "Pursuit after Diarmuid ODuibhne and Graine, daughter of Cormac Mac Airt;" edited by Mr. Standish H. O'Grady. It is to be regretted, however, that the Society should have selected so bad a copy of this tale for their text; they had not of course, at that time, access to the excellent and ancient copy now before us; but in the "Book of Ballymote," in the Library of this Academy, there is a copy much fuller and better than that which they have published.

Fol. 62. *b. col.* 1. A legend entitled Ɑcᵖo anc a�643bᵖaᵖ ᵖanabaᵖ bomnach cᵖom bubh, "This is the reason why Crom Dubh Sunday was so called," beginning Laᵗ . . . . ᵖobe caimbeach naeṁ anoilen ᵖoᵖa [cᵖe] . . . . "One day that Saint Cainnech was in the island of Roscrea," he saw a great legion of demons flying over him in the air. One of them came down to the island, and Cainnech asked him where the devils were going. He replied that a good friend of theirs, named Crom-dubh, had died that day, and they were going to take possession of his soul. 'Go,' said the saint, 'but I charge you to return to me here on your way back, and tell me how you have fared.' The demon after some time returned, but limping on one leg

---

* He is better known as the founder of Ath-cross-Molaga (now Aghacross, n. of Fermoy), and Temple-Molaga.

† *Society.* Transact. vol. iii. (1855), p. 212.

‡ The MS. is here illegible.

and groaning with pain. 'Speak,' said the saint; 'what has happened to you?' 'My Lord,' said the demon, 'we seized upon Crom-dubh, certain that our claim to him was good, but suddenly St. Patrick, with a host of saints and angels, appeared, who assailed us with fiery darts, one of which struck me in the leg, and has left me lame for ever. It seems that Crom-dubh's charities and good works were more than a balance for his sins; so the saints took possession of his soul, and put us to flight.'"

(VII.) The seventh stave contains now ten leaves, foll. 63-72 ; numbered as before; written in double-columns.

Fol. 63. *a. col.* 1. A tract beginning Ochcepin uȝupc ba haipopi an bomain anb po ȝeinip Cpipc, &c., "Octavianus Augustus was emperor of the world when Christ was born, &c." This is a history of the birth, life, and death of our Lord, with the succession and acts of the Roman emperors, to the destruction of Jerusalem under Titus. The lower margins are much injured; on the upper margin of fol. 63. a. col. 2. is some writing in a hand of the sixteenth century, now nearly illegible. On the left-hand margin of fol. 64. a. is scribbled the name "uill ua heaȝpa, 1805," i. e. William O'Hara, and on the lower margins of fol. 70. a. and b. is the same name without the date. On the upper margin of fol. 72. a. is written "Emanuel," but not in the hand of the original scribe.

This tract ends fol. 72. a col. 1. line 10.

Fol. 72, *a. col.* 1. (line 11). A tract beginning Apoile oȝlach bo bi m abbaine bpumanaiȝ, "A certain youth was in the abbey of Drumanach," now Drimnagh, county of Dublin. This is a foolish story. The youth, at Easter time, with a sword in his hand, lay down on the side of the hill upon which the abbey was built, and there fell asleep; when he awoke he found himself transformed into a comely maiden.

Fol. 72. *b. col.* 1. A tract beginning Oa bpon placha nime, "The two sorrowful ones of the kingdom of heaven," viz., Enoch and Elias. This is a tale of which we have other copies. There is one, slightly defective at the beginning, in the "Leabhar na hUidhri."

(VIII.) The eighth stave contains four leaves only. It is evidently very defective. The first page is marked 73, in a modern hand ; the remaining leaves are numbered in red pencil, in Mr. O'Curry's hand, 74, 75, 76 ; but there are traces of the older pagination which seems to have been 79, 80, 81, and 82. This Mr. O'Curry found to be wrong, and altered it accordingly.

Fol. 73. *a. col.* 1, to *col.* 2. line 10, seems to be the conclusion of the tract on Enoch and Elias. See fol. 72. *b.*

Fol. 73. *a. col.* 2. from line 11 to the end is in a different hand. It is a collection of extracts translated into Irish from St. Ambrose. It begins, bpiachpa annpo o Ambpopiup, "These are the words of Ambrose."

Fol. 73. *b.* is blank.

Fol. 74. *a.* The remainder of this stave is written across the pages at full length, and not in double columns.

On this page begins a poem of which the Academy possesses a complete copy in the O'Gara MS. From this it appears that the author was Donnchadh Mór O'Daly,* abbat of Boyle, in the first half of the thirteenth century. The subject of the poem is religious; it consisted originally of seventy-one stanzas (284 lines), as appears from the O'Gara MS., but there now remain in the present copy only thirty-one stanzas, owing to a loss of several leaves between fol. 74 and 75. The poem begins—

Ɉabum bechmab ap nbana
Do Dia map ap biñɈmala.

"Let us give tithe of our poems
To God, as it is meet."

Ends imperfect ; fol. 74. *b.*

Fol. 75. *a.* A poem on the Signs of the Day of Judgment, by the same author.† It wants nine stanzas at the beginning, as appears

* *O'Daly.* See O'Reilly, "Transact. Iberno-Celtic Soc," p. lxxxviii.   † *Author.* See O'Reilly, *ibid.* p. xc. no. 17.

from the O'Gara MS.; but twenty-six stanzas remain, ending on the present page, ninth line from bottom. This poem began

ᵹaᵽb eiᵽᵹe ıᵶna an bᵽaᵵa

" Fierce the uprising of the Signs of the Judgment."

Ibid. Line 8 from bottom. A poem in praise of the B. V. Mary, beginning,

ᗋ ṁuıᵽe, a maᵵaıᵽ aᵽ naᵵaᵽ
ᵽo ᵵaᵵaıᵹ ᵹaᵶ ᵶoᵶuᵽ,

" O Mary, O Mother of our Father,
Who hast appeased all grief."

This poem is anonymous; no other copy of it is known. It is of considerable length, and ends fol. 76. b. line 10. Several words in the last few lines are rubbed and illegible.

Fol. 76. *b.* line 11. A poem headed Mıanna Coᵽmaıc mıc ᗋıᵽᵵ, " The Desires of Cormac Mac Airt." It begins—

Mıan Coᵽmaıc ᵵıᵹı ᵵemᵽa, oᵹlaᵶ ᵵlaıᵵ ᵽe ᵵıᵹeᵽna,

· "The desire of Cormac of the house of Tara, a soldier mild towards his Lord."

The poem consists of twelve stanzas, and is here anonymous; but O'Reilly* attributes it to Flaithri, son of Cormac's brehon Fithil, which is ridiculous. Copies of it are common, but this is an old and valuable one.

Ibid. line 12 from bottom. A poem of eleven stanzas, headed, ᵹeᵽoıᵶ ıaᵽla ᵶoᵵum na ᵽuaᵵa beᵹa ᵽoᵽıᵽ, " Earl Gerald that composed the little hateful things down here." This was Gerald, fourth Earl of Desmond, who succeeded his half-brother in 1349. He died, or was murdered, 1397.†

The poem, which is anonymous, begins—

ᵽuaᵵh lem ᵽuaᵵha mıc mıc Cuınn,

" Hateful to me what was hated by the son of Conn's son."

It is very much rubbed, and difficult to read.

---

* *O'Reilly. Ibid.* p. xxiv.
† He was celebrated for his learning, and was surnamed the Poet. Lodge,

Peerage, vol. i., p. 65. The Four Masters call him *Geroid an dana*, " Gerald of the poems." (A. D. 1588, p. 1796.)

(IX.) The ninth stave contains four leaves. The pagination has been altered as before, by Mr. O'Curry, who has marked the leaves in black pencil in the upper margin, changing to 77, 78, 79, 80, what were before 74 [an attempt seems to have been made to erase this number, and it is evidently not in the same hand as the other old pagination] 74, [repeated in the old hand], 75, 76. We shall here follow Mr. O'Curry's pagination. This stave is written in double columns, as before.

Fol. 77. *a. col.* 1. A poem beginning O mnaıb aınmnıξceɲ eɲı, "From women Eri is named," alluding to Fodla, Banba, and Eri, the wives of the Tuatha De Danann Kings, whose names are frequently given by the bards to Ireland. The poem ends on the following page, col. 1, line 14. It is in many places illegible; but it seems to be a panegyric on the daughter of O'Brien, who was married to David,* son of Morris Roche.

Fol. 77. *b. col.* 1. line 15. A poem headed eoξan mac conchobaıɲ hı ɓalaıξe. c̄c̄., "Eogan, son of Conchobhair O'Dalaighe, cecinit." This poet, Eoghan, or Owen, son of Connor O'Daly, is not mentioned by O'Reilly, or elsewhere, as far as I can find. The present poem is a panegyric on the same wife of David, son of Muiris Roche, to whom the preceding relates; but it gives us the additional information that her name was *Mór,* and that she was the daughter of Mathgamhain (or Mahon) O'Brien, of the county of Clare. The poem begins—

    Ní ɲɑ́ hınɓṁe ıɲ meaɲca mór,

    "Not for her wealth [only] is Mór to be estimated;"

so that she was probably a great heiress in her day. The poem ends fol. 78. a. col. 1.

Fol. 78. *a. col.* 1. line 7 from bottom, a poem with the heading Ceɲɓall mac conchobaıɲ ı ɓalaıξe .c̄c̄., "Cearbhall, son of Conchobhair O'Dalaighe, cecinit." This poet must have been the brother of the preceding; but I can find no account of him. The poem is an

---

    * *David.* See above, fol. 56. a.

elegy on the death of the above-mentioned Mór, daughter of Mahon O'Brien. It begins—

Olc an cumchaċ an cuṁa,

" An ill covering is sorrow."

This poem ends fol. 78. b. col. 2.

Fol. 79. *a. col.* 1. An anonymous poem of sixty stanzas (240 lines), beginning—

Ɑ ceġ beġ ciaʒaıp a ceġ móp.

" From a small house people go to a big house."

This is a panegyrical poem on Diarmait O'Brien, son of the celebrated Torrdealbhach, or Torlogh, the hero of the well-known historical romance called the " Wars of Torlogh," or " Wars of Thomond."[*]

The margins are greatly injured, and in many places illegible; but there is an excellent copy of it in the O'Conor Don's MS. where the authorship is ascribed to Godfrey Fionn O'Daly,[†] a poet who died in 1386, or 1387.

Fol. 79. *b. col.* 2. A prose tract entitled Caċ alṁaıne ro, " The battle of Almhain here." It begins boı cocaḃ mop ecıp caċal ṁc pınʒuıne pı leċe moḋa ⁊ peṗʒal mac maeıleḃuın pı leċe cuınḃ pı pé cıan, " There was a great war between Cathal mac Finguine, King of Leth Mogha [Munster], and Ferghal, son of Maelduin, King of Leth Cuinn [K. of Ireland]; during a long time." This famous battle was fought A. D. 722 (see Tighernach in anno), at the Hill of Almhain, now the hill of Allen, in the county of Kildare. See " Four Masters," and " Chron. Scotor." ad ann. 718.

There is another copy of this tract in the Library of Trin. Coll., H. 2. 16.

Fol. 80. *b. col.* 2. A legend of Longarad of Disert-Longarad, in Ossory, beginning, Lonʒapaḃ coıpṗınḃ amuıʒ cuachac : the story is, that Longarad refused to allow St. Columbcille to see his books, whereupon the saint of Hy prayed that the books might become useless to every one after the death of their owner; accordingly, on the night of Longarad's death the satchels fell from their racks, and the books be-

---

* *Thomond.* See O'Curry's Lectures, p. 233, *sq.*

† *O'Daly.* O'Reilly mentions this au-

thor, and notices several of his productions, but not the present poem, *ubi supra*, p. ciii.

came illegible for ever. See Mart. Donegal, 3 Sept. p. 234. Reeves,
Adamnan, p. 359, n. Book of Obits of Christ Church, Introd., p. lxxi.

(X.) There is a loss of some leaves between this and the foregoing stave. The tenth stave contains eight leaves, numbered
in the old hand from fol. 85 to 92, written in double columns.

Fol. 85. *a. col.* 1. A prose tract beginning Ƒeaȼȼ naen ꞁan-
ꞁeachaꞁ piuȼna pinꞁ mac baeꞁain meic muꞃceꞃȼaiᵹ mc muꞃe-
ꞁaiᵹ mc eoᵹain ṁeic neill aheiꞃinꞁ amach co painic a loȼlanꞁaiꞁ.
"Once upon a time Fiacna Finn, son of Baedan, son of Muirchertach,
son of Muredach, son of Eoghan, son of Niall, went forth from Ireland until he came to the Lochlanns." This is a copy—the only known
copy—of the life of Mongan, son of Fiachna, King of Ulidia in the
sixth century. It is mentioned in the list of ancient tales published by
Mr. O'Curry,* from the "Book of Leinster," under the title of Ꞓȼȼꞃa
Monᵹain mic Ƒiachna, "Adventures of Mongan, son of Fiachna."
The first part of the tract is occupied by the adventures of Fiachna,
Mongan's father, who in his youth had visited the country of the Lochlanns, or Scandinavia, where Eolgharg Mor, son of Maghar, was then
king, and lying ill of a fatal disease. The physicians declared that nothing could cure him but the flesh of a perfectly white cow, with red
ears; after searching the whole country, only one such cow was found,
the property of an old woman,† whose sole possession it was. She agreed
to accept four of the best cows in exchange for her own, provided the
Irish prince Fiachna became security for the performance of the promise.
To this the king's steward induced Fiachna to agree; but soon after,
the death of his father compelled him to return with haste to Ireland, to
take possession of his inheritance as King of Ulidia. He had been
scarcely settled on his throne when the old woman appeared before him,

* *O'Curry.* Lect. p. 589. Mr. O'Curry
adds in a note, "This tale is not known to
me." But there is an abridged copy of it
in Trin. Coll. Library.

† *Woman.* The original word cailleaꞁ
(cucullata) may signify either *a nun,* or
an old woman wearing a hood, or cowl.
White cows with red ears are mentioned
more than once in Irish History. Cathair
Mór, in his will, bequeathed 100 such cows
to Nia Corb (*Mart. Donegal, Introd.* p.
xxxvi.); and Matilda, wife of William de
Braosa, is said to have offered 400 cows, all
milk white, but with red ears, to Isabelle,
the queen of King John of England, in
order to purchase her intercession with
John. *Leland, Hist. of Ireland,* i., p.
191, quoting Speed (8vo. Dublin, 1814).
For these references I am indebted to Mr.
Hennessy.

to complain that the king's word had been broken, and that she had
never received the promised cows. Fiachna offered her eighty cows to
make good her loss, but she refused to receive any such compensation,
and demanded that he should invade Scandinavia with an army, and
take signal vengeance on the king for his breach of faith. This Fiachna,
in consequence of his promise, considered himself bound to do, and
landed with an army in the kingdom of the Lochlanns, challenging the
false king to battle. In a series of battles the Irish were defeated,
owing to Druidical influences which were brought to bear against
them; for we are told that flocks of poisonous sheep, who were really
demons, issued every day from the Lochlann King's pavillion and
destroyed the Irish soldiers. Fiachna, therefore, resolved to take the
field against these strange enemies, and did so notwithstanding all his
people could say to dissuade him. When he appeared at the head of
his troops he beheld a knight approaching him in rich and gorgeous
apparel. The knight promised him victory over his Druidical enemies,
provided Fiachna would give him a gold ring which he wore on his
finger. Fiachna gave him the ring, and the knight produced from
under his cloak a small hound with a chain, which he gave to the
Irish king, saying, that the hound if let loose upon the magical sheep
would soon destroy them all. The stranger knight then said that he
was Manannan Mac Lir, the celebrated Tuatha de Danann Navigator
and Necromancer, and instantly vanished; immediately after, however,
he appeared in Fiachna's Court in Ireland, and presented himself to
the queen in the exact likeness of her husband, wearing also his signet
ring. The queen never doubted his identity, and admitted him
without scruple to her bed. Fiachna, having vanquished his enemies,
returned home, and found his wife pregnant from the stranger, but he
had no difficulty in conjecturing from her story who the stranger was.
In due time a son was born, and named Mongan, but three nights
after his birth he was carried off by Manannan, who kept him, and
educated him until he was sixteen years of age. At that time Fiachna
was deposed and slain by a pretender to the throne, and Manannan
brought back Mongan to receive his reputed father's crown. What
follows is the most curious part of this tale, containing the history of
Mongan's dealings with Brandubh, King of Leinster, and recording
several curious and seemingly authentic historical facts, with the origin
of many legends and superstitions, frequently alluded to elsewhere, but
of which this valuable tale contains the only ancient explanation.

This tract is well worthy of publication. It occupies eight pages of the MS., and ends fol. 88. b. col. 2.

Fol. 89. *a. col.* 1. A tract begining Ⱀeachⱅ naen ba ⱀoiⰱe conn .c. cachaó mac Ⱀeiblimiჳ ⱀecⱅmaiⱀ mic Ⱅuachail cechⱅmaiⱀ mic Ⱀeⱀabaiჳ ⱀinb ⱀechⱅnaiჳ, &c.

Conn of the Hundred Battles, when in the midst of his glory as King of Ireland (at the close of the second century), lost by death his wife Eithne Taebhfada [of the long side, i. e., the tall], daughter of Bris-lind Bind [the melodious], King of Lochlann, or Scandinavia. To dispel his grief, he repaired to the hill of Howth, and derived some consolation from watching the sea. One day he beheld a boat approaching with rapidity without the agency of any rowers. It soon arrived, when a beautiful woman, in splendid garments, who seemed to have been its only occupant, stepped ashore, advanced to Conn, and sat fami-liarly beside him. She proved to be Becuma Cneisgel [of the fair skin], daughter of Eoghan, of Inbher [now Arklow], a famous Tuatha de Danann chieftain, and wife of Labbraidhe Luaith-clamh-ar-cloidem [of the swift hand at the sword], another chieftain of the same race who dwelt at Inis Labhrada, in Ulster. Her history was this : she was found guilty by her tribe of a too great intimacy with the son of Manannan Mac Lir, whereupon, on the very day when she ap-peared before Conn, she had been expelled from her people by the great assembly of the Tuatha de Danann, who sentenced her to be sent adrift upon the sea in a self-moving boat ; and she was carried, as we have seen, to the place where Conn was sitting. After some con-versation, Conn proposed to make her his queen, but she declared that she preferred to marry his son Art, of whose fame she had heard, and whom she loved, although she had never seen him. Conn pressed his own suit, and the lady at length consented, on the condition that Art was to be banished from Ireland for a year. This was done, but on his return at the end of the year, Art was challenged by Becuma to play with her a game of chess. Art won, and imposed upon his stepmother the task of procuring for him the magical wand which the great Irish legendary hero Curoi Mac Daire used to carry in his conquests. Then are described the travels of Becuma through all the fairy mounds and mansions of Ireland in search of the wand, which at last she discovered, and brought to Art. This is a very curious portion of the tale, as illus-trating the fairy mythology of the Irish. Art, on receiving the wand, challenged her to another game, but this time he lost, and his stepmother imposed upon him the task to seek for, and bring home with him, Delbh-chaemh [beautiful form], a lady of transcendent beauty, daughter of Mongan. Art inquired where Delbh-chaemh was to be found, but the only information he could get was, that she resided in an island of the sea. With this clue he set out in search of her, and his adventures are described. He brings her home with him at length; and the tale concludes with the repudiation and banishment of Becuma.

This tract is valuable, and ought to be carefully studied, if ever the history of the legendary lore and fairy mythology of Ireland should be written.

Fol. 92. *b.* A poem headed ꞃaelmuıꞃe maꞡꞃaıꞇ .cc., "Mael-muire Magrath cecinit." This poet flourished about 1390, according to O'Reilly, who does not, however, mention the present poem, which begins, ꞃıꞃı a aımı aꞃ hınꞇaıꞇ ꝑeın, "I put myself, O Emma, upon thine own protection."

This is a panegyric upon Emma, daughter of the Earl of Desmond, and was evidently written during her lifetime. This was Maurice, the first Earl, who was married in 1312 to Margaret, fifth daughter of Richard de Burgo, the red Earl of Ulster. At the end of the poem the scribe has signed his name ꞃıꞃı ꝺoṁnall oꞇeıꞡ . . . . . . "I am Domhnall O'Leig . . . . . " the rest of the name is illegible.*

(XI.) The eleventh stave contains four leaves only, written across the page, and not in double columns. They are numbered in the old hand, fol. 93-96. This stave is very much injured, and in many places utterly illegible; the application of tincture of galls by some former possessor has blackened altogether several passages.

Fol. 93. *a.* This is a poem of thirty-eight stanzas, written in a most beautifully regular hand. It is anonymous, and seems to be a panegyric on David Roche of Fermoy. The first line is illegible.

Ibid. (fifth line from bottom). A poem in the same hand, with the following heading, which gives the author's name: Comaꞃ, mac ꞃuaıꞇꞃı ṁc ꝺıaꞃmaꝺa ṁecꞃaıꞇ .cc., "Thomas, son of Ruaidhri (or Rory), son of Diarmaid Magrath, cecinit." The poem begins,

* *Illegible.* The name was probably O'Leighin, now Lyons. We find the name of a scribe Domhnall hua Leighin in another place. See fol. 96. a.

Ceic oıρbeρc an ınṁeρıᵹ,
Um oıρbeρc ρe hınoıne aᵹ oıaℓℓ.

" The wealth of royal nobility,
    With the nobility of wealth contends."

This poem seems to be a panegyric, probably on the same David
Roche, who is the subject of the preceding. It is greatly injured at
the margins.

Fol. 83. *b.* (14th line from bottom). A poem (anonymous) of thirty-
three stanzas, in praise of the same David Roche, of Fermoy. The first
line is illegible; it is in the same beautiful hand as the foregoing.

Fol. 84. *a.* (line 20). A poem in praise of David, son of Muiris
Roche. It is anonymous, and in the same hand as the preceding, consisting of thirty-one stanzas, beginning,

ᵹeρρ ᵹo ℓaıbeoρaıo an ℓıa ρáıℓ,

" It is short until the Lia Fail speaks."

This means that the claims of David Roche to be King of Ireland
will soon be acknowledged by the voice of the Lia Fail, or Druidical
Stone of Destiny, at Tara, which was fabled to utter a peculiar sound
whenever the true heir to the crown of Ireland was placed upon it.

Fol. 94. *b.* (line 8). An anonymous poem of twenty-eight stanzas,
in the same hand, in praise of the same David, son of Muiris Roche.
The first line is illegible.

Fol. 94. *b.* (line 9 from bottom). A poem whose author is recorded
in the heading, which is now nearly illegible, Ɗonchao mac Coᵹaın
O Ɗaℓaıoe .c̄c̄., "Donogh, son of Owen O'Daly, cecinit." It is in
praise of the same David Roche, but the first line is illegible. The first
half of the next page is blackened and rendered utterly illegible by
tincture of galls. I cannot say whether it contains a continuation
of O'Daly's poem, or a different article.

Fol. 95. *a.* (half down the page). An anonymous poem of thirty-
four stanzas in praise of the same David Roche, of Fermoy, beginning
oa ρıoı ρeoℓca aρ ρen nᵹaℓℓ, "In two ways is woven the property
of the foreigners." This poem ends on the next page, the second part
of which is blank.

Fol. 96. *a.* Here is a very curious and valuable list of lands which once formed part of the vast estates of the Roches of Fermoy. It is in many places now totally illegible, but enough might still be recovered to be of considerable interest; especially if it were decyphered with the aid of a local knowledge of the names of the places mentioned. The first line is illegible, with the exception of the words 18 ιρα. . . . . The last nine lines of this page are less obliterated than the rest, and were thus translated for me by Mr. O'Curry, soon after I obtained possession of the MS.; they are curious, as fixing the date of this inventory of the lands of the Roche family.*

"[It was in the time of] Daibith mor mac Muiris do Roidsigh [David the great, son of Morris Roche], that Domhnall h. Leighin† wrote this first; and I, Torna, son of Torna h. Maoilconaire‡ wrote this present chart for David, son of Muiris, son of David, son of Muiris, son of Daibith mor; and for Oilen, daughter of Semus, son of Semus, son of Eman, son of Piarois [Pierce], at Baile Caislean an Roitsigh,§ the fortress of the authors and ollavs, and exiles, and companies of scholars of Ireland; and from which none ever departed without being grateful,

---

* From this curious document it appears that an inventory of the lands belonging to the Roche family was made in the time of David Mór, or the Great, son of Morris Roche, by Donnell O'Leighin, or Lyons. Of this older document the present page is a copy made by Torna, son of Torna O'Mulconry, for another David, whose descent from David Mór mac Muiris is thus given:—

David Mór mac Muiris.
|
Muiris.
|
David.
|
Muiris.
|

David, who was, therefore, the great-great grandson of David Mór; he was married to Oilen, or Ellen, daughter of James, son of James, son of Edmund, son of Pierce Butler; and it would seem that this branch of the Butler family bore the name of Mac Pierce, to distinguish them

from other branches. The chart, or charter, as it is called, was transcribed in the year 1561, at Castletown Roche, then the seat of the Roche family, where scholars, poets, ollaves, exiles, &c., were received with hospitality, and invited to consider it as "their fortress." The names of the witnesses who were present at the transcription of the document are then appended to it. These are, William, son of James, who is called Sionanach, or of the Shannon; Edmund Bán (or the white), son of John Ruaidh (or the red), son of . . . . Garoid (or Gerald), son of Edmund, who is called the Ceithernach, or Kerne [i. e. soldier or champion] of the House of Roche; Godfrey O'Daly, son of Cerbhaill (or Carroll) Beg (the little), "with many others;" whose names are not given.

† Domhnall O'Leighin, now Lyons.
‡ Mulconry.
§ Now Castletown-Roche, barony of Fermoy, county of Cork.

according to the laws* of *Laoich-liathmuine*, to this couple, i. e., to the
Roche and to the daughter of Mac Piarois; and may God give them
counsels for prosperity and for light a long time in this world, and the
Kingdom of God in the next, without termination, without end.   And
these are the witnesses that were present at the writing of this out of
the old charter, namely, the Sionanach,† i. e. William Mac Semuis, and
Emann Ban, mac Seain Ruaidh, mac [a name erased here], Garoid mac
Emaind, i. e. Ceithernach of the House of Roitsech; and Diarmaid h.
Leighin, i. e. the Ollav of the Roitsech; and Gotfraid h. Dalaighe, mac
Cerbhaill beg, and many others along with them.   Anno Domini 1561
is the age of the Lord at this time.''

On the next page is a similar document in the same handwriting,
considerably damaged at the margins; it appears to be a schedule of
the rents in cash payable to the Roche, for certain denominations of
lands enumerated.

A careful search ought to be made amongst our MSS., both in the
Academy and in Trinity College, for another copy of these curious documents.   A second copy would materially assist in decyphering them,
and they are of great interest and curiosity, not only to the family history of the Roche, but to the local topography of the country.

Fol. 97 is wanting.

(XII.) The twelfth stave contains five leaves (including one leaf
loose), numbered 98–102.   This stave is in double columns.

Fol. 98. *a. col.* 1. The first five or six lines are injured by the application of galls.   In the first line the following words are legible:—
. . . . . bc. ap mile iappin poṛgab paṛtalan. . . . . .

The tract begins imperfectly; it gives an account of the early colonists of Ireland, and of Tuan mac Cairrill, who survived the deluge, and
remained in Ireland to the coming of St. Patrick.   The tract ends fol.
98. b. col. 1.

----

* The laws of Laoch Liathmuine, i. e.,
the laws of the most unbounded hospitality.
Onana, son of Ailcen or Cailchine, lord of
Fermoy, was called *Laoch Liathmuine*,
or Hero of Cloch Liathmuine, in the parish
of Kilgullane, barony of Fermoy. See *Four
Masters*, A. D. 640, and O'Donovan's
notes.

† This seems a kind of nickname, signi-
fying " of the Shannon."

Fol. 98. *b. col.* 1. A poem of ten stanzas (anonymous), on the relative length of life of man and other animals, as well as the time allowed for the duration of fences and tillage in fields. It begins:—

> bliaꝺan ꝺon cuaılle co cept
> Q cpı ꝺon ᵹupc na ᵹlapbepc
> Na ċup ⁊ na aċ cup
> Qn cpep na cpepcup.

> " A year for the stake by right,
> Three for the field in its green bearing,
> In fallow and in second fallow,
> And the third in its third fallow."

Fol. 99. *a. col.* 1. There is here a loss of one or more leaves, not noticed in the pagination. On the corner of the upper margin is the number 208, which would seem to show that more than 100 pages of the volume are lost. Fol. 99. a. contains the last page of the tale of the Lady Eithne, daughter of Dichu, of whose history we shall speak at fol. 111. a. *infra*.

Fol. 99. *b. col.* 1. An anonymous poem, of which the first thirty-four stanzas now remain, a leaf or more having been lost between what are now fol. 99 and 100, although not noticed in the pagination. It is a dialogue between the aged Eagle of Ecaill (Achill island) and Fintan, who had preserved the history of Ireland since before the Deluge,[*] in which Fintan gives an account of the primitive history of Ireland and its early colonists. The poem begins:—

> Qppaıꝺ pın a eóın eacla!
> ınꝺıp ꝺuın aꝺꝺup heaċcpa
> aca aᵹam ᵹan cpéna
> ċaᵹulluım a heın bepla,

> " It is old thou art, O Bird of Eacaill,
> Tell me the cause of thy adventures;
> I possess, without denial,
> The gift of speaking in the bird language."

Fol. 100. *a. col.* 1. The last seven stanzas of a poem, imperfect, owing to the loss of the leaves already noticed. The names of " Cormac," and also that of " Diarmaid mag Carthaigh," occur in it.

---

[*] *Deluge.* See above, fol. 57, a. col. 1.

Ibid. Then follows a collection of eighteen short poems, ending on fol. 103. b., intended, apparently, for the instruction of Cormac, son of Diarmaid Mac Carthy. These poems are driftless and unintelligible; Mr. O'Curry thought that they may have been school lessons, or exercises for the young Mac Carthy, for the author seems to have been his tutor. They are not worth the time it would take to catalogue them more minutely. In some of these poems the O'Briens of Cluain-Ramh-fhada, now Clonrood, near Ennis, are mentioned. On the corner of the margin of fol. 100. a. is the number 2012, probably intended for 212. On the corresponding margin of fol. 101. b. is what seems the number 204; and there is a similar pagination which seems to be 209 on fol. 102. a.; but the last figure in all these paginations is very uncertain.

(XIII.) The thirteenth stave contains eight leaves, numbered foll. 103 to 110; the folios 105 to 110 have a second pagination in the upper margin, 154 to 159. The first two leaves of this stave are written across the pages, and not in double columns.

Fol. 103. *a.* A poem whose author is announced in the following heading:—Muιρcheaρτach O Ploιnn .cō., "Muircheartach (or Murtoch) O'Flynn, cecinit." This poem is in praise of two ladies, Mór and Johanna, who appear to have been the daughters of Owen Mac Carthy, and to have been in some way connected with the family of Roche, of Fermoy. It begins, Ceac ba bansan paιc Caιριl. "The Rath (or fort) of Cashel is a house of two fortresses." Ends next page.

Fol. 103. *b.* A poem of fifteen stanzas, headed, Eosan mc aensuρ ιbalaιs .cō., "Eoghan, son of Aongus O'Daly, cecinit." This poem is in praise of Johanna, wife of David Roche, of Fermoy. It begins, Nel ριsna óρ paιc lusaιne, "There is a queenly cloud over Rath Ugaine."

Fol. 104. *a. & b.* Here are six more of the short, meaningless poems which were already noticed, fol. 100. a., and which Mr. O'Curry thought were written for Cormac son of Diarmaid Mac Carthy. These are in the same handwriting, and relate to Diarmait's son as well as to some female of the family who is not named. Except for the language, they are quite worthless.

Fol. 105. *a. col.* 1. Here begins an ancient religious tale, or legend,

known under the name of lmpuim óupaiᵹ ua coppa, "Navigation*
of the curach [canoe or boat] of O'Corra." It begins Ρlachῦpuᵹaiῦ
ceῦach compamaó póóineapap ῦo cuiᵹeaῦ conaóc.

As Mr. O'Curry has given a full and minute account of the contents
of this tale (Lect. xiii. p. 289. sq.), it will be unnecessary to say anything on the subject here. The O'Corra, and the company of nine
who formed the crew and passengers in their boat, are invoked in the
Litany of Aongus the Culdee. If that work be genuine, and written,
as Mr. O'Curry supposed, about 780 (a date scarcely credible), this
would give a very high antiquity to the legend; not that the tale or
legend, as here given, can pretend to such antiquity, for it is manifestly
of a much later date, but Mr. O'Curry's argument is, that the O'Corra,
if they have been invoked as saints in a litany of the end of the eighth
century, must have lived long before that time; this, however, assumes
the litany to have been written at the date he assigns to it, and that we
have it now uninterpolated, and in its original state; both these as-
sumptions, I need hardly say, are extremely improbable.

109. col. 1. A short tract entitled, Riᵹaῦ nell noiᵹiallaiᵹ op
clann Echaó, añpo, "Inauguration of Niall of the Nine Hostages over
the clann Eochaidh here." It begins, ῦoi Eochaῦ muiᵹmeῦin pi
Epenn maῦun i cpich conacht i comῦoccup ῦo lochuiῦ Epne. The
object of this tract is to show how it came to pass that Niall succeeded
his father as King of Ireland, although he was the youngest of his
father's sons.

The original ink having become faint, has been gone over in some
places with black ink.

Fol. 110. *a. col.* 2. A tract headed Cepta ᵹpeᵹa anῦpo, "Greek
questions here." This seems a silly and worthless production.

(XIV.) The fourteenth stave contains six leaves, numbered from
111 to 116, written in double columns.

Fol. 111. *col.* 1. A tract without title, beginning Αpῦpiᵹ cpoῦa
copᵹpach clann. It contains the legend of Eithne, daughter of Dichu,
a very curious addition to the Tuath De Danaan mythology of Ireland;

---

* *Navigation.* Lit. rowing. In the list   entitled lmpam hua Coppa. "Row-
of ancient tales published by Mr. O'Curry,   ing [or Navigation] of O'Corra." Lect.
from the Book of Leinster, this tale is   p. 587.

for this tract has hitherto been unknown to us, and no other copy of it is known to exist.

The tale opens by an account of the Milesian invasion of Ireland, and their overthrow of the Tuatha De Danaan, the joint reign of the brothers Heber and Heremon, and the battle of Geisill, in which Heber fell, and Heremon became sole monarch of Ireland. After this the chiefs of the Tuath De Danaan appointed over themselves two supreme chiefs, viz., Bodhbh Dearg and Manannan Mac Lir. The latter being the great astrologer and magician of the tribe, was entrusted with the duty of selecting for them habitations where they might lie concealed from their enemies. Accordingly he settled them in the most beautiful hills and valleys, drawing round them an invisible wall impenetrable to the eyes of other men, and impassable, but through which they themselves could see and pass without difficulty. Manannan also supplied them with the ale of Goibhnenn, the Smith, which preserved them from old age, disease, and death; and gave them for food his own swine, which, although killed and eaten one day, were alive again, and fit for being eaten again, the next, and so would continue for ever.

The story then goes on to tell how the great Tuatha De Danaan mansion of Brugh na Boinne, near Slane, on the banks of the Boyne, had passed from the possession of Elcmar, its true owner, into that of Aengus, youngest son of the Daghda Mór, or great king of the Tuatha De Danaan. Elcmar was the foster-father of Aengus, and Manannan Mac Lir suggested to him to ask his foster-father for the palace. Meanwhile Manannan, by his art, deprived Elcmar of the power of refusing, and drove him forth, with all his family, to seek other habitations. Thus Aengus took undisputed possession of the palace, and there he dwells to this day, surrounded by an impenetrable and invisible wall, drinking Goibhnenn Smith's ale of immortality, and eating the never-failing pigs.

But it so happened that when the spell was put upon Elcmar and his family, which compelled them to abandon their home, part of the household was absent. This was Dichu, Elcmar's chief steward, with his wife and son. They had gone to seek some additional dainties for the distinguished company that Elcmar was then entertaining, one of whom was Manannan himself. The steward finding his old master gone, entered into the service of Aengus, and things went on as before.

Soon after this a daughter was born to Manannan, to whom he gave the name of "Curcog," from a tuft of golden hair which appeared on the crown of her head when she was born. On the same night a daughter was also born to the steward, Dichu, and she was named Eithne.* Aengus, according to the old fosterage customs, received both daughters to be brought up at his court.

When the girls grew up, Eithne was appointed one of the maids of honour to wait upon Curcog; but she refused to eat; and nevertheless continued in good health and plumpness. This was a great mystery, and gave much uneasiness to her friends; but Manannan discovered the cause. It appeared that on a former occasion she had received an insult from Finnbar, a Tuatha De Danaan chieftain of the hill Cnoc Meadha, who had been on a visit at her foster-father's. Her pure soul so resented this insult that her guardian demon fled from her, and was replaced by a guardian angel sent by the true God. From that time she was unable to eat any pagan food, and was miraculously sustained by the power of God.

Aengus and Manannan had at this time two lovely milch cows, giving an inexhaustible supply of milk. These cows they had brought home from India, whither they had gone on some necromantic voyage; and as India was then a land of righteousness, it was proposed that Eithne should live on the milk of these cows, which she consented to do, milking them herself.† Things went on so, and Eithne continued to live with, and wait upon the lady Curcog, at Brugh na Boinne, from the days of Heremon to the reign of King Laeghaire, son of Niall, and the coming of St. Patrick,‡ a period of about 1450 years.

At this time, St. Patrick still living, Curcog and her ladies, finding the weather sultry, went to bathe in the Boyne, after which they returned home, all except Eithne, whose absence they did not at first perceive, as neither did Eithne perceive that she had wandered from them. Her astonishment was great, when she returned to the shore, to find her companions gone. The fact was, that the influence of the true faith

---

* *Eithne.* "Sweet kernel of a nut."

† *Herself.* It seems that she was wont to milk her two cows in two golden *medars*, or methers; and that this tale was, therefore, called Altrom tige da medar, i. e. "The fosterage of the house of the two medars." But the medars do not seem to occupy a very prominent place in the story, as it is told in the Book of Fermoy.

‡ *St. Patrick.* In the text he is called incailgin, "the shaven head," fol. 115. a. col. 2. line 8 and 17; in another place (ibid. line 5 from bottom), he is called Patrick Mac Alpuirn." St. Patrick, *Apost. of Ireland*, p. 411.

was now in the land, and had destroyed the power of her *feth-fiadha*, or veil of invisibility, when she threw it off with her other garments on going into the river. She therefore became an ordinary woman, unable to see through, or penetrate the invisible wall which protected her former associates from mortal gaze. She wandered on the north side of the Boyne, in great perplexity, ignorant of the cause of her dilemma; every thing to her eye was changed, and she could no longer find those paths and places which had been for so many centuries familiar to her. At length she came to a walled garden, in which stood what seemed to her a dwelling-house. A man, in a garb which was new to her, sat at the door and was reading in a book. He proved to be a recluse, and was sitting at the door of his church. She spoke to him, and told him her history. He received her kindly, and brought her to St. Patrick, by whom she was instructed and baptized.

One day she was sitting at the church of the recluse on the Boyne, when a great noise and clamour, as of a great multitude surrounding them, was heard, but it was not seen from whence the voices proceeded. Eithne, however, at once recognized her former friends, and discovered that Aengus and his household had gone forth in search of her, and when they could not discover her (for she was now invisible to them) they set up a loud wail and lamentation. At this she was so deeply affected that she swooned away, and was at the point of death. This shock she never recovered. She died, her head leaning on St. Patrick's breast, and was buried with due honour in the little church of the recluse, which from that time received the name of Cill-Eithne, or Eithne's Church.

The hermit's name was Ceasar; he was son of the King of Scotland, and one of St. Patrick's priests. He abandoned his little church on the death of Eithne, and retired to the wood of Fidh-Gaibhle, in Leinster, where he cleared for himself a field, in which he built another hermitage, called, from his name, Cluain-Ceasair.

The story of Eithne is continued on fol. 115. a. col 1, in a quite different hand, and ends fol. 116. b. col. 1, line 12 from bottom.

Several poems are inserted into the latter part of the tale, viz. :—

Ɖena ḃaṁ a cana ꝑen.   Fol. 115. a. col. 1. line 7 (a poem of three stanzas).

Ɖenum impoḋ iniṙniṁuch.   Fol. 116. a. col. 1, line 28 (seven stanzas).

ᵹoιρι'ᵒ ṁe α muιnᴄιρ nιṁe. "Call me, ye people of Heaven."
Fol. 116. a. col. 2, line 14 (six stanzas).

Cluιᴄᴄιρ lιb ρeρᴄ ριαιl eᴄne. "Let the generous Ethne's grave
be dug by you." Fol. 116. b. col. 1. line 30 (thirteen stanzas).

Fol. 116. *b. col.* 1. (line 10 from bottom). A poem with the title
Goᵹαn moρ u ᴅαlαιᵹ .ᴄᴄ̄., "Eoghan mor O'Daly cecinit." It begins
Ceαᵹαρᴄ mιρι α Muιρe, "Teach me, O Mary." The first four or
five stanzas are greatly rubbed, and in part illegible; the entire poem
seems to have consisted of nineteen stanzas.

(XV.) The fifteenth stave contains seven leaves, numbered from
fol. 117 to fol. 123. On the upper margin of fol. 117, a. col.
1, are the words ιhρ mαρια, "Jesus Maria."

Fol. 117. *a. col.* 1. A poem of thirty-seven stanzas (anonymous),
on the Crucifixion of our Lord, His descent into Hell, His Resurrection, and His Ascension into Heaven, accompanied by the souls whom
He had delivered from the Limbus patrum. The poem begins,

Gιρeιρᵹι ᴅo eιριᵹ Dια,

"A resurrection in which God arose."

It is written in a very beautiful and remarkable hand.

Fol. 117. *b. col.* 2. A poem with the heading bριαn o huιᵹιnn .ᴄᴄ̄.,
"Brian O'Higgin, cecinit." This is a panegyric on David, son of
Muiris, or Maurice Roche, of Fermoy, enumerating all the places in
Munster from whence he had carried off plunder and spoil. The poem
contains sixty-two stanzas; it begins, Cιnᴅuρ ιᴄᴄαρ ρeᴅ ρuιρᵹι,
"How is a gift of courtship paid." Brian O'Higgin is not mentioned
by O'Reilly. But the Four Masters record the death of Brian, son of
Fergal Ruaidh Ui Uiccinn, or O'Higgin, "head of his own tribe,
oιᴅe, or Superintendent of the Schools of Ireland, and preceptor in
poetry,"—on Maundy Thursday, 1477. He seems to have been a Connaught poet. The poem ends fol. 119. a col. 1.

Fol. 119. *a. col.* 1. A poem (of thirty-six stanzas), whose author is
given in the following title: Seααn oᵹ mαᴄ ραιᴄ .cc., "Shane (or

---

* *Magrath.* Not mentioned by O'Reilly.

John) Óg [i. e. Junior] Mac Raith, or Magrath,* cecinit." It begins,

ᵹach ꝼonn ᵹuꝼeꝓuıꝺ muıᵹe,

" All lands *are good until* [compared with] Fermoy."

This is a poem in praise of the territory of Fermoy and its lord, David, son of Morris Roche, and his wife Joan. It ends fol. 120. a col. 1.

Fol. 120. *a. col.* 1. A poem headed, OⅯaoᴄhaᵹan .c̄c̄., " O'Mao-thogan, cecinit." This poet is not mentioned by O'Reilly, but he was certainly of Munster. His poem begins, ꝼaꝺa ıꝼ mnᴅ maıᴄı mnᴅ Ⅿuṁan, " Long have the women of Munster been noble women." It is a panegyric on Cathilin, who seems to have been the mother of David, son of Morris Roche, of Fermoy. The poem consists of thirteen stanzas of an unequal number of lines. It ends fol. 120. b. col. 2.

Fol. 121. *a. col.* 1. A poem headed Coꝛmac mac Eoᵹaın u Dalaıᵹ, .cc., " Cormac, son of Eoghan O'Daly, cecinit." A panegyric on Cathilin, daughter of Tadhg Mac Carthy, and on David, son of Morris Roche, who seems to have been her son. The poem begins,

Dlıᵹım ıc aꝼ mꝑeaꝓaᴄᴄ ᵹꝛᴅıꝺ,

" I am entitled to payment in right of my office."

This poem consists of thirty-nine stanzas of the usual number of four lines each.

Fol. 121. *b. col.* 1. (eight lines from bottom). A poem headed, Ua maeᴄaᵹan, .c̄c̄., ı ꝓeaan "OMaethagan, cecinit, i. e. John." This is a panegyric on Morris, son of Morris Roche, of Fermoy, and his son David. It begins, ꝼoꝛmaꝺ aᵹ caᴄ le clu Ⅿuıꝓıꝓ, "All men envy the fame of Muiris." It consists of twenty stanzas of an unequal number of lines, and is written in a good hand, but in faint ink. The poem ends fol. 122. a. col. 2. After which, in a space that was origi-nally blank, is written, apparently by the same hand that wrote the pagination, these words in English: " The former pages of this Book, from the beginning to this page, was 288."

Fol. 122. *b.* This page was originally blank, but is now covered with idle scribbling. Amongst these are the following: ꝺo ꝺı an leabaꝓ ꝓo aꝓ na aꝓcꝓıbaꝺ le uıllıam ua heaᵹꝓa anno ꝺꝼı 1805, ambaıle aᴄa clıaᴄ, " This book was re-written by William O'Hara,

A. D. 1805, in Baile-atha-cliath, i. e. Dublin." Again, 'ᴜᴉᄔ. ᴜᴀ heᴀᵹᵱᴀ Ꮐ.Ꮯ. 1806, Jan. 29, 1806."

I am sorry to be obliged to add that Mr. O'Curry condescended to write his respectable and honored name amongst such wretched scribbling, thus:

Є6ᵹᴀn 6 Coᵯᵱᴀᴉᴆe,
ᵯᴃccᴄᴌuᴉᴉ.

Another note is this: Ceᴀᴆᴀᴉᵱ ᴃeᴀnnᴀᴆᴄ ᴀᵱ ᴀnᵯᴀᴉn ᵱᵱoᴉnᵱᴉᴀᵱ ᴜᴉ ᴌoᴄᴉᴆe ᴀᵱ ᵱon ᴆe ᵱnᴀ ᴄᴄeᴀᵱᵱᴀᴆ, "Give a blessing on the soul of Francis O'Hickey, for the sake of God, and his friends (?)."

Fol. 123. *a.* (written across the page, without columns). An anonymous poem of fifty-two stanzas, in praise of Cathilin, daughter of Tadhg Mac Carthy, who has been already mentioned. It begins,

Ꭺᴉᴌeᵱ ᵹᴀᴄ en ᴆuᴉne ᴀ eᴉᴃᵱeᴆᴄ, "Every one has a right to his inheritance."

Fol. 123. *b.* (13 lines from bottom, very much rubbed, and in many parts illegible), is a poem of which the author is named in the title, ᵯᴀᴉᴄᴴᴉᴀᵱ ᵯ6ᵱ o ᴄᴉᴌᴌᴉn .ᴄ̄ᴄ̄., after which we have the words in a later, but contemporary hand, uᴉᴌe ᴄᵱᴉoᴆ oᵱ ᵱᴀᵱ.

The writing is so effaced that neither the number of stanzas nor the first line can be ascertained.

(XVI.) The sixteenth stave consists of five leaves, numbered by Mr. O'Curry (in entire disregard of the old pagination), fol. 124, 125, 126 [127 omitted], 128, 129. On fol. 125 the old pagination seems to have been 77; on fol. 126 it is clearly 94, and on 128, 78. On the other leaves it is obscure. This stave is written in double columns.

Fol. 124, 125, 126, contain fragments of the ancient tale Coᴆᵯᴀᵱᴄ Єᴉᵯᴉᵱe, "Courtship of Eimire," or Eimer, by the celebrated Ulster champion Cuchullainn (ob. AD. 2). Mr. O'Curry gives a full abstract of this tale (Lectures, p. 278, *sq.*) A perfect copy of this curious legend is in the British Museum, from which Mr. O'Curry tells us he made a careful transcript for his own use (ibid. p. 282). Two other copies belong to the Royal Irish Academy, one in the Leabhar na h-Uidhré, and the other partly on paper and partly on parchment. Both are imperfect, as is also the copy now before us. There is also in the Royal Irish Academy an indifferent modern copy made from the British Museum text.

Fol. 127. Mr. O'Curry appears to have omitted to number this page by mistake. It is not likely that a leaf could have been lost since his pagination was written, as the book has never since been out of my possession.

Fol. 128, 129. These leaves contain a fragment of the old historical tale of bpuıʒeɑn bɑ beɑpʒɑ ("Palace of Da-Dearga"), or the death of Conaire Mór, King of Ireland, at the house of Da-Dearga, a farmer of Leinster of noble birth, who kept a mansion celebrated for hospitality, at a place in the upper valley of the Dodder, the name of which is yet partly preserved in that of Bothar na Bruighne, "Road of the Bruighean, or Palace," on the River Dodder, near Tallaght, in the county of Dublin. At this place Conaire Mór was slain, and the palace burned by a party of pirates, in the 60th year of his reign (A.D. 60, according to O'Flaherty's date, *Ogyg.* p. 138, 273).*

The remainder of the volume consists of some fragments of medical MSS. in a very much injured condition. These fragments do not appear to have formed any part of the collection now called the Book of Fermoy.

(XVII.) This stave consists of four leaves marked on the lower margins ℮ 1, ℮ 2, ℮ 3, ℮ 4. The upper margins are greatly injured throughout, and no traces remain of any older pagination.

This is a fragment of a medical MS. imperfect at beginning and end. It never formed a part of the Book of Fermoy. We have found the

----

* O'Curry, (*Lect.* xii. p. 258, *sq.*).   O'Donovan's note, p. 90.
Conf. Four Masters, A.M. 5160, and

name of O'Hickey scribbled more than once on the margins and elsewhere in the Book of Fermoy, and, as the O'Hickeys were hereditary
physicians, we may fairly conjecture that this is a fragment of one of
their professional MSS. which has got mixed up with the Book of
Fermoy.

(XVIII.) A fragment in a small and beautiful medical hand,
consisting of two leaves, marked both on the upper and
lower margins, e 5, and e 6.

This fragment seems to contain part of a treatise on the liver and
organs of generation. On page 2 of e 5, begins a tract, the first
sentence of which (as is commonly the case in medical MS.) begins
with some words in Latin: be epace [hepate] ec be eius
uarecace [sic] complexiones [sic] loquamur; the tract
then translates this into Irish, and proceeds in the same language.
Perhaps these Latin sentences may indicate that the work was translated from some Latin original. It would be of great importance to
philology, and enable us, no doubt, to fix the true meaning of many
old Irish names for plants and medicines, if the original Latin could
be discovered.

On page 2 of e 6 is a tract beginning, be membRoRum
generaciuorum [opera]cionibus e[c eorum] qua-
licacibus, which then proceeds in Irish, as before.

(XIX.) A fragment imperfect at beginning and end, consisting
of two leaves, in a good medical hand. Mr. O'Curry did
not put any paging on these leaves, nor are the remains of
any former pagination now visible.

On the first page of the second leaf begins a tract on the liver, with
these words: uIRcus Nacuralis esc IN epace que cum
peR uenar ab membra in cher biuibicur uircucer ꝝc.

(XX.) A fragment, five inches by four, containing the conclusion
of what seems to have been a religious tract. It was evidently
cut from the upper part of the leaf of some book for the sake
of the blank parchment that surrounded it.

It contains twenty lines, ending with the word pinic, and is written
in a very good and scholarlike hand.

The back of this fragment was originally blank, and now contains
some scribbling, of which I can read only the following words:—

> Gn ainm Dia [sic] don. . . . .
> cen Conpbelbach ui Domnaill maille . . . . .
> le peil rhaichecae popc . . . .

INDEX TO THE BOOK OF FERMOY.

Finall, of Ciariaghe Luachra [now Kerry] was his family," 20.

Molaᵹa ᵭı. ᵭꝼeꝛaıᵭ muıᵹı ꝼene a cenel, .ı. ᵭe uıᵭ cuꝛcꝛaıᵭ, ꞇc., "Now Molaga, his race was of the men of Magh Fene, i. e. of the Hy Cusgraighe," 30.

Molaᵹa ᵭın ᵭꝼeꝛaıᵭ muıᵹe ꝼene a oenel, .ı. ᵭe uıᵭ cuꝛcꝛaıᵭ, 30.

Molaga (St.), Life of, 29.

Mongan, son of Fiachna Finn, adventures of, 86.

Moꝛ oıceꝛ luchc an ınᵭluıᵹ, "Much do slandering people destroy," 11.

Mór-Mumhan, legend of, 8.

Mór, daughter of Owen Mac Carthy, poem in praise of, 44.

Mór, daughter of Mathgamhain (or Mahon) O'Brien, wife of David, son of Morris Roche, panegyric on her, 34 ; elegy on, ib.

Muircheartach, son of John O'Neill, poem urging him to assert his right to the throne of Connacht, 10 ; his mother's genealogy, ib.

Muile, isle of (now Mull), 11.

Mull. See Muile.

Nı ꝼá hınᵭme ıꝛ meaꝛca Móꝛ, "Not for her wealth only is Mór to be estimated," 34.

Nel ꝛıᵹna óꝛ ꝛaıc luᵹaıne, 44.

Niall of the Nine Hostages, why he succeeded his father, although the youngest of his father's sons, 45.

O'Briens of Cluain Ramhfhada, 44.

O'Brian, Diarmaid, son of Torrdealbach (or Torlogh), panegyrical poem on, 35.

O'Brian (Mahon), daughter of, married to David, son of Morris Roche, 34. See Mór.

O'Cillin, Mathias [or Mathew], mór, poem by, 51.

O'Conor Don, his MS. of historical poems, 35.

O'Corra, navigation of, 45 ; one of the ancient tales enumerated in the Book of Leinster, ib., n. ; the O'Corras and their nine companions invoked in the Litany of Aengus, 45 ; Mr. O'Curry's inference as to their date, inconclusive, ib.

Octavian Agustus, 31.

Ochceꝼın uᵹuꝛc ᵭa haıꝛᵭꝛı an ᵭomaın anᵭꝛo ᵹeınıꝛ Cꝛıꝛc, ꞇc., "Octavianus Augustus was emperor of the world when Christ was born," &c., 31.

O'Dalaighe. See O'Daly.

O'Daly, or O'Dalaighe, Cearbhall, son of Conchobhair, poem by, 34.

O'Dalaighe, or O'Daly, Eoghan, son of Aonghus, poem by, in praise of Johanna, wife of David Roche, 44.

O'Dalaigh, or O'Daly, Eoghan mór, poem by, in praise of the B. V. Mary, 40.

O'Daly, Godfrey Fionn, poem ascribed to, 35.

O'Daly (Donchad, son of Eoghan), poem in praise of David Roche, by, 40.

O'Daly, Cormac, son of Eoghan, panegyric on Cathilin, daughter of Tadg Mac Carthy, 40.

O'Daly (Donnchadh mór), abbot of Boyle (13th century), poems by, 32.

O'Daly (or O'Dalaighe), Cearbhall, son of Conchobhair, poem by, 34.

O'Flynn, or Ua Floinn (Eochaidh), poems by, 7 ; Muircheartach, poem by, in praise of Mór and Johanna, daughters of Owen Mac Carthy, 44.

Ogham, 7.

O'Grady (Standish H.), 30.

O'Hartigan (Cineadh), poem by, 19 ; date of his death, ib.

O'Heagra, or O'Hara, 31 ; chieftain of Luigne, Sligo, 20 ; William, writes his name on a margin of the MS. MS. in 1805 and 1806, 20, 50, 51 ;

II.—Some Account of the Irish MS. deposited by the President De Robien in the Public Library of Rennes. By the Rev. James H. Todd, D. D., F. S. A., Senior Fellow of Trinity College, Dublin.

It is now upwards of one-and-twenty years since I laid before the Academy a detailed account of an Irish MS. in the Bibliothéque Impériale of Paris*, which had been described, and a very beautiful *fac-simile* of a page of it engraved, by M. Silvester, accompanied by letter-press from the pen of M. Champolion Figeac, in the fourth volume of the "Palæographie Universelle." In the description accompanying this engraving M. Champolion maintains the opinion that the Paris MS. is the same which was sent from Britanny, upwards of a century ago, by the President de Robien, to the Benedictines of the Congregation of St. Maur, compilers of the "Nouveau Traité de Diplomatique," of which they have given a full account in that learned work†.

On comparing this description, however, with the MS. in Paris, I saw reason to doubt the opinion of M. Champolion, and in my former paper I endeavoured to show that the Paris MS. must have been a different book from that which the learned authors of the "Traité de Diplomatique" have described as the MS. of the President de Robien‡. My arguments were drawn from the fact that the description of this latter MS. given by the Benedictines, and the *fac-similes* of portions of it engraved in their plates, did not at all agree with the Paris MS. I concluded, therefore, that there were two Irish books, distinct from each other, although containing some of the same matter—the one, that described by Champolion, and now in the Library at Paris, of which the Benedictines make no mention; the other, the MS. which had been sent to them from Britanny by M. de Robien, of which they have given a minute description.

---

* See "Proceedings of the Royal Irish Academy," vol. iii., p. 223.

† Tom. iii., p. 200.

‡ Christophe Paul Gantron de Robien, President a mortier au Parlement de Bretagne. Mort de 1751 a 1756. (Querard, "La France Litteraire," tom. viii., p. 82, where see an account of his writings). He was the founder of the public Library of Rennes, to which he left all his books.

When I read to the Academy, one-and-twenty years ago, my former paper on this subject, I was ignorant of the existence of this latter MS.*; but afterwards I found reason to believe that it was preserved in the town Library of Rennes, in Britanny; and during my very agreeable visit to that country, in August last, I went to the Library in search of it. I remained at Rennes for three or four days, for the express purpose of examining this MS.

I found that my former conclusion was fully borne out; the Rennes MS. agreed exactly in every particular with the description given of it by the Benedictines. It had been given to the Library by the President de Robien, about the middle of the eighteenth century; and in its contents it coincided partially with the MS. at Paris. Clearly, then, there were in France two distinct Irish MSS., as I had formerly concluded, and M. Champolion was wrong in his conjecture that the MS. now in the Bibliothéque Impériale was the same as the De Robien MS. which had been sent from Britanny to the Benedictines.

But before I proceed to speak of the contents of this latter MS., I must return my grateful thanks to M. de la Bigne Villeneuve, Librarian of Rennes, for his courtesy in affording me every possible facility for examining it; although I had called upon him without any introduction, he received me with the greatest kindness, assisted me to the utmost of his power, and permitted me to transcribe from the MS. whatever was necessary for my purpose.

The volume in size is what would probably be called a small folio, and is thus described by the authors of the "Nouveau Traité de Diplomatique" (Dom Tassin, and Dom Toustain):—

"La notice† de ce MS., tres difficile à lire, porte, qu'il contient des fragmens de piété

---

* I ought to have known that this MS. is mentioned by M. de Vaines in his "Dictionaire raisonnée de Diplomatique," vol. i., p. 456. He follows the errors of his predecessors in regarding the MS. as of the 11th or 12th century. It has been more recently noticed by Mr. C. P. Cooper, in the Appendix A. to his (not yet published) "Report on the Records" (Supplement to App. A., p. 44), where he has printed a very inaccurate and imperfect account of the MS. by one of his foreign correspondents. See also another very useless notice of this MS., "The Literary Remains of the Rev. Thomas Price:" *Llandovery*, 1854, vol. i., p. 20.

† The "Notice" here alluded to is a MS. paper inserted at the beginning of

et de morale, plusieurs traductions soit en vers, soit en prose, des sermons de S. Ambrose,
et de son Traite de la Confession, la Genéalogie des anciéns Rois et des prémières familles
d'Irlande.   Cette partie du MS. est une des plus considérables.   Sa largeur est de sept
pouces et demi, sa hauteur de neuf et plus.   Il est a deux colones et l'on y rencontre de
tems en tems quelque lignes de latin avant les genéalogies.   L'écriture en est toute sem-
blable a l'anglo-saxone. Beaucoup de lettres initiales des ouvrages et des chapitres sont
dans le meme goût que celles du MS. de S. Ouen de Rouen, d'on nous avons tiré l'al-
phabet saxon de lettres initiales serpentines.   On trouve dans le commencement du MS.
irlandois beaucoup d'articles, qui commencent par *labrvm* en plus grosse écriture saxone*."

The Benedictines speak of this MS. (that is to say, of the first portion of it) as written " vers la fin du xii° ou commencement du xiii°
siècle," and notice certain contractions (such as $\overline{\text{7c}}$ for " et cætera;" .ı.
for *id est ;* 2 for *est*), which the antiquaries of the period regarded as
characteristic of that date.   Their words are these :—

   " S. Bernard y est cité de cette sorte : *Ut dixit Bernardus in sermone de beata Maria
Virgine, &c.* Cette abbreviation, 7c., qu'on trouve plusièurs fois dans ce mſ. est remarkable, ainsi que les autres abbreviations de cette écriture saxone de la fin du xiie siècle, ou
du commencement du suivant.   Les antiquaires qui donnent† au moins neuf cent ans a
des mſſ. en lettres saxones, nous sauront gré d'en avoir produit un plus recent d'environ
trois siécles et demi‡."

To this it may be added that S. Thomas Aquinas and S. Bonaventure are quoted, who flourished in the middle and latter half of the
thirteenth century, and that the character of the writing, to every one
acquainted with Irish palæography, indicates unmistakeably the end of
the fifteenth century as the period at which the MS. was written.

With respect to the contractions alluded to as indications of the date

---

the Rennes volume, giving a description of
its contents in English, written about the
middle of the seventeenth century, by a
person who was very imperfectly acquainted with the Irish language, and
wholly ignorant of its palæography. He
attributes to the MS. a much higher antiquity than it really possesses, and his
opinion has evidently been the cause of the

mistakes made by later writers on the subject.
   * " Nouv. Traité de Diplom.," tom. iii.
p. 200.
   † " Journal Historique," Avril, 1755,
p. 289.
   ‡ " Nouv. Traité de Diplom.," tom. iii.,
p. 228.

of the MS., the Benedictines further say (they are speaking of what they call the " demi-uncial" Saxon square character, followed by the "minuscule :")—

"Le MS. de M. le président de Robien nous a donné le modèle suivant* : *Zelus dommus tue cometit me, id est.* Le z a été laissé en blanc comme lettrine dans le MS. L'm est redoublée en *domus,* l'e simple est mis pour *æ* dans *tue,* et le *t* prend la place du *d* dans le mot suivant; en sorte qu'on lit *cometit* au lieu de *comedit*—mais rien n'est plus singulier que l'abreviation des mots *id est,* signifiés par un *i* ayant deux points à ses cotést."

But the contractions which these learned writers deemed so peculiar are to be found in all the later, as well as in the earlier Irish MSS., and indeed are in use with the Irish scribes to the present day, so that they are no criterion of age whatsoever. With respect to the use of *e* for *æ,* the double *m* in *dommus* for *domus,* and the *t* for *d* in *cometit,* it will be enough to refer to the valuable remarks of Dr. Reeves, on the orthography of Latin in Irish MSS., in the preface to his edition of Adamnan's "Life of St. Columba‡."

I believe the foregoing extracts from the "Nouveau Traité de Diplomatique" contain all that the learned compilers of that work have said as descriptive of the MS. of the President de Robien. A comparison of these extracts, and of the *fac-similes* in the plates, renders it quite certain that their MS. was the book now at Rennes, and not the volume preserved in the Paris Library.

I proceed now to give some account of the contents of the de Robien MS.; but in quoting from it I shall not attempt to preserve the contractions. To represent them accurately would require an especial fount of types.

The book is not all written in the same hand. It consists of fifteen portions—or, as printers would now call them, *signatures* or *staves*—containing an unequal number of leaves. This inequality may arise from the loss of some leaves of the original MS.; but this is not always the case. The following is a Table of these " signatures:"—

---

* Alluding to a *fac-simile* of this passage given in one of their plates, *Planche* 47.

† Ib., p. 229.

‡ Reeves, *Adamnan,* p. xvi., xvii.

No. 1 contains .... 10 leaves.	Then begins another hand, and the re-
,, 2 ,, ... 8 ,,	maining signatures of the volume are
,, 3 ,, ... 8 ,,	numbered thus—
,, 4 ,, ... 10 ,,	No. 10 [bis] containing ... 8 leaves.
,, 5 ,, ... 10 ,,	,, 11 [bis] ,, ... 8 ,,
,, 6 ,, ... 10 ,,	,, 12 ,, ... 8 ,,
,, 7 ,, ... 10 ,,	,, 13 ,, ... 6 ,,
,, 8 ,, ... 8 ,,	,, 14 ,, ... 8 ,,
,, 9 ,, ... 10 ,,	
,, 10 ,, ... 5 ,,	
,, 11 [not numbered] .. 5 ,,	

So that the total number of leaves now in the volume is 132 ; unless I have made a mistake in the number of leaves I have assigned to the signature No. 11 (not numbered), which in my notes is, I am sorry to say, somewhat obscure.

Fol. 1. 22 b. col. 1.—This portion of the MS. is all in the same hand-writing, and contains a series of short religious tracts or sermons on the Christian virtues or duties. To these is prefixed a preface, which begins :—

Deo pacṗi caṗiṗṗimo Peṫṗo beı   Deo Patri carissimo Petro Dei gratia
ṡṗacıa Poṗcuṗenṗı .ı. an onoıṗ bıa   Portusensi, i.e. in honour of God the Father
aċaṗ ⁊ peabaṗ baṗ cınbṗcnab an   and of Peter, for whom this book was
leabaṗ ṗo.   begun.

I know not who the Peter here spoken of was. We should probably read *Portuensi* instead of *Portusensi*; and, if so, he was probably a bishop of Porto, or Portus Augusti, at the mouth of the Tiber, near Rome ; but the transcriber, in the Irish translation which follows the Latin words, seems to have imagined that S. Peter the Apostle was intended. There was a Peter bishop of Porto at the beginning of the twelfth century, to whom S. Bruno, bishop of Segni and abbat of Monte Casino, addressed one of his epistles*, on the forced investiture of the Emperor Henri by Pope Paschal, A. D. 1111.

Then follow the short religious tracts or sermons, each beginning with the words Labṗum anoıṗ, "Let us now speak . . . ." The

---

* Ceillier, "Hist. des Auteurs Eccles.,"   trum," (Lugdun.), tom. xx., p. 738.
tom. xxi., p. 102, 107; "Biblioth. Pa-

Benedictines, in a passage already quoted, have mentioned these words, which they did not understand, but which attracted their attention, because of their frequent occurrence, and because they are written in a larger and peculiar character. They serve to identify the Rennes MS. with that which had been sent to the Benedictines by the President de Robien, inasmuch as they do not occur at all in the Paris MS.

Fol. 23. a. col. 1.—A tract beginning

Ƒouec ın pρıncıρıo uıρȝo maρıa meo .ı. coƒ[u]ρcaócaıȝı muıρe ban-cıȝeρna bam a coρach mobeıρcı. oıρ abeıρ auȝ. naem . . . .

Fovet in principio virgo maria meo, i. e. May the Lady Mary comfort me in the beginning of my work, for Saint Augustine says . . . .

This tract occurs also in the Paris MS., and it was one of the evidences on which M. Champolion relied in support of his opinion of the identity of that MS. with the volume described by the Benedictines. He has given a very correct *fac-simile* of it[*], in which it will be observed that the words " virgo maria meo" are so much contracted as to be decy-phered with difficulty—in fact, I myself, in my former paper, failed to decypher them[†]. Twenty years ago I was not so well skilled in reading the contractions of such a MS., as I am now; and I am glad to have this opportunity of acknowledging my error. But in the Rennes MS. the words are written without contractions, and are quite easily read. I neglected to transcribe the passage quoted from St. Augustine; for my notes were necessarily made in great haste. The Tract was probably translated from the Latin, and the passage from St. Augustine would possibly have helped us to identify or discover the original work.

The Tract ends fol. 24. 1.

Fol. 25. a. col. 1.—A Tract beginning " Ut dixit Bernardus in ser-mone de beata Maria Virgine ⁊c." The rest is in Irish; but I unfortu-nately omitted, as before, to transcribe the quotation. Ends fol. 27. a. col. 2.

Similar religious tracts follow to fol. 35. a. col. 2., where we have a

[*] See the "Palæographie Universelle;" tom.iv., Planche, 130 (Sir Fred. Madden's Translation, vol. ii., p. 641).

[†] "Proceedings of Royal Irish Aca-demy," vol. iii., p. 227.

Treatise on Confession, which begins thus [a space is left in the margin for an initial ornamented ı or a]:—

[I] Siad so na se cumgill dege dligis an faeisidin do beiṫ inti amail adeir sanctus tomas, sa .u. deis-ding don lebar ren abarar supra quartum summarum decima quin-ta de intencione.

"These are the sixteen conditions that confession requires to have in it, as Saint Thomas says in the 5th Distinction of the book which is called Supra quartum, the fifteenth of the Sums, De intentione."

The reference here is to the great works of St. Thomas Aquinas on the Sentences (in Librum Quartum Sententiarum Distinct. xvii. 39. 4. 4. 1., according to the present mode of citing; and 3 Summ. q. 9. 4. 4. 1.)* where the sixteen conditions of confession are given in these verses:—

> "Sit simplex, humilis, confessio; pura, fidelis,
> Atque frequens, nuda, discreta, libens, verecunda,
> Integra, secreta, lacrymabilis, accelerata,
> Fortis, et accusans, et sit parere parata."

Fol. 37. b., in the margin, in the handwriting (as I believe) of old Charles O'Conor, of Belanagare, is the following note:—

Is terc duine an Erinn do nis [for gnis] a faeisind mar adeir an leabar so.

"Scarcely a man in Erinn makes his confession as this book directs."

Fol. 44. b. col. 2.—There is here a note, in a very bad hand, difficult to read, and in very ignorant spelling, to the effect that the writer had here inscribed his name (which is now illegible) in the year 1755. He adds "Nannetiis," which, I presume, signifies that his name was written here at Nantes.

Fol. 45. a. col. 1.—A collection of sayings gathered from the works of St. Augustine, beginning

Adeir Au. cidbe b3. . . . "Augustine says that whoever is . . ."

Fol. 47. a. col. 2.—Here are continued the short tracts or sermons noticed by the Benedictines, beginning

Labrum anos don trocaire. . . . "Let us now speak of mercy."

---

* These references do not agree with the number of the distinctions and questions as given in the text. But it is not worth while to attempt to reconcile such discrepancies, which are probably only evidence of the ignorance or carelessness of transcribers.

In this Tract are quoted SS. Augustine, Gregory, Isidore, Ambrose, Bonaventure.

Fol. 52. a. col. 2.—We have here the following very curious note:—

Loce don lebapra Rorr bpom a cnich .h. nechach Muman, 7 peapra do Seon Mandauil, pibepi do muind-cip piz Saxan do paccaib Saxa la peile Michil, 7 do piblaiz mopan do cipicaib in domuin, map aca an Fpainzo 7 an almain, 7 ancplizeb appm co hlapuralem: 7 cib bé lé bub ail dol depechain an cipe pin ap pon cup cog Cpirc da popul pein hi map cip caipngepi, 7 do cpiblaiz da chopaib naemca pein hi, 7 con-depna mopan penmopa 7 cecaipce da popul innci, 7 cop cog a machain 7 hé pein do bpec 7 do ablacab innci; 7 map a dubaipc pe cup bé pein pi .na iudaize; ap pon pebup an copaz pin cuc an cip, 7 ap pon naemhcache an ci do cpiblaiz hí, 7 do cog a páip do pazbail a pongc cepc medóin an domain in nlapuralem, innup comab zap dá pzelaib 7 da cpeibim pochcain ap an mad pin paip 7 piap, buddear 7 bud cuaib; 7 ip ann do chuip pé an ppipacc naem docum a appcal domnach Cinzcióipi, 7 do chuip po cecpib haipbib an domain iac do cpilad cpeibim 7 cpabab do chinedaib an domain; 7 cib bé le bub ail a píp do beic aizci inc plizeb bud penn do bul ap each cip co hlappuralem 7 na loco naemca acaib na cimcill, mbeo-paib Finzin mac Diapmaca mic Domnaill mic Finzin mic Diapmaca moip hí Maczamna hí, óip ippe do chuip an lebupra a beplai 7 a laibin,

"The place of this book is Ross-Broin in the territory of Ui-Echach-Mumhan and the person [i. e. author] of it, John Mandavil, a knight of the people of the king of the Saxons, who left Saxon-land on Michaelmas day, and traversed many of the lands of the world, as France and Germany, and the way from thence to Jerusalem. And, whoever has a desire to go to see that land*, because Christ had selected it for His own people as a Land of Promise, and traversed it with His own holy feet, and uttered many sermons and instructions to His people in it, and chose that His Mother and Him-self should be born and interred in it, and as He said that He Himself was King of the Jews—or because of the excellence of the produce the land furnished, and the ho-liness of Him who traversed it, and who chose to receive His passion in the very central point of the world—in Jerusalem—so that it might be convenient for His fame and His faith† to reach from that place eastwards, and westwards, southwards and northwards. And it was in it that He sent the Holy Spirit to His Apostles on Pentecost-sunday, and sent them to the four quarters of the world, to sow the seed of faith and devotion in the tribes of the world;—and whosoever would wish to know the best way to go from every country to Jerusalem, and to the Holy places that are around it, Finghin son of Diarmait, son of Domhnall, son of Finghin, son of Diarmait Mor O'Math

---

* The Holy Land.   † That is Faith in Him, or His Religion.

a ʒпеıʒο ⁊ a haḃna a nʒaeıḃılʒe, ḃo
τреοlaḃ na рlıʒeḃa aп muıп ⁊ aп τíп
οο hıeпuраlem, ḃa ʒaó aen le ḃuó
mıan ḃοl ḃa οılıτпı ann, ⁊ co рпuḗ
Oпптannaın, ⁊ co рlíaḃ рıοın, ⁊ cach
рlıʒeḃ no ʒaḃaıр рeon oпın amach,
⁊ ḃo ınḃıрın cach ınʒnaḃ ḃo con-
naıпcc рeon aп ḃaeınıḃ ⁊ aп τıп-
cḣaıḃ an ḃomaın a coıτchınne; ⁊ ḃoḃ
ı aoıр an Cıʒeпna an τan ḃo пınḃı
рeon a eachτпa .ı. mılı ḃlıaḃan ⁊
τпı ceḃ, xxıı ḃlıaḃna. A aoıр ın
τпach ḃo cuıр Fınʒın a nʒaoıḃılʒc
ро ḃeıпeḃ hé .ı. mılı cocc. lxx. ıı.
ḃlıaḃna; ⁊ ḃo ḃı рeon ceıτпı ḃlıaḃna
.x. aп .xx. ıc cuaпτuʒaḃ an ḃomaın;
⁊ aп nımpoḃ ḃo ḃo пoım ḃo ḃaınʒ-
nıḃ ın pápa a leaḃaп.

Iр ıacc ро na τıʒeпnaḃa ḃo ḃı
oр cınn ʒaoıḃel ın uaıп ḃo cuıр
Fınʒın ро a nʒaoıḃılʒc. ı. Caḃʒ
mac Ḋomnaıll oıcc mıc Caıḃʒc na
maınıртпech mıc Ḋomnaıll oıcc ınna
Mac Caпτhaıʒ mór, ⁊ Ḋıaпmaıc
mac Caıḃʒc mıc Aṁlaıḃ ına .h. æSu-
laḃaın ḃeппe, ⁊ Ḋonncḣaḃ mac Ḋıaп-
maτa mıc Ḋomnaıll mıc Fınʒın, ⁊
Ḋomnall cona mḃпaıτпıḃ, oр cınḃ
.h. nEchach; ⁊ Coпmac mac Ḋonn-
cḣaḃa mıc Ḋomnaıll пıaḃaıʒ oр cınn
.h. Caıпппe; ⁊ Ḋıaпmaıc mac Ḋomnaıll пıaḃaıʒ ana mac Caпτhaıʒ
Caıпппech; ⁊ Ḋomhnall mac Ḋomh-
naıll mıc Ḋomnaıll cluaпaıʒh oр cınn
τ⸗lechτa Ḋıaпmaḃa пeṁuıп; ⁊ Fınʒın mac Meıc Con meıc Mıc Con
ṁıc Fınʒeın ına O Eıḃeпрceoıl mór;
⁊ Coпmac mac Caıḃʒ mıc Coпmaıc
oр cınn Muпʒпaıḃı; ⁊ Ḋonncḣaḃ

gamhna (O'Mahony) will tell it ; for it was
he that put this book from English, and
from Latin, from Greek, and from He-
brew, into Irish, to show the ways on
sea and on land to Jerusalem, to every
one who may wish to go in pilgrimage thither, and to the river Orrthan-
nan [i.e. the Jordan], and Mount Sion ; and
[to describe] every way that John*
proceeded from that out; and to relate
every prodigy that John saw amongst
the peoples and countries of the world
in general. And the age of the Lord
when John made his journey was one
thousand years, and three hundred and
thirty-two years. His age†, when Finghin put it ultimately⸗ into Irish was
one thousand, four hundred and seventy-
two years. And John was thirty-four
years visiting the world, and on his return
to Rome the Pope confirmed his book.

"These are the Lords who⸗were over
the Gaeidhel when Finghin put this into
Irish, viz :—Tadhg‡, son of Domhnall óg,
son of Tadhg of the monastery, son of
Domhnall óg, as Mac Carthaigh Mór; and
Diarmait, son of Tadhg, son of Amhlabh,
was the O'Sullivan Berre; and Donnchadh,
son of Diarmait, son of Domhnall, son of
Finghin, and Domhnall, with their brothers,
over Ui-Echach; and Cormac§, son of
Donnchadh, son of Domhnall Riabhach,
over Ui-Cairpre; and Diarmait, son of
Domhnall Riabhach, as the MacCarthaigh
Cairbrech ; and Domhnall, son of Domh-
nall, son of Domhnall Cluasach over
Slicht-Diarmada-Remhair‖; and Finghin,
son of Mac Con, son of Mac Con, son

---

* i. e. Sir John Mandeville.

† i. e. Our Lord's age, or the era of A. D.

‡ This was Tadhg, called Liath, or the
grey. See " Life and Letters of Florence
MacCarthy," by Daniel MacCarthy, p. 452.

§ See 4. M. 1477, and " Life of Florence
MacCarthy," p. 453.

‖ " The descendants of Diarmait Remhair," or the Fat.

oᵹ mac Coippbealbaıᵹ mıc bpıaın mıc Machᵹamna ınna .h. bpıaın; ⁊ enpı mac eoᵹaın mıc Neıll oıᵹ ına .h. Neıll, ⁊ cpen cpeana Conᵹaıl aᵹ Conn mac aeða buıðı mıc bpıaın ðallaıᵹ, ⁊ ðepbpachaıp a achap ına .h. Neıll buıðı; ⁊ aeð Ruað mac Neıll ᵹaıpb mıc Coippðelbaıᵹ an fına ına .h. Oomnaıll; ⁊ cpen ıchcaıp Connachc aıᵹcı; ⁊ feıðlım mac Coippðelbaıᵹ mıc aeða mıc Coippðelðaıᵹ ına .h. Concuðaıp; ⁊ caðᵹo caoch ma c Uıllıam ıCellaıᵹ ına .h. Cellaıᵹ; ⁊ Uıllıam mac aeða mıc bpıaın ına aᵹaıð ðon caoð caıp ðo fucca; ⁊ eoᵹan mac Mupchaða hí Maðuᵹaın ap cpıl nanmchaða; ⁊ Mupchað mac Muıpcepcaıᵹ mıc Oonnchaða Caemanaıð na pıᵹ ap laıᵹnıb; ⁊ Cachaıp mac Cuınn mıc an Calbaıᵹ ap ıbh Conðuðaıp; ⁊ caðc mac laıᵹen mıc puaıðpı ına .h. Ouınn; ⁊ Sean mac Maolpuanaıᵹh mıc Caıðᵹo mıc Caıðᵹo na pıᵹ ap 'eılıb; ⁊ ᵹılla na naomh mac Caıðᵹ mıc ᵹılla na naomh ap ıb Meachap; ec alıı mulcı an eıpınn o punn amach nach pımcap ap ðaıᵹ chuımne.

of Fingbin, as O'Edirsceoil [O'Driscoll] Mór; and Cormac, son of Tadhg[*] son of Cormac, over Musgraidhe; and Donnchadh óg, son of Torrdealbach, son of Brian, son of Mathgamhain, as the O'Brien; and Henry, son of Eoghan, son of Niall og, as the O'Neill; and the power of Trian-Conghail† was with Conn, son of Aedh Buidhe, son of Brian Ballagh; and the brother of his father was the O'Neill Buidhe; and Aedh Ruadh, son of Niall Garbh, son of Torrdelbach-an-fhina, was the O'Donnell, (and he had the power of lower Connacht) ; and Feidhlim, son of Torrdelbach, son of Aedb, son of Torrdelbach, was the O'Concobhair; and Tadhg Caoch, son of William O'Cellaigh, was the O'Cellaigh; and William‡, son of Aedh, son of Brian, was opposed to him on the eastern side of the Succ; and Eoghan§ son of Murchadh O'Madughain [O'Madden] was over Sil-Anmchada; and Murchadh, son of Muirchertach, son of Donnchadh Caembanach, was king over Leinster; and Cathair, son of Conn, son of the Calbach [the Bald] over the Ui Conchobhair|| ; and Tadhg, son of Laighen, son of Ruaidhri, was the O'Duinn; and John, son of Maol-ruanaigh, son of Tadhg, son of Tadhg, was king over the Eile¶; and Gilla-na-naemh, son of Tadhg, son of Gilla-na-naemh, over the Ui Meachair** ; et alii multi in Erinn from that time forth, who are not reckoned for commemoration.

Then follows the Irish translation of Sir John Mandeville's travels to fol. 68. b. col. 2.

---

* Slain, 1495, 4. M.

† A name for the district of Clanaboy, or inheritance of Clann-Aedha-buidhe.

‡ See Geneal. Table, No. 32, in O'Donovan's "Hy Many," p. 96.

§ Ibid., No. 31.

|| That is, the O'Connor Failghe.

¶ That is, the Eile-O'Carroll.

** The Cineal Mechair, whose tribe name was Uí-Cairin, whence the barony of Ikerrin, Co. of Tipperary. The name is now Meagher.

, I have decyphered and translated from my rough notes the fore-going very curious document, by the able assistance of my friend Mr. W. M. Hennessy. We learn from it that this book was transcribed at Rossbroin, "in the country of Hy nEchach Mumhan," now Ivaugh*, the territory of O'Mahony, in the county of Cork. Rossbroin, now Ross-brin, was a castle of the O'Mahonys, in the parish of Skull, barony of West Carbery.

"The person," that is to say, the author of the original work of which this MS. contains an Irish translation, was Sir John Mande-ville, "a Knight of the people of the King of the Saxons," whose well known travels in the Holy Land were so popular in England, and in-deed in Europe, in the 14th and following centuries. It has not, I be-lieve been hitherto known that there was an Irish version of this re-markable book, made at the close of the 15th century, by an eminent Irish chieftain, Finghin O'Mathgamhna, or O'Mahony. This is no doubt the same Finghin, or Florence (as the name is generally angli-cized) O'Mahony who died in the year 1496, according to the Chrono-logy of the Four Masters, and who is described by them as Finghin O'Mahony of Fonn-iartharacht†, "general supporter of the humanity and hospitality of West Munster, a wise man, learned in the Latin and the English." The Annals of Ulster (Dublin MS.) called him "a man of understanding, penetration, learning, and knowledge in the history of the world, τοιρ η αβαρ, "in the east and here."

This description agrees very well with what we may conceive to have been the character of a man who had executed such a work as a translation into Irish of Sir John Mandeville's Travels. The writer then gives us the genealogy of this Fingin O'Mahony, up to Diarmait Mór; and the Four Masters mention another Diarmait, "a truly hos-pitable man, who never refused anything to any one," who died in 1427. This was perhaps the father of Fingin, the translator of Sir John Mande-ville. The early genealogy of Mathgamhain, son of Cian, who was a contemporary of Brian Borumha, will be found in the Append. A. to

---

* Ivaugh or Iveagh, is an attempt to soften for English pronunciation the Irish *Ibh* [ablative plural of *Ui* or *Hy*] *Eoch-adha*. See Wars of the Gael and the Gall, p. 243, Table IV., No. 8, Intr., p. clviii., n. 5.

† *Fonn-iartharach*, i. e. the western land; the name given to the territory of Hy nEachadho, the patrimony of this branch of the O'Mahonys. See Dr. O'Do-novan's note on the Four Masters, at A. D 1496.

the Danish Wars, Table V., The generations between him and the
Fingin who translated Sir John Mandeville are as follows :—

```
Mathgambain son of Cian
      |          a quo O'Mahony.
Diarmaid.
      |
Conchobhar.
      |
Diarmaid.
      |
Domhnach of the Ui n Eochad
      |
Conchobhar.
      |
† Diarmait Mór.
      |
† Fingin.
      |
† Dmbnall.
      |
Diarmait, ob. 1427.
†     |
† Fingin*, ob. 1496.
```

The Irish author of the memorandum just quoted further tells us that
Sir John Mandeville set out on his travels on Michaelmas day, 1332,
that he was thirty-four years "visiting the world;" that on his return to Rome "his book was confirmed by the Pope;" and that Fingin
O'Mahony "put it into Irish," in the year 1472.

The importance of this translation into Irish of the famous travels
of Sir John Mandeville can scarcely be exaggerated. If it were
transcribed and printed, it would probably add considerably to our
Irish vocabulary; and it would also establish the state of the text of
Sir John's work at the close of the 15th century, which is suspected
of having been corrupted by many interpolations of the monks, with
a view to promote pilgrimages to the Holy Land. That Sir John's book
was "confirmed by the Pope," is expressly stated by himself. See
Halliwell's edition, Lond. 1860, pp. 314, 315.

It is worthy of notice that the earliest printed edition of the work,
with a date, was that in Italian, by Pietra de Cornero, Milan, 1480,
4to. which was followed by the edition in English, printed at West-

---

* The names marked (†) are given in
the passage just quoted from the Rennes
MS. They will also be found, with the
earlier portion of the genealogy, in Cron-
nelly's Hist. of the Eoghanachts, in a note,
quoted from a Lambeth MS., p. 225.

minster, by Wynkyn de Worde, 1499, 8vo.; the Irish version of the work, written in 1472, was therefore earlier than any printed edition*.

Then we have a very curious and interesting list of the chieftains of the principal Irish tribes in this latter year. It speaks for itself, and cannot fail to be of great value to the genealogist. It will be seen that, although some preponderance is given to the southern tribes, yet the list extends to all Ireland.

It may be convenient to some readers to have here, in a tabular form, the names of the above-named chieftains under their respective clans or kingdoms :—

1. *Mac Carthy mór*. TADHG [called *Liath*, the Grey], son of Domhnall óg, son of Tadhg na Mainistrech, son of Domhnall óg.

2. *O'Sullivan Beare*, or *Berre*. DIARMAIT, s. of Tadhg, s. of Amhlaibh [or Olaf].

3. *Ui Echach.* DONNCHAD, s. of Diarmait, s. of Domhnall, s. of Finghin, and DOMHNALL, with their brothers. [The family name, after surnames were established, was O'Mathgamhna, or O'Mahony. Book of Rights, p. 256, *n.*, Topograph. Poems of O'Dubhagain and O'Huidhrin, p. lxviii. *n.* (588)].

4. *Ui Cairpre*. CORMAC, s. of Donnchadh, s. of Domhnall Riabhach [or Reagh].

---

* According to some authorities there was a Latin version of Sir John Mandeville's travels, printed at Liége, in 1455; but others tell us that this edition is without date. The truth is, that this Latin version was made from the original French, in 1355, at Liége, but printed at Venice, perhaps about the year 1455, although the date of printing is not given. See the colophon at the end of it. A fine copy of this rare book is in the Library of Trinity College, Dublin. It forms one of a series of five Tracts, bound together, which were all evidently printed at the same time, and were probably issued in the same volume. The book has no pagination. The tracts it contains are (1) S. Bonaventuræ animæ et hominis interioris dialogus, *sign.* a— (in eights); (2) Proverbia in theutonico primo deinde in Latino sibi invicem consonantia, *sign.* a—d; (3) Liber cujus auctor fertur Joannes de Mandeville, *sign.* A—H; (4) Ludolphi de itinere ad terram sanctam (1336), *sign.* aa—hh; (5) Liber Marci Pauli de Veneciis, De Consuetudinibus et conditionibus orientalium regionum, *sign.* a—k.

Sir John Mandeville died at Liége, 17 Nov., 1372. Many MSS. of his Travels exist in our public libraries; but as Sir John died before the invention of printing, it is not wonderful that a century should have elapsed after his death before the book was printed.

5. *Mac Carthy Cairbrech.* DIARMAIT, s. of Domhnall Riabhach [or Reagh]. See the genealogy, *Life of Florence Mac Carthy,* by Daniel Mac Carthy, p. 453.

6. *Slicht Diarmada Remhair.* DOMHNALL, s. of Domhnall, s. of Domhnall Cluasach.

7. *O'Eidirsceoil* (or *O'Driscoll*) *mór.* FINGHIN, s. of Mac Con, s. of Mac Con, s. of Finghin.

8. *Musgraidhe* (or *Muskerry*). CORMAC, s. of Tadhg, s. of Cormac.

9. *The O'Brien.* DONNCHAD óg, s. of Tordealbach [or Turlogh], s. of Mathgamhain [or Mahon].

10. *The O'Neill.* HENRY, s. of Eoghan, s. of Niall óg.

11. *Trian Conghail,* or *Clann-Aedha-Buidhe* [now *Clanaboy*]. CONN, s. of Aedh Buidhe, s. of Brian Ballagh.

12. *O Neill Buidhe.* The brother of Aedh Buidhe (see No. 11).

13. *The O'Donnell* (with the power of lower Connacht). AEDH RUADH, s. of Niall Garbh, s. of Tordealbach an Fina.

14. *The O'Conchobhair* [or *O'Conor*]. FEIDHLIM, s. of Tordealbach, s. of Aedh, s. of Tordealbach.

15. *The O'Cellaigh* [or *O'Kelly*]. TADHG CAOCH, s. of William O'Cellaigh; but William, s. Aedh, s. of Brian, was opposed to him on the Eastern side of the river Suck [i. e. in Dealbhna Nuadhat].

16. *Sil Anmchada* [the *O'Madughain,* or *O'Madden*]. EOGHAN, s. of Murchad O'Madughain.

17. *King of Leinster.* MURCHADH, s. of Muircheartach, s. of Donchadh Caemhanach [Kavenagh].

18. *O'Conchobhar* [*Failghe*]. CATHAIR, s. of Con, s. of the Calbach.

19. *O'Duinn* (*O'Dunne*). TADHG, s. of Laighen, s. of Ruaidhri.

20. *King of Eile* [i. e. *Eile* or *Ely O Carroll*]. TADHG, s. of Tadhg.

21. *O'Meachair.* GILLA-NA-NAEMH, s. of Tadhg, s. of Gilla-na-naemh.

Fol. 69. a. col. 1.—Here follows a religious tract of no historical interest, to fol. 74 a.

Fol. 74. b.—was originally blank, but now contains the following note:—

"Ambitiosus honos, luxus, turpisque voluptas
Haec tria pro trino Numine mundus habet.

Miri emainn óg o Cealluiʒ bo
reniob an nanb laibni ri ain baile
puirc an nibeni .i. anra Ʒleanb, an
reireb la bo mi Auʒurc, 1599, an
ceb bliabain bo coʒab Muimneb a
naiʒaibi ʒall ; ┐ ʒo ma leoran cneo-
bar rin ma ca coil bia [*read* Dé] linn
bocum na ʒuiʒi rin bo benam.

" I am Edmond óg O'Kelly who wrote*
this Latin verse in Baile-Puirt-an-Ridéri*,
i. e. in the Glenn, the sixth day of the
month of August, 1599; the first year of
the war of the Munstermen against the
Foreigners; and may this plundering fall
upon them, if the will of God be with us in
making this prayer.

The " Foreigners" here spoken of are of course the English. A
full account of the " war" alluded to will be found in the Four Masters
(1599, 1600), O'Sullevan Beare, *Hist. Catholicor. Ibern. Compend.* (tom.
iii. lib. 5. c. ix.), and other authorities. The unfortunate expedition of
the Earl of Essex in Munster is no doubt intended.

Fol. 75. a. col. 1.—The Life of St. Colman, son of Luachan, com-
mencing " Viriliter agite et confortetur cor vestrum omnes qui speratis
in Domino :" the rest is in Irish ; it occupies fifteen leaves. I am not
aware of the existence of any copy of this Life in Ireland. Colgan does
not appear to have had it in his possession. He makes no mention of
it, and has made up a short life, compiled by himself, from the various
notices of St. Colman mac Luachain, and of his half brother, who was
also named Colman. *Acta SS.* 30 *Mart.*, p. 792.

There is great confusion between these two saints, in consequence
of their having had the same name, as well as from the similarity in the
names of their churches. Lassar, their common mother, had two
sons, both named Colman, but by different fathers. One of these, called
also *Mo-Colm-og* (with the diminutive affix *og*, little or beloved, and
the devotional prefix *mo*, my, that is to say, " my special saint or patron"), was venerated on the 30th March. He was of the tribe of Hua
Guala, whose territory was Gail-fhine in Ulster ; his church was *Lann-
mocholmog* [church of St. Mocholmog] now Magheralin or Maralin, in
Dalaradia in Ulster. The other Colman, *mac Luachain*, or son of

---

* " The town of the Knight's port in
the Glenn." Dr. Reeves suggests that this
must be Glin, or Glenn-Corbraighe, in the
N. W. of the Co. of Limerick, where there
is a good harbour on the Shannon, where
the *Knight of Glin* resides, and from which
he takes his title ; in Irish, *Ridire an Gle-*
anna. The castle of Glin was called Cloch-
Glenna. It was surprised and sacked, and
every soul within it put to death, including
some women and children, by Sir George
Carew, President of Munster, aided by the
Earl of Thomond, in 1600. See *Four
Masters*.

Luachan, was venerated on the 17th of June, at a place in Meath, called also *Lann*, and *Lann-mic-Luachain* [church of the son of Luachan], to distinguish it from the *Lann*, or church of his half-brother. This Luachan was son of Aedh, son of Maine, son of Fergus Cearbhaill, son of Conall Crimhthann, son of Niall of the Nine Hostages. Both the brothers Colman flourished at the close of the 7th century. See Colgan, *ubi supra*, and Four Masters, at A. D. 699.

It is probable that the Irish Life of St. Colman mac Luachain preserved in the Rennes MS., would effectually remove this confusion between the two brothers; and I regret very much, for that reason, that it was not in my power, during my stay at Rennes, to transcribe it; but it would have taken at least a fortnight's hard work to do so; and as I was ordered abroad for relaxation, and to escape hard work, this was to me impossible.

Fol. 90. a.—Here follows, in a most beautiful hand, a copy of the Dinnsenchus, or History of the Forts of Ireland. This part of the volume is certainly as old as the close of the 13th or beginning of the 14th century.

It commences thus :—

Senchair bind Erend inro do ꞃiᵹne amonᵹein mac amalᵹa inꝼile dona deirib cemꝧach . . .

The history of the forts of Erinn begins here, which Amorgein, son of Ambalgaidh, the Poet of the Deisi of Tara, wrote . .

Of this tract we have several copies—a very good one (although imperfect) in the book of Leinster in Trinity College, and others in the Library of this Academy. But the Rennes copy exceeds in beauty of penmanship almost any MS. of its date that I have ever seen.

With this the volume terminates.

It is unfortunately impossible, as I have been informed, consistently with the rules of the Rennes Library, to obtain a loan of this, to us, singularly interesting volume; but if any competent Irish scholar, who could spend some weeks at Rennes, would transcribe the Irish version of Sir John Mandeville's Travels, and the Life of St. Colman mac Luachain, he would confer a most important benefit on Irish literature.

DE QUIBUSDAM EPISCOPIS.

BODLEIAN MS.; RAWLINSON, No. 480.

[See Proceedings of the Royal Irish Academy, vol. ix. (1865) p. 184.]

ISU Cpirc, Mapia, Pacpaic, Colum Cille, bpiʒiʒ.—Cuimpe cuimniʒċe punna ap apoile ʒo eappoccaiʒ Epenn ʒa naċ áipmcep puiʒe earpocʒa anopa, ʒé ʒombaʒ áipmeʒa ina puiʒiʒ aʒur peiʒ uʒepne.

Ċuiʒ a léʒċóip na púiʒe ap copaċ, ir na heappoico iapccain.

Mipi an Duʒalcaʒ mao ṗipʒipiʒ eʒrap po 17 Mapċii anno Chpircı 1665 no 1666.

Aċaʒ Caoin.—Caċbaʒ mac Pepʒupa eprcop Aċaiʒ caoin cenceppimo anno aecacir puae obiıc.

Noca: ʒo maʒ ıonann Aċuʒ caoin aʒur cinn annpo.

Achaʒ Cinn.—Caċʒub mac Pepʒupa eprcop Aċaiʒ Cinn, anno Chpircı 554. Caoʒa ap céʒ bliaʒna apaoʒal.

Aċaʒ Coʒapċa.—bpiʒiʒ inʒen Dallbponaiʒ, ¬ Diapmaiʒ, aʒur Aonʒur, aʒur Eprcop Eoʒan—ʒo Pocapcaiʒ ʒóiʒ. Icé pil in Achaʒ Coʒapċa i ccpich Ua nDuach muiʒe hAipʒeʒpoip.

Aipʒ Ṁóip—Deacclan Aipʒe Moipe, eprcop aʒur conferróip; ʒo piól Péʒleimıʒ peaċcmaip pi Epenn. Dona heappoccaiʒ baʒap pia bPacpaic in Epinn in Declan pin.

---

[1] For the annotations the translator is indebted to W. M. Hennessy, M.R.I.A.

[2] *Achadh-Caoin* (or *Achadh-cinn*). This place has not been satisfactorily identified. Colgan (*Trias Thaum.*, p. 182) thought that it was the same place as Achadh-na-Cille (Aughnakilly, barony of Kilconway, county of Antrim). See Reeves's *Down and Conner*, p. 89, note [n], and O'Donovan's *Four Masters*, A.D. 554, note [o].

[3] *Oathbadh—Cathdubh.* Different names of the same person, who is called *Cathub* in the Martyrologies of Tallaght and Donegal, where his obit is entered under April 6. The Four Mast. (A. D. 554) also write the name *Cathub;* but the Chron. Scotorum (A. D. 555) has

ON SOME BISHOPS OF IRELAND,

BY DUALD MAC FIRBIS.[1]

TRANSLATED BY D. H. KELLY, M. R. I. A.

———◆———

JESUS, MARY, PATRICK, COLUMB CILLE, BRIGIT.—Brief memorials here of certain Bishops of Erinn, for whom episcopal sees are not now reckoned; although they were reckoned in their own times and sees.

Take notice, reader, that the sees are placed first, and the bishops after.

I am Duald Mac Firbis who arranges this, the 17th March, Anno Christi 1665 or 1666.

ACHADH-CAOIN.[2]   Cathbadh,[3] son of Fergus, bishop of Achadh-Caoin; in the one hundred and fiftieth year of his age he died.

NOTE: Haply Achad-Caoin and [Achadh]-Cinn are identical.

ACHADH-CINN.—Cathdubh,[3] son of Fergus, bishop of Achadh-Cinn, Anno Christi 554; fifty and one-hundred years his age.

ACHADH-TOGARTHA.—Brigid, daughter of Dallbronagh, and Diarmaid and Ængus, and Bishop Eoghan; they were of the Fotharta.[4] It is they who are in Achadh-Togartha,[5] in the territory of Hy Duach of the plain of Airgedros.[6]

ARDMORE.[7]—Declan of Ardmore, bishop and confessor, of the race of Fedhlimidh Rectmhar, king of Erinn. This Declan was of the bishops that were in Erinn before Patrick.

Cathbadh. The latter authority also gives his age as 150 years.

[4] *Fotharta :* now the barony of Forth, county of Carlow ; called *Fothartha-Ui-Nolain*, or O'Nolan's Fothartha, to distinguish it from other districts called Fothartha.

[5] *Achadh-Togartha.* See next note.

[6] *Airgedros.* Ui-Duach, or Hy-Duach, is represented by the present parish of Odogh, barony of Fassadineen, county of Kilkenny. But, according to an Inquisition taken in the year 1635, the district of Ui-Duach was then considered co-extensive with the said barony. See O'Donovan's note, Four Masters, A. D. 850, note e, and MS. 24, C. 6., R. I. A.

[7] Barony of Decies-within Drum, Co. Waterford.

Cipeʒal Muaꝺain. .i. Muaꝺan eprcop ó ꝺipeʒal Muaꝺain; 30 Auʒurc.

Cipiuꝺ Ionꝺuiʒ.—Ꝺiapmaiꝺ eprcop ó Oipiuꝺ Ionꝺuiʒ.

Cipʒiall.—Qoꝺ O Ceallaiꝺe eprcop Cipʒiall, ir cenn cananać Epenn, quieuic 1182.

Maoliopa O Cepꝫaill, eprcop Cipʒiall, quieuic 1187.

Maoliopa mac an eprcoip mic Maoilćiapain, eprcop Cipʒiall, ꝺo ćcc 1195.

Niocol mac Cacapaiʒ, eprcop Cipʒiall, floruit anno 1356.

Ꝺpian mac Cacmail, eprcop Cipʒiall, ꝺo ćcc 1358.

Qoꝺ Ua hЄóćaiʒ, eprcop Cipʒiall, quieuic 1369.

Cipćep aćaiꝺ.—Luʒaiꝺ eprcop Cipćep aćaiꝺ.

Cipćep Laiʒen.—Flaićeṁ Ua Ꝺuiꝺiꝺip, eprcop aipćep Laiʒen, ꝺo ecc 1104.

Ꝺaʒꝺan inꝺip Ꝺaoile, .i. eprcop, in aipćep Laiʒen aca in Inꝺep Ꝺaoile. 13 Sept.

Cipćep Maiʒe.—Ꝺiapmaiꝺ mac Mećaip eprcop ó Cipćep maiʒe, i cCuaić paća i ꝼꝼepaiꝺ Manach.

Qolmaʒ.—Seóc neprcoip ó Qolmúiʒ .i. in Ꝺomnach mór .i. un. neprcoip Ꝺomnaiʒ móip Qolmuiʒe. Már 6 ro aca Qolmaʒ i mꝺpeipne Ui Ruaipc.

Ꝺallan Qolmuiʒe eprcop, 14 December.

Qonꝺpuim.—Cuimine eprcop nQonꝺpoma, quieuic cipca annum 661.

Oeʒeććaip eprcop nQonꝺpoma, pausat 730.

Colman eprcop nQonꝺpoma, quieuic 871.

Cponan beʒ, eprcop nQonꝺpoma, anno Cpirci 642. Ʒo maꝺ 6 ro le ccuipcep Caenꝺpuim; ꝼec Caonꝺpuim.

Mochoma eprcop nQonꝺpoma.

---

[1] Errigal, county of Monaghan.

[2] *Airiud-Ionduigh*, not identified.

[3] Airgiall (Oriel), i. e. bishopric of Clogher.

[4] *O'Cellaigh*. The Four Mast. and the Ann. L. Cé, &c., call him O'Caellaighi, or O'Kealy; but in Ware's list of the bishops of Clogher, he is called O'Kelly.

[5] Ann. L. Cé, and IV. M.

[6] IV. M.; but Ware says in 1184.

[7] Ware.

[8] Ob. 1356, Four Masters.

[9] IV. M.

[10] *Aedh O'Heothaigh :* i. e. Hugh O'Hoey. His name is not in Ware's list of the bishops of Clogher. The IV. M. have the death of Aodh O'Neill, bishop of Clogher, at the year 1369, as also the Annals of Loch Cé; and the name Ua Heothaigh is probably a mistake for

AIREGAL-MUADHAIN.[1] — Muadhan, bishop of Airegal-Muadhain, 30th August.

AIRIUD-IONDUIGH.[2]—Diarmaid, bishop of Airiud-Ionduigh.

AIRGIALL.[3]—Hugh O'Cellaigh,[4] bishop of Airghiall, and head of the canons of Erinn, quievit 1182.[5]

Maolisa O'Carroll, bishop of Airgiall, went to his rest 1187.[6]

Maolisa, son of the bishop Mac Maelchiaran, bishop of Airgiall, died 1195.[7]

Nicholas Mac Cathasaigh, bishop of Airgiall, flourished 1356.[8]

Brian Mac Cathmail, bishop of Airgiall, died 1358.[9]

Aodh O'Heothaigh,[10] bishop of Airgiall, quievit 1369.

AIRTHER-ACHAIDH.[11]—Lughaidh, bishop of Airther-achaidh.

AIRTHER-LAIGHEN.[12] — Flaithemh O'Dwyer, bishop of Airther-Laighen, died 1104.[13]

Dagdan of Inbher-Daile,[14] id est bishop; in Airther-Laighen he is, in Inbher-Daile, 13 Sep.[15]

AIRTHER-MAIGHE.[16]—Diarmaid, son of Mechar, bishop of Airther-Maighe, in Tuath-ratha[17] in Fermanagh.

AOLMAGH.[18]—Seven bishops from Aolmagh, id est in Domhnach-mor ; viz., seven bishops of Domhnach-mor-Aolmaighe. If this be so, Aolmagh is in Breifne-O'Ruairc.

Dallan of Aolmagh, bishop, 14 December.[19]

AONDRUIM.[20]—Cummine, bishop of Aondruim, quievit circa annum 661.[21]

Oegetchair, bishop of Aondruim, pausat 730.[22]

Colman, bishop of Aondruim, quievit 871.[23]

Cronan Beg, bishop of Aondruim, anno Christi 642.[24] Perhaps this is he with whom Caendruim is placed. See Caendruim.

Mochoma, bishop of Aendruim.

---

that of O'Neill.

[11] Airther-Achaidh, not identified.

[12] Airther-Laighen ; East Leinster.

[13] Four Masters.

[14] Inbher-Daile ; Ennereilly, county of Wicklow.

[15] Mart. Taml. and Mart. Doneg.

[16] Airther-Maighe. Armoy, Co. Fermanagh.

[17] Tuath-ratha. Tooraah in Fermanagh.

[18] Aolmagh. Donaghmore, barony of Dromahaire, county of Leitrim.

[19] Mart. Doneg.

[20] Aondruim. Mahee Island, in Strangford Lough.

[21] Four Masters, 658 : Tig. and Chron. Scot. 659.

[22] IV. M.

[23] IV. M.

[24] Ob. IV. M.

Cpiocan eppcop nαonopoma, anno Cpipci 632.

Cuimen eppcop nαonopoma, anno bomini 698.

αpa.—θccnech comapba θnna αipne, eppcop azup ancoipe, anno 916.

αelchu bapab ainm pupa αipne, mac Paolcaip mic θbαluiz; azup pa pí Oppuize in Paolcaip pin. αp uaio píol Paolcaip la hOppaize. Uime abbepap bo pupa .i. papa; ó po zab abbaine na Roma cap óip nZpezoip, azup poppacaib a abbaine azup bo luio bo iappuio a maizipbpech caipip zo hiapcap θoppa, azup zo hαpuinn na nóem; zonab í an cpep pelic ainzil αipne pelic Þupa mic Paelcaip mic θabaluiz.

bpecan (nó bpacan) eppcop: zo mab ó po bpecan αipme i ccill bhpecáin i ncuao Muinan.

αpo bpecain.—αelznao eppcop aipo bpecain, mopcuup 776.

Maoluma eppcop aipo bpecain, ob. 823.

bpecan eppcop (aipbe bpecain Mibe), no abb Maize bile, 6 December.

αpo capna.—beoaio eppcop αpba capna, quieuic 523. α péil ap an 8. lá bo Mapca.

αpo ppaca.— eppcop θozan αpba ppaca.

Mopp Maoilpozapcaiz, eppcop αpba ppaca, 678.

Coibben eppcop αpba ppaca, quieuic 705. Ooiz zup ionann ip Coibbenac eppcop αpba ppaca, cepba anno Cpipci 706, pa péil aca ap an 26 la bo November.

αc-ba-laapz.—eppcop Coinne ó ach ba laapz (1° Decʳ.) i ccaob chenannpa i Mibe.

---

¹ 638, Chron. Scot. and IV. M.

² *Cuimen.* This Cuimen is not referred to in any of the Irish Annals;
and the editor does not know where Mac
Firbis found the date of his obit.

³ The Great island of Aran, in Galway
Bay.

⁴ Four Masters.

⁵ *Pupa.* In the Life of S. Endeus,
published by Colgan, a note occurs relative to this Pupa, or Papa, of which
the following is a translation :—

"Three holy men went from Ireland
into Britain, &c.; after some time they
went to Rome. At this time the Roman
pontiff died, and the people and clergy
sought to make S. Pupeus, one of the
three, pope, but which he refused to
consent to, and St. Hilarius was made
comarb of Peter. . . . At length the
three return to Ireland, and go to
Aran."—Act. SS. p. 708, cap. 19.

⁶ *Cill-Breeain;* now Kilbreckan, barony of Upper Bunratty, county of Clare.

Criotan, bishop of Aondruim, [ob.] anno Christi 632.[1]

Cuimen,[2] bishop of Aondruim, [ob.] anno Domini 698.

ARA.[3]—Eccnech, comarb of Enna of Ara, bishop and anchorite, [ob.] anno 916.[4]

Aelchu, who was named the Pope of Ara, the son of Faolchar, son of Edalach; the said Faolchar was king of Ossory, and from him descend the race of Faolchar in Ossory. The reason why he was called Pupa[5] (Pope), was because he obtained the abbacy of Rome after Gregory; and he vacated the abbacy, and went in search of his master (i. e. Gregory), across to the west of Europe, and to Ara of the saints; so that the third angelical cemetery of Ara is the cemetery of Pupa, son of Faolchar, son of Edalach.

Brecan, or Bracan, bishop. Perhaps this is Brecan of Ara, who is [venerated] in Cill-Brecain[6] in Thomond.

ARD-BRECAIN.[7]—Aelgnad, bishop of Ard-Brecan, died 776.[8]

Maoluma,[9] bishop of Ard-Brecain, ob. 823.

Brecan, bishop (of Ard-Brecain in Meath), or abbot of Magh-Bile,[10] 6 December.[11]

ARD-CHARNA.[12]—Beo Aedh [Aedus vivus], bishop of Ard-Carna, quievit 523.[13] His festival is on the eighth day of March.[14]

ARD-SRATHA.[15]—Owen, bishop of Ard-Sratha.

Death of Maelfogharty, bishop of Ard-Sratha, 678.[16]

Coibden, bishop of Ard-Sratha, quievit 705. Probably this is the same as Coibdenach, bishop of Ard-Sratha, who died A. D. 706,[17] whose festival is on the 26th day of November.[18]

ATH-da-laarg.[19]—Bishop Coinne from Ath-da-laarg (1st December), near Cenannus, in Meath.

---

[7] *Ard-Brecain*, county of Meath.

[8] Four Masters.

[9] *Maoluma*. The Four Masters record, under A. D. 823, the death of a Maelrubha, bishop of Ard-Brecain.

[10] *Magh-Bile*. Moville, county of Down. The festival of Brecan, abbot or bishop of Magh-Bile, is set down in the Calendar at 29 April.

[11] Mart. Doneg.

[12] *Ard-Charna;* Ardcarne, barony of

Boyle, county of Roscommon.

[13] Four Masters; 518, Chron. Scot.

[14] Mart. Doneg.

[15] *Ard-Sratha.* Ardstraw, county of Tyrone.

[16] IV. M. Chron. Scot.

[17] Ann. Ulster and Chron. Scot.

[18] Mart. Doneg.

[19] *Ath-da-laarg.* "Ford of two forks;" near Kells, county of Meath.

Ⱥⱦ ⱄⱆⱁⱃⱀ.—Ⰼⱁⱀⱀⱑⱄ ⱄⱆⱁⱃⱀ, eppcop Ⰿⰹⰾⰾe Ⰼⰹⱀⱀⱆe, ⱁ Ⱥⱦ ⱄⱆⱈⱃⱀ ⰹⱀ Oppⰰⰹⰶe 2 Feb.

Ⱥⱦh ⱂⰰⱄⰰⱄ.—Ⰻⱄ eppcop o Ⱥⱦ ⱂⰰⱄⰰⱄ ⰹ Lⰰⰹⰷⱀⰹⱴ, 14 Julii.

Ⰰⱆh ⱄⱃⱆⰹⱞ.—Ⰼoⱃⱞⰹⱄⰰⱄⰹo Coⱃⱞⰰⰹⱆ eppcop Ⰰⱆhⰰ ⱄⱃⱆⰹⱞ, 741.

Ⰼoⰹⱃⱆeⱃⱀ eppcop (ⱄⰹⱃⰶⰹⱴⱆⰾ Ⰼⰰⱄⱃⰰⰹⱆⱆ), ⱁ Ⰰⱆ ⱄⱃⱆⰹⱞ ⰰ Lⰰoⰷⰰⰹⱃe, ⰼⰹ Oⱆⱄoⱴeⱃ.

Cennⱂⰰeⰾⰰⱄ eppcop Ⰰⱆhⰰ ⱄⱃⱆⰹⱞ, ⱨⱆⰹeⱆⰹⱆ 819.

Loⱞⰰⱀ, eppcop ⱁ ⰰⱆh ⱄⱃⱆⰹⱞ (ⱄⰹⱃⰷⰹⱴⱆⰾ Ⰼⰰⱄⱃⰰⰹⱆ) ⰼⰹ Oⱆⱄoⱴeⱃ.

Ⱞⰰoⰾⱑⱆⰹⱀ eppcop ⰰⰷⱆⱃ ⰰⱀⰷⱆoⰹⱃe ⰰⱆhⰰ ⱄⱃⱆⰹⱞ, 929.

Coⱃⱞⰰⱆ eppcop Ⱥⱄⰰ ⱄⱃⱆⰹⱞ, ⰰⰷⱆⱃ coⱞⰰⱃⱴⰰ Ⰼⰰⱄⱃⰰⰹⱆ; anno 496, 17 February.

Oⱃⱃⰰⰹⱀ eppcop o Rⰰⰹⱄ Oⱃⱃⰰⰹⱀ ⱂⱃⰹ Ⰰⱆh ⱄⱃⱆⰹⱞ ⰰⱀⰹⰰⱃ; anno Cⱃⰹⱃⱆⰹ 686 ; February 17.

Cⱆⰹⱞen eppcop ⰹⱀ Ⰰⱆ ⱄⱃⱆⰹⱞ; February 17.

Lⰰⱆhⱄⰰⱀ eppcop ⰹⱀ Ⰰⱆ ⱄⱃⱆⰹⱞ; February 17.

ⱴⰰⰹⰾe Slⰰⰹⱀe.—eⰰⱃⱆ Slⰰⰹⱀe eppcop Lⰹoⰾⱆⰰⰹⰷ, ⰹⱃ ⱁ Ⰼeⱃⱄⰰ ⱂeⱃ ⱂeⰷ ⰹ ⱄⱆⰰoⱴ Sⰹoⱴⰰ Ⱄⱃⱆⰹⱞ ⰰⱀⰰⰹⱃ ; anno 512 ⰰⱀ ⱄⰰⱀ ⱄeⱃⱴⰰ, ⰾⱆ. ⰰ ⱄoⰹⱃ. Ⰰⱃ ⱁ ⰰⱄⰰ ⰹ ⱞⱴⰰⰹⰾe Slⰰⰹⱀe et cetera.

ⱴennⱆoⱃ.—Ⰼⱆⰹⱴⰹⱀⱃⰹ, ⱃⰰoⰼ ⰰⰷⱆⱃ eppcop ⱞⱆⰹⱀⱆⰹⱃe ⱴennⱆⰰⰹⱃ, 951.

Ⰼⰹⰰⱃⱞⰰⰹⱴ O Ⱞⰰoⰹⰾⱆeⰾⱆhⰰ, coⱞⰰⱃⱴⰰ Choⱞⰷⰰⰹⰾⰾ, eⰰⱆⱆⱀⱆⰹⱴ ⱂoⰹⱃⱆⱆe, ⱃⰷⱃⰹⱴⱀⰹⱴ ⰰⰷⱆⱃ eppcop, ⱴo ⱁⰷ 1016.

Ⰼⰰⱀⰹeⰾ eppcop ⱴenⱴⱆⰰⰹⱃ, 11 Septembris.

Ceⰾe Ⰼⰰⱴⰰⰹⰾⰾ ⱞⰰⱆ Sⰷⰰⱀⱴⰰⰹⰾ, eppcop eⱆ ceⱆeⱃⰰ, ⱴo ⱁⱆ 927. Ceⰾe Ⰼⰰⱴⰰⰹⰾⰾ ⱞⰰⱆ Sⰷⰰⱀⱴⱆⰹⰾ ⱴo ⱴⱆⰾ ⱴon Roⰹⱞ ⰰ hⰰⱴⱴⰰⰹⱀe ⱴenⱴⱆⰰⰹⱃ, 926.

---

[1] *Ath-Duirn*, i. e. "the *Ford of Dorn*." The Mart. of Donegal adds that *Dorn* was the name of a hill in Magh-Raighne. It was probably near or at Cill-Finnche.

[2] *Cill-Finnche;* the church of Finneoh, now Killinny, in the parish and barony of Kells, county of Kilkenny.

[3] *Ath-fadat;* Aghade, or Ahade, barony of Forth, county of Carlow.

[4] Mart. Doneg.

[5] *Ath-Truim;* Trim, county of Meath.

[6] Four Masters; 745, Ann. Ult.

[7] *Laoghaire,* or Ui-Laoghaire, the ancient name of a district comprising the greater part of the present baronies of Upper and Lower Navan, county of Meath.

[8] Mart. Doneg.

[9] IV. M.

[10] Mart. Doneg.

[11] *Maolécin.* This name is written Maeleoin (Malone) by the Four Masters. He was probably the same as Maeloin,

ATH-DUIRN.[1]—Finnech-Duirn, bishop of Cill-Finche[2] from Ath-duirn in Ossory, 2 Feb.

ATH-FADAT.[3]—Id, bishop of Ath-fadat, in Leinster, July 14.[4]

ATH-TRUIM.[5]—Dormitatio of Cormac, bishop of Ath-truim, 741.[6]

Fortchern, bishop (disciple of Patrick), from Ath-truim, in Laoghaire,[7] 11 October.[8]

Cennfaeladh, bishop of Ath-truim, quievit, 819.[9]

Loman, bishop, from Ath-truim, a disciple of Patrick, 11 October.[10]

Maolécin,[11] bishop and anchorite of Ath-Truim, ob. 929.[12]

Cormac, bishop of Ath-truim, and comarb of Patrick, [ob.] anno 496,[13] 17 Feb.[14]

Bishop Ossan, from Rath-Ossain,[15] to the west of Ath-truim, anno Christi 686,[16] 17 Feb.[17]

Cuimen, bishop in Ath-truim, 17 Feb.[18]

Lachtan, bishop in Ath-truim, 17 Feb.[19]

BAILE SLAINE.[20]—Erc of Slane, bishop of Liolcagh, and from Ferta-fer-feg, at the eastern side of Sidh-truim. It was the year 512[21] when he died: his age was 90. It is he that is (venerated) in the town of Slane, &c.

BENNCHOR.[22]—Duibhinsi, a most eminent man, and bishop of the community of Bennchar, 951.[23]

Diarmaid O'Maeltelcha, comarb of Comghall, a perfect wise man, scribe and bishop, died in 1016.[24]

Daniel, bishop of Benncha, 11 September.[25]

Ceile-Dabhaill, son of Scannall, went to Rome from the abbacy of Benncha, 926.[26]

bishop and anchorite, whose festival is given in the Mart. Dung. at the 20th of October.

[13] Four Masters.

[13] IV. M. and Chron. Scot.

[14] Mart. Doneg. and Mart. Taml.

[15] *Rath-Ossain.* This was the name of a place a little to the west of Trim. In the Annals of Ulster and of the Four Masters, Ossan, or Osseni, is called bishop of Monasterboice.

[16] Ann. Ult.

[17] Mart. Doneg. and Mart. Taml.

[18] Mart. Taml.

[19] Mart. Taml.

[20] *Baile Slaine.* Slane, county of Meath.

[21] Four Masters; 513, Chron. Scot.

[22] *Bennchor;* Bangor, county of Down

[23] IV. M.

[24] IV. M.; 1017, Chron. Scot.

[25] Mart. Taml. and Mart. Doneg.

[26] IV. M.

beʒ Épe.—Eppcop Iubap baoi in Epinn na eppcop puil caíniʒ Paopaiʒ na eppcop ince, oo oiciʒ ipin inip (ap muip laim le Laiʒnib) oana hainm beʒ Épe. Cepoa anno Chpipci 500. A pel 23 Appeil.

Cponnmael abb beʒ Epenn, eppcop ip pep leʒino Camlabca, 964.

bioppa.—Oooiu, eppcop bioppa, 842.

Plaichnia eppcop bioppa, mortuus 851.

Oó clúain.—Ppaocan eppcop ó oó clúain i Laoiʒip, ó chluain ·ironech paip, nó ap oeulaib plebe blaoma in oó clúain, nó ó Inip mic Eapca, no o Inpi mic Eapca.

boch conaip.—Céle Cpipc, ó cill Cele Cpipc; in Uib Oun-chaoa, i ppocapcuib a Laiʒnib aca Cill Cele Cpipc ó boich conuip, 3 Marta.

bpecmuiʒ.—Aiobce eppcop ip abb éipe oa ʒlaip.

Aiobe .i. aoobeó, uaip ba beó epén a bpeapcaib aʒup a míopbuilib. Aca a ceall ppi hímlec anoep, no i mbpeemuiʒ a cCepa in iapcap Connachc.

bpepne.—Aób O Pino, eppcop na bpepne, oo óʒ in Inip Clo-cpainn, 1136.

Plann Ua Connachcaiʒ eppcop na bpepne, quieuic 1132.

Siomon o puaipc, eppcop na bpeipne, quieuic 1285.

Maca maʒ Ouibne, eppcop na bpeipne, quieuic 1314.

Eppcop na bpeipne .i. O Cpiobacain, quieuic 1328.

Concobap mac Connama, eppcop na bpeipne, quieuic 1355.

[1] Beg-Eri; Beggery Island, Wexford Harbour.

[2] Four Masters, and Chron. Scot.

[3] Mart. Doneg. and Mart. Taml.

[4] IV. M.

[5] Biorra; Birr, King's County.

[6] IV. M.

[7] IV. M.

[8] Bo-chluain, "Cow's lawn or (meadow)." From the description, it would appear that two places in Laighis (Leix, Queen's County,) were so called—one to the east of Clonenagh, and the other somewhat to the west of it, or in front of Sliabh-Bladhma. The one here re-ferred to is a couple of miles to the west of Maryborough.

[9] Both-Chonais, pronounced Bo-cho-nais. This establishment is now repre-sented by the old grave-yard in the townland of Binnion, parish of Clon-many, barony of Inishowen, and county of Donegal.

[10] Hy Dunchadha. This was the name of the tract of land extending between the River Liffey and the Dublin moun-tains, the patrimony of the family of Mac Gilla Mocholmog, for an account of whom see Gilbert's "History of Dublin," vol. i. pp. 230, 403.

BEG-ERI.[1]—Bishop Ibhar, who was in Erinn as a bishop before Patrick came as a bishop into it, dwelt in an island (in the sea near to Leinster), which is named Beg-Eri. He died A. C. 500.[2] His festival is on the 23rd April.[3]

Cronmael, abbot of Beg-Eri, bishop and lector of Tamlacht; [died] 964.[4]

BIORRA.[5]—Dodiu, bishop of Biorra, 842.[6]

Flaithnia, bishop of Biorra, mortuus 851.[7]

BO-CHLUAIN.[8]—Fraechan, bishop of Bo-chluain, in Laighis, to the east of Cluain-eidhnech, or right before Sliabh-Bladhma, in Bo-chluain, or from Inis-mic-Erca, or from Inei-mic-Erca.

BOTH-CHONAIS.[9]—Cele-Christ, of Cill-Cele-Christ, 3 March; in Hy Dunchada,[10] in the Fotharts[11] of Leinster, is the church of Cele-Christ of Both-Chonais.

BRECMUIGH.[12]—Aidhbche, bishop and abbot of Tir-da-glais.[13]

Aidbhe i. e. Aedh-beo (Aedus vivus), for he was active in prodigies and in miracles. His church is to the south of Imlech, or in Brechmagh, in Cera, in the west of Connaught.

BREIFNE.[14]—Aedh O'Finn, bishop of the Breifne, died in Inis-Clothrainn,[15] 1136.[16]

Flann O'Connaghty, bishop of the Breifne, quievit 1132.[17]

Simon O'Ruairc, bishop of the Breifne, quievit 1285.[18]

Matthew Mac Duibhne, bishop of the Breifne, quievit 1314.[19]

The bishop of the Breifne, i. e. O'Criodachan,[20] quievit 1328.[21]

Conor Mac Connamha, bishop of the Breifne, quievit, 1355.

[11] *In the Fotharts*; ı ꝼꝋᴛᴜᴀᴛᴀıꝺ. This should probably be ı ꝼꝋᴨᴛᴜᴀᴛᴀıꝺ, "in the Fortuathas (or border lands)," as the *Fortuatha* of Leinster included the southern part of the county of Dublin, and was not confined to the territory of Ui-Mail, in Wicklow, as O'Donovan thought. (*See* "Book of Rights," p. 250, *note*.)

[12] *Brecmuigh*. Breaffy, barony of Carra, county of Mayo.

[13] *Tir-da-glais*. Terryglass, barony of Lower Ormond, county of Tipperary.

[14] *Breifne*, i. e. the present diocese of Kilmore.

[15] *Inis-Clothrainn*. Now Inisdoghran, in Lough Ree.

[16] Ann. Loch Cé, and IV. M.

[17] 1231, Ann. Four Masters, Ult., and Loch Cé.

[18] IV. M., Ann. Loch Cé, and Ware.

[19] IV. M., Ann. Loch Cé, and W.

[20] *O'Criodachan*. This seems to have been the same as the bishop who is called "Patrick" in Ware's list of the bishops of Kilmore. (Harris's ed. of "Ware," vol. i. p. 227).

[21] IV. M.; Ann. Ult.

Riccapd O Raiᵹilliᵹ, eppcop na bpeipne, do ecc 1369.

Comap mac Cindpiu meᵹ bpáduiᵹ, eppcop aᵹup eipóinneć an vd bpepne pe pó 30 bliaban, quieuic 1511.

Copmac maᵹ Sampabain, vap ᵹaipeb eppcop ip in mbpepne, quieuic 1511.

bpicania.—Ceobopup eppcop bpicanae, quieuic 689.

Caipiol loppae.—bpón eppcop ó caipiol loppae in lb Fiaópać muaibe, anno Domini 511; luin 8 la.

Caonopuim (Fopce Conopuim). — Quiep Cponain eppcop Caonopoma, cipca annum 639. Fec Conopuim.

Capn Fupbuibe.—Muaban eppcop o Capn Fupbuibe, mapca 6 mopcuup.

Ceannanup.—Maelpinnen mac Neccain, eppcop Cenannpa, comapba Ulcain aᵹup Caipniᵹ, 967.

Cillachaib, no aichib. — Reććabpa, eppcop Cille haćaib, 952.

Cillachaib bpaiᵹniᵹe.—Dubapcać, eppcop Cille achaib, quieuic 869.

eppcop Dappcać ó Cill achaibh bpaiᵹniᵹe.

Mac epc Cille achaibh, eppcop.

Cill aip.—Aeb mac bpic, eppcop, ó Cill áip i Mibe, aᵹup ó Sliab liaᵹ i ccíp bóᵹuine i ccenel Conaill, quieuic anno Cpipci 588. Q pel ꝟ⁰ Novemb.

Cill achaib bpoma poca.—Sinćell, abb Cille achaib bpoma poca, .i. an pen Sinćell, 548; 330 bliabna a aoip.

baccap 12 eppcop ip 12 oilicpeć, ᵹo niomab ele, a cCill achaib bpoma poca, in lb Failᵹe, áic ambái Sinćell popap paᵹapc, aᵹup Sinćell pinpip eppcop.

---

[1] Four Masters.

[2] IV. M.

[3] IV. M.

[4] 690 Angl. Sax. Chron.

[5] *Caisiol-Iorra;* Killaspagbrone, barony of Carbury, county of Sligo.

[6] IV. M.; 510 Chron. Scot.

[7] Mart. Doneg. and Mart. Taml.

[8] *Caondruim;* this was one of the ancient names of the hill of Tara. See next note.

[9] *Cronan.* This is apparently the Cronan mentioned under the head of Aondruim, for which Caondruim seems to be a mistake.

[10] *Carn-Furbaidhe.* It is stated in the Dinnsenchus, "Book of Lecan," fol. 231, that this was the name of a large carn on Sliabh-Cairbre, or the Carn mountain, in the north of the county of Longford; and Colgan (AA. SS., p. 253) observes that Cill-Modani was "juxta Carn-fur-

Richard O'Reilly, bishop of the Breifne, died 1369.[1]

Thomas, son of Andrew Mac Brady, bishop and herenech of the two Breifnes during 30 years, quievit 1511.[2]

Cormac Mac Samhradhain, styled bishop in the Breifne, quievit 1511.[3]

BRITANNIA.—Theodorus, bishop of Britannia, quievit 689.[4]

CAISIOL-IORRA.[5]—Bron, bishop of Caisiol-Iorra, in Hy-Fiachrach of the Moy, anno Domini 511.[6] His festival is on the 8th of June.[7]

CAONDRUIM[8] (Forte Aondruim).—Quies of Cronan,[9] bishop of Caon-druim, ob. circa annum 639. *See* Aondruim.

CARN-FURBAIDHE.[10]—Muadan, bishop of Carn-Furbaidhe, March 6 mortuus.[11]

CEANNANUS.[12]—Maolfinnen, son of Nechtan, bishop of Cennanus, comarb of Ultan[13] and of Cairneeh,[14] 967.[15]

CILL-ACHAIDH (or ACHIDH).[16]—Rechtabra, bishop of Cill-achaidh, 952.[17]

CILL-ACHAIDH-DRAIGHNIGHE.[18]—Dubhartach,[19] bishop of Cill-achaidh, quievit 869.[20]

Bishop Darrtach, from Cill-achaidh-draighnighe.

Mac Erca, bishop of Cill-achaidh.

CILL-AIR.[21]—Aedh Mac Bric, bishop of Cill-air in Meath, and from Sliabh-Liag in Tir-Boghuine, in Cinel-Conaill, quievit anno Christi 588.[22] His festival on 10th November.

CILL-ACHAIDH-DROMA-FOTA.[23]—Sinchell, abbot of Cill-achaidh-droma-fota, i. e. the Elder Sinchell, 548;[24] 330 years was his age.

There were 12 bishops and twelve pilgrims, with many others, in Cill-achaidh-droma-fota, in Ui-Failghe, where Sinchell junior was priest, and Sinchell senior bishop.

baidhe."

[11] Mart. Taml. and Mart. Doneg.

[12] Kells, county of Meath.

[13] *Ultan;* founder of Ard Brecan, in Meath.

[14] *Cairnech.* St. Cairnech of Tulen, or Dulane, near Kells, in Meath.

[15] Four Masters, Chron. Scot.

[16] *Cill-achaidh;* Killaghy, county of Fermanagh.

[17] IV. M.

[18] *Cill-achaidh-draighnighe,* the same as Cill-Achaidh of note [16].

[19] *Dubhartach.* This name is written Dubhtach by the Four Masters.

[20] IV. M.

[21] *Cill-air;* Killare, county of West-meath.

[22] Chron. Scot.; IV. M.

[23] *Cill-achaidh-dromo-fota;* Killeigh, King's County.

[24] IV. M.; Chron. Scot. 551.

Cill (poñce cairbre in) ᵹaire.—Somad Cairppe epꞃcop aca Nouembꞃiꞃ 1, do bec iꞃin cill ꞃin.

Cill aiꞃċeꞃ.—Ioain (.ı. Eóin) epꞃcop Cille aiꞃċeꞃ.

Cill baiꞃꞃinn, ꞃe hEꞃ ꞃuaid [acuaid]. — baiꞃꞃionn epꞃcop, 8 Maı.

Cill Chaꞃcuiᵹ.—I ꞇꞇiꞃ boᵹuine, 6 Maꞃca; Caꞃċaċ epꞃcop, mac Aonᵹuꞃa mic Naꞇꞃꞃaic, ꞃiᵹ Eoᵹanaċca Caiꞃil.

Cill bıa.—Neman epꞃcop ó ċill bıa, 1 Sepc.

Cill bꞃacain.—bꞃacan no bꞃecan, epꞃcop, Aiꞃꞃil 1.

Cill Cele Cꞃiꞃc.—Cele Cꞃiꞃc, epꞃcop ó cill Cele Cꞃiꞃc in 1ᵇ Dunċada ıl Laiᵹniᵇ.

Cill Cuanna.—Epꞃcop Ꝑecmeċ ó ċill Chuanna, .ı. Ꝑecmeċ ó ċill Cuama no Coama.

Cill-cuilınn.—Mac Caıl Cille cuilınn; epꞃcop eꞃide, aᵹuꞃ Eoᵹan a ainm, 548. Maoı 11.

Suıbne mac Seᵹonain, epꞃcop aᵹuꞃ ꞃiaᵹloiꞃ Cille cuilınn 962.

Cuachal Ua Ꝣaꞃbain, epꞃcop Cille cuillinn, do ecc 1030.

Cill cunᵹa.—Dabnan epꞃcop Cille cunᵹa, 11 Aꞃꞃil.

Cill da leꞃ.—Sanccan, epꞃcop, ó ċill da leꞃ, 9 Maói.

Cill duma ᵹlinn.—Moᵹenoᵹ, epꞃcop, o Cill duma ᵹluinn ı ndeꞃᵹiꞃc bꞃeᵹ, Decemb. 26.

Cill eanᵹa.—Epꞃcop Diomba ó Cill eannᵹa. Cill eꞃᵹa, poꞃce Cill poꞃᵹa.

Cill epꞃcop Sanccain.—Epꞃcop Sanccan mac Cancoin ꞃiᵹ bꞃecan.

Cill epꞃcop Dꞃonain.—Epꞃcop dꞃonan ı Cill eꞃꞃuic Dꞃonain.

---

[1] *Cill . . . ingaire.* The Compiler suggests that this might be " Cill-Cairbre." The Mart. Doneg. commemorates a bishop Cairbre at 1 November, and adds that there was a Cill-Cairbre near Assroe, in the county of Donegal.

[2] *Cill-airther ;* in Ulster.

[3] Kilbarron, county of Donegal.

[4] 21 May, Mart. Donegal and Mart. Taml.

[5] Kilcarr, barony of Banagh, county Donegal.

[6] *Tir-Boghuine.* Now the barony of Banagh, county of Donegal.

[7] 5 Mar., Mart. Doneg. and Mart. Taml.

[8] *Cill-Bia ;* not identified.

[9] Mart. Donegal.

[10] 1 May, Mart. Doneg. and Mart. Taml. ; and see above under Ara.

[11] *Cill-Cele-Christ.* See under Both-chonais.

[12] *Hy Dunchadha. See* note [10], ꞃ. 90, *supra.*

Cill- (perhaps Cairbre) Ingaire.[1]—Perhaps it is Cairbre, the bishop, who is [commemorated] Nov. 1, that is in this church.

Cill-Airther.[2]—Joain (i. e. John), bishop of Cill-airther.

Cill-Bairrinn.[3]—To the north of Es-ruadh. Bairrion, bishop, 8 May.[4]

Cill-Carthaigh.[5]—In Tir-Boghuine ;[5] 6 March,[6] Carthach, bishop, the son of Aongus, son of Nathfraech, king of the Eoghanacht of Cashel.

Cill-Bia.[9]—Nemhan, bishop of Cill-Bia, 1 September.[9]

Cill Bracan.—Bracan, or Brecan, bishop, April 1.[10]

Cill-Cele-Christ.[11]—Cele-Christ, bishop of Cill Cele-Christ, in Hy Dunchadha,[12] in Leinster.

Cill-Cuana.[13]—Fethmech, bishop of Cill-Cuana, i. e. Fethmech, bishop of Cill-Tuama, or [Cill]-Toama.

Cill-Cuilinn.[14]—Mac Tail of Cill-Cuilinn : (he was a bishop, and his name was Eoghan); 548.[15] May 11.[16]

Suibhne, son of Segonan, bishop and ruler of Cill-Cuilinn, 962.[17]

Tuathal O'Garvan, bishop of Cill-Cuilinn, died, 1030.[18]

Cill-Cunga.[19]—Dadnan, bishop of Cill-Cunga, 11 April.[20]

Cill-da-les.[21]—Sanctan, bishop of Cill-da-les, 9 May.

Cill-Duma-Glinn.[22]—Mogenog, bishop of Cill-duma-glinn, in the south of Bregia, December 26.[23]

Cill-Eanga.[24]—Bishop Dioma, from Cill-Eanga. Cill-Erga, forte Cill-Forga.

Cill-Espuc-Sanctan.[25]—Bishop Sanctan, son of Canton, king of Britain (i. e. Wales.)

Cill-Espuc-Dronan.[26] — Dronán, bishop of Cill-Espuc-Dronan.

[13] Cill-Cuana. Cill-Tuama. The former would now be written Kilquan, and the other Kiltoome. There are many places in Ireland bearing these names.

[14] Cill-Cuilinn; Old Kilcullen, county of Kildare.

[15] Four Masters; 551 Chron. Scot.

[16] May 11; recte June 11. Mart. Doneg. and Mart. Taml.

[17] IV. M.

[18] IV. M.

[19] Cill-Cunga; not identified.

[20] Mart. Doneg. and Mart. Taml.

[21] Cill-da-les; not identified.

[22] Cill-Duma-Glinn; Kilglynn, barony of Upper Decie, county of Meath.

[23] Mart. Doneg.

[24] Cill-Eanga. The Compiler adds, "Cill-erga, forte Cill-forga;" Killarga, barony of Dromahaire, county of Leitrim.

[25] Cill-Espuc-Sanctan; Kill-Saint-Anne, county of Dublin.

[26] Cill-Espuc-Dronan; not identified.

Cill Opoṅaın. Oponan epṛcop ó cıll Opoṅaın, Oecemb. 12.

Cill Ḟınnċe.—Ḟınneċ ⁊buıṛn, epṛcop Cılle Ḟınnċe o aċ Ouıṛn ın Oṛṗaıȝe, Feb. 2.

Cill Foıṛccepn, ın Uıḃ Oṛona. Foıṛccepn epṛcop, ⁊ırȝıbal Paċṛaıc, Occ. 11.

Cill poıċıṛḃe.—Fec Cuıl poıċıṛḃe.

Cill poṛȝa no Cill eaṛȝa.—Fıonnċaḃ epṛcop, Nouemb. 11.

Cill Ȝṛeallaın.—Epṛcop Ȝṛeallan (acaıḃ ⁊d ċıll Ȝṛeallaın ı ccıṛ ṗıachṛach muaıḃe), Sepc. 7.

Cill Ian.—Epṛcop Aoḃ ı Cill Ian.

Cill ınṛı.—Aılltín, epṛcop, aȝuṛ an óȝ (no ınȝen óȝ) o Cıll ınṛı. Noca.—Cıll Aılltın ın ınıṛ Sȝṛeobuınn ı ccíṛ Fıaċṛaċ Muaıḃe; maıṛıḃ múṛ na heaȝlaıṛı ṛın ṗoṛ. Nouemb. 1.

Cill maıȝnenn.—Maıȝnen epṛcop ıṛ abb cılle Maıȝnenn, la caob Aċa clıaċ, Oecemb. 18.

Cill Maınċın.—Epṛcop Manċan, no Maınċaın, ı cıll. M.

Cill moıṛ Enıṛ.—Cṛunnmael epṛcop, ab Cılle moıṛe Enıṛ, quıeuıc 765.

Cill Muıne.—Oauıḃ epṛcop, Cılle Muıne, ıṛ aıṛḃ epṛcop ınṛı ḃṛecan uıle, Maṛ. 1.

Cill Moḃıuıc.—Sımpleȝ, epṛcop .ı. Moḃıuıc ó Cıll Moḃıuıc ı Soȝuın, Feb. 12.

Cill paċaın.—(Blank in original).

Cill ṛıȝmanaḃ ın Albuın. Caınneċ abb, Occ. 11.

Cill ṛuaıḃe.—Colman mac Caċbaḃa, epṛcop Cılle ṛuaıḃe ı nOaılaṛaıḃe, aṛ bṛú Loċa Laoıȝ ın Ulcoıḃ, Occob. 16.

1 *Dronan.* The form Drunan is also suggested by the compiler.

2 Mart. Doneg.

3 Killinny, in the parish and barony of Kells, county of Kilkenny.

4 Mart. Doneg. and Mart. Taml.

5 Idrone, county of Carlow.

6 Mart. Doneg. and Mart. Taml.

7 Killarga, county of Leitrim.

8 Nov. 11, *recte* 12 ; Mart. Doneg.

9 *Tir-Fiachrach.* Now the barony of Tireragh, county of Sligo.

10 17, Mart. Doneg.

11 *Cill Insi.* See text.

12 *Inis-Sgreobuinn,* otherwise Eiscirabhann, now Inishcrone, in the parish of Kilglass, barony of Tireragh, and county of Sligo.

13 Mart. Doneg.

14 Kilmainham, near Dublin.

15 Mart. Doneg.

16 Kilmanaghan, barony of Kilcoursey,

CILL-DRONAN.   Dronan,[1] bishop, from Cill-Dronan, December 12.[2]

CILL-FHINNHCE.[3]—Finnech-Duirn, bishop of Cill-Fhinnche, from Aith-duirn, in Ossory, Feb. 2.[4]

CILL-FORTCHERN IN UI-DRONA.[5]—Fortchern, bishop, disciple of Patrick, Oct. 11.[6]

CILL-FOITHIRBHE.   See Cuil-Foithirbhe.

CILL-FORGA, or CILL-EARGA.[7]—Finnchad, bishop, Nov. 11.[8]

CILL-GREALLAN.—Greallan, bishop (there are two Cill-Greallans in Tir-Fiachra[9] of the Moy), Sept. 7.[10]

CILL-IAN.—Bishop Aedh, of Kill-Ian.

CILL-INSI.[11]—Ailltin, bishop, and the virgin (or the young maiden) of Cill-insi.   Nov. 1.[12]

NOTE.—Ailltin's church is in Inis-Sgreobbhuinn,[13] in Tir-Fiachra of the Moy.   The walls of that church are still in existence.

CILL-MAIGHNEN.[14]—Maighnen, bishop and abbot of Cill-Maighnenn near Dublin, Dec. 18.[15]

CILL-MAINCHIN.[16]—Bishop Manchan, or Mainchin, in Cill-Man-chan.

CILL-MOR-ENIR.[17]—Crunnmael, bishop, abbot of Cill-mor-Enir, quievit 765.[18]

CILL-MUINE.[19]—David, bishop of Cill-Muine, and archbishop of the isle of Britain, Mar. 3.[20]

CILL-MODIUT.[21]—Simplex, bishop, i.e., Modiut of Kill-modiut in Soghan,[22] Feb. 12.[23]

CILL-RATHAIN.—(Blank in original.)

CILL-RIGHMANAD, IN ALBA.[24]—Cainnech,[25] abbot, October 11.[26]

CILL-RUADH.[27]—Colman, son of Cathbadh, bishop of Cill-ruadh in Dal-Araidhe, on the brink of Loch-Laegh[28] in Uladh, Oct. 16.[29]

King's Co.

[17] Kilmore, three miles east of Armagh.

[18] Four Masters.

[19] Cill-Muine; St. David's, Wales.

[20] Mart. Doneg.

[21] Kilmude, in Hy-Many.

[22] Soghan, in Hy-Many, the district of the enslaved tribes, near the Suck.

[23] Mart. Doneg.

[24] Cill-Righmanad, in Alba; St. Andrew's, Scotland.

[25] Cainnech.   St. Canice of Achadh-bo, Queen's County; also founder of Cill-Cainnigh, i. e. Kilkenny.

[26] Mart. Doneg. and Mart. Taml.

[27] Kilroot, barony of Lower Belfast, county of Antrim.

[28] Loch-Laegh, the ancient name of Belfast Lough, which Adamnan Latinizes Stagnum Laous Vituli.   See Reeves' "Adamnan."

[29] Mart. Doneg. and Taml.

Cill Sȝanḃuil, no cill ḃian. Ferȝur eprcop Cille Sȝanḃuil, no ḃian ; aȝur ir fiór rin.

Cill Sȝire. Roḃarcaḃ (Fionnȝlairi), eprcop; Conull eprcop Cille rȝire, 865.

Cill rleḃe. Fiacc (eprcop Sleḃce) cille rleḃe.

Cill Ciḃill. Eprcop Fuirceḃal (i cill Ciḃil), mac Cail, mic Deȝa, mic Cuirc mic Luiȝḃeḃ. Seḃc nereop cille Ciḃil, no ḃroma Ciḃil, Nouemb. 1.

Cill cuama (no coama). Ninniḃ eprcop cille cuama. 1 Miḃe. Nouemb. 13. Fec cill Cuanna.

Cill Uraille. Uuaraille, eprcop, mac ua Ḃairḃ. Auȝ. 27. Aca cill Uraille a Laiȝniḃ.

Cenel Eoȝain. Cacaraḃ mac Ailche, eprcop cenel Eoȝain, 946. Fec cir Eoȝain.

Ua Coḃcaiȝ, arḃ eprcop cenel Eoȝain, quieuic, 1173.

Ȝiolla an ḃoimḃeḃ Ua Cerḃallain, errcop cire Eóȝuiṁ, 1279.

Floirinc Ua Cerḃallain, eprcop cire hEeoȝain, quieuic, 1293.

Cinḃ Ȝalarac. Iolan, eprcop Cinḃ ȝalarac, quieuic, 687.

Cinḃ ȝaraḃ. Daniel eprcop, anno 659; Feb. 18. Aca Cill Ȝaraḃ anḃ, ec cecera.

Ḃlaan eprcop ó cinḃ ȝaraḃ, i nȝallȝaoiḃelaiḃ; Duḃḃlaan a priom cacaoir ; ir ḃe ȝaircer "ḃlaan ḃliaḃaḃ ḃrecan." Auȝ. 10.

Cinriolaiȝ. Anc eprcop Ua Caeccain, i. arḃ eprcop Ua Cenrelaiȝ, quieuic, 1135.

Iorep Ua hAeḃa, eprcop Ua cCinriolaiȝ, 1183.

Clochor, Pilip, Mar. 4.

Ailill eprcop, quieuic, 867.

<hr/>

1 Not identified.

2 Killakeery, co. Meath.

3 Four Masters ; and 867, Chron. Scot.

4 *Cill-sleibhe.* This is apparently a mistake, for *Cill-slebhte*, or Slatey, in the Queen's Co., as *Cill-sleibhe* is Killeavy, Co. Armagh.

5 Probably Kilteel, barony of Salt, Co. Kildare.

6 Mart. Doneg.

7 Kiltome, barony of Fore, Co. Westmeath.

8 Mart. Doneg.

9 Killossey, near Naas, Co. Kildare.

10 Mart. Doneg.

11 *Cenel-Eoghain*, i. e. the diocese of Derry.

12 Four Masters.

13 O'Coffey, Ua Cobhthaigh. His Christian name was Murrough (Muiredhach).

14 IV. M. ; and Ann. Loch-Cé.

15 *Gilla-an-Choimdedh.* This is Latinized Germanus by Ware.

CILL-SGANDAIL, or CILL-BIAN.[1]—Fergus, bishop of Cill-Sgandail, or Cill-Bian, and that is true.

CILL-SGIRE.[2]—Robhartach of Finglas, bishop; Conall, bishop of Cill-Sgire, ob. 865.[3]

CILL-SLEBHE.[4]—Fiach (bishop of Sleibhte) of Cill-Slebhe.

CILL-TIDIL.[5]—Bishop Foirceadal of Cill-Tidil, son of Tal, son of Dega, son of Coro, son of Lughaidh. The seven bishops of Cill-Tidil (or Druim Tidil), Nov. 1.[6]

CILL-TUAMA (or TOMA).[7]—Ninnidh, bishop of Cill-Tuama in Meath, Nov. 13.[8] See Cill-Cuanna.

CILL-USAILLE.[9]—Usaille (Auxilius), bishop, son of Ua Baird, Aug. 27.[10] Cill-Usaille is in Leinster.

CENEL-EOGHAIN.—Cathasach, son of Ailche, bishop of Cenel-Eoghain,[11] 946.[12]

O'Coffey,[13] archbishop of Cenel-Eoghain, quievit 1173.[14]

Gilla-an-Choimdedh O'Carolan,[15] bishop of Tir-Eoghain, 1279.[16]

Florence O'Carolan, bishop of Tir-Eoghain, quievit 1293.[17]

CIND-GALARAT.[18]—Iolan, bishop of Cinn-Galarat, went to his rest 687.[19]

CIND-GARAD.[20]—Daniel, bishop of, A°. 659,[21] 18 Feb.[22] There is a Cill-Garad, &c.

Blaan, bishop, from Cinn-Garad in Gall Gaeidhela. Dunblane is its chief city. He is named Blaan the virtuous of Britain, Aug. 10.[23]

CINNSIOLAIGH.[24]—The bishop O'Caettain, i. e., the chief bishop of Hy-Cinnsiolaigh, quievit 1135.[25]

Joseph O'Hea, bishop of Hy-Cinnsiolaigh, 1183.[26]

CLOCHOR. Philip,[27] March 4.

Ailill, bishop, quievit 867.[28]

---

[16] Four Masters, and Ann. Loch-Ce.

[17] IV. M., and Ann. Loch-Cé.

[18] *Cind-galarat.* This is a mistake for Cind-garad, or Cenn-garad. It is written Cinngarad in the Chron. Scot., but Cindgalarat by Tigernach.

[19] 688, IV. M.; 685, Chron. Scot.

[20] Kingarth, Bute, Scotland.

[21] IV. M.; 656-660, Chron. Scot.

[22] Mart. Doneg. and Mart. Taml.

[23] Mart. Doneg. and Mart. Taml.

[24] *Cinnsiolaigh. Rectè* Hy-Cinnsiolaigh. Now the diocese of Ferns.

[25] Four Masters.

[26] IV. M.; Ann. Loch-Cé.

[27] Philip. In the Mart. Doneg. he is Philip of Cluain-Bainb; and in the Mart. Taml. the place is called Clochar-Bainni.

[28] IV. M.

Cluain aiccen. Eprcop Lugaó a ccluain Aiccen a Laiẓioṛ, Occ. 6.

Cluain bainb. Pilip eprcop Cluana bainḃ, no naoiṁ eprcop ó Chloċoṗ, Maṗc. 4.

Cluain caoin. Apuin eprcop Cluana caoin, Auẓ. 4.

Cluain Conaiṗe comain. Maoinenn eprcop i ccluain Conaiṗe comaim, i ccuaiṛẓeṗc Ua pƑaolain, Sept. 16.

Cluain cua. uii. neprcop Cluana cua, Occ. 3.

Cluain cṗema. Oṛṗḃṛan eprcop Cluana cṗema, quieuic 747. Laeẓaiṛe eprcop Cluana cṗema, Nou. 10.

Cluain cióneó. Cellaó mac Eṗoṗain, eprcop Cluana heióneó, 940.

Muiṗebaó Ua Concaḃaiṗ, eprcop, aẓuṗ comaṗba Ƒionncain Cluana heiónió, 970.

Ciobṛaibe, eprcoṗ Cluana heiónió, 909.

Ƒioncan coṗaċ, eprcop cluana ṗeṗca bṗenainb, aẓuṗ a ccluain heióneċ beoṛ, Ƒeb. 21.

Munba, eprcop aẓuṗ ab Cluana heiónió i Laoiẓiṗ; anno Domini an can ceṛba, 634. Occ. 21.

Cluain eoiṗ. Ciẓeṗnaċ mac Caiṗppi, ṗanccuṗ epiṗcopuṗ Cluana eoiṗ, quieuic 548; Appil 4.

Caencompac mac Caṗṗain, ṛui eprcop, aẓuṗ ab Cluana heo- aiṗ, 961.

Ƒlaiċbeṗcaċ Ua Cecnen, comaṗba Ciẓeaṗnaiẓ, ṛenoiṗ aẓuṗ ṛui eprcop, bo ẓoin ó ṗeṗaib bṗéẓ, aẓuṗ a éoc iaṗṛin ina ćill ṗén a cCluain Eoaiṗ, 1012.

Cluain eaṁuin. Ailill (eprcop Aṗbmaċa anno Cṗiṗci 535); aliceṗ eprcop Cluana emuin.

Cluain ṗoca. Eprcop Ecóen (ó cluain ṗoca) mac Maine eccir bo ṛiol Concoḃaiṗ aḃṗac ṛuaib.

---

¹ Clonkeen, Queen's Co.
² Mart. Doneg. and Mart. Taml.
³ *Cluain-bainbh.* Not identified.
⁴ Mart. Doneg. and Mart. Taml.
⁵ Clonkeen, Co. Louth.
⁶ August 1. Mart. Doneg. and Mart. Taml.
⁷ Cloncurry, Co. Kildare.
⁸ Mart. Doneg. and Mart. Taml.

⁹ *Cluain-Cua ;* in the Queen's Co.
¹⁰ Mart. Doneg. and Mart. Taml.
¹¹ Clooncraff, near Elphin, Co. Roscommon.
¹² Four Masters.
¹³ Mart. Doneg.
¹⁴ Cloncnagh, Queen's Co.
¹⁵ IV. M.
¹⁶ IV. M.

CLUAIN-AITCHEN.[1]—Bishop Lugach, in Cluain-Aitchenn in Leix, Oct. 6.[2]

CLUAIN-BAINBH.[3]—Philip, bishop of Cluain-bainbh, or holy bishop of Clogher, March 4.[4]

CLUAIN-CAIN.[5]—Aruin, bishop of Cluain-Cain, Aug. 4.[6]

CLUAIN-CONAIRE-TOMAIN.[7]— Maoinen, bishop in Cluain-Conaire-Tomain, in the north of Hy-Faolain, September 16.[8]

CLUAIN-CUA.[9]—Seven bishops of Cluain-Cua, Oct. 3.[10]

CLUAIN-CREMHA.[11]—Ossbran, bishop of Cluain-cremha, rested 747.[12]

Laeghaire, bishop of Cluain-cremha, Nov. 10.[13]

CLUAIN-EIDHNECH.[14]—Cellach, son of Eporan, bishop of Cluain-eidhnech, 940.[15]

Muiredhach O'Conchobhair, bishop, and comarb of Finntan of Cluain-eidhnech, 970.[16]

Tiobraide, bishop of Cluain-eidhnech, 909.

Finntan Corach, bishop of Clonfert-Brendan, and at Cluain-eidnech also, Feb. 21.[17]

Munda, bishop and abbot of Cluain-eidnech, in Laighis; in A. D. 634[18] he died, Oct. 21:[19]

CLUAIN-EOIS.[20]—Tighernach, son of Cairbre, holy bishop of Cluain-eois, quievit 548,[21] April 4.[22]

Caencomrac, son of Carran, eminent bishop and abbot of Cluain-eois, 961.[23]

Flaithbhertach O'Cetnen, comarb of Tighernach, a senior, and distinguished bishop, was wounded by the men of Bregia,[24] and he died afterwards in his own church at Cluain-eois, 1012.[25]

CLUAIN-EAMHUIN.[26]—Aillill, bishop of Armagh, A. D. 535[27]; otherwise bishop of Cluain-Eamhuin.

CLUAIN-FOTA.[28]—Bishop Etchen (from Cluain-fota), son of Maine the poet, of the race of Conchobar Abrat-ruadh.

[17] Mart. Doneg. and Mart. Taml.
[18] Four Masters. Chron. Scot.
[19] Mart. Doneg. and Mart. Taml.
[20] Clones, Co. Monaghan.
[21] IV. M. 545 Chron. Scot.; 550 Keating.
[22] Mart Doneg. and Mart. Taml.
[23] Chron. Scot., IV. M., and Ann. Ult.

[24] Bregia. The Annals generally attribute this violence to the men of Breifne.
[25] Chron. Scot.; Ann. Ult.; and Four Masters.
[26] Cloonowen, Co. Roscommon.
[27] IV. M. Chron. Scot.
[28] Clonfad, bar. of Farbill, Co. West-meath.

Noca. Ecchen eprcop cluana poca baobain aba, floruit cinca annum 576.

Cluain poba pepa bile. Ecben eprcop (Cluana poba pepa bile ı Mıbe); apé cuʒ ʒpaba paʒaıpc ap Colum cílle, Peb. 11.

Cluain poba pine. Senaċ eprcop ó Cluain poba pine a pepaıb culach .ı. Cluain poba Lıbpen; comapba Pınnen cluana hepaıpb, aʒup a berʒebul, ın Senaċ eprcop po.

Cluain mór. eprcop Colman ó Ċluain mór.

Cluain popca. berchan eprcop aʒup páıb ó Cluain popca, ın ſb Paılʒe, Dec. 4.

Cluain uaır. Iopep eprcop cluana uaır, 839.

Comann. Corʒpaċ mac Maoılmocaınʒe, eprcop cıʒe Moċua aʒup na cComann, 951.

Conmaıcne. Maelpeaċluınn ó Perʒal, eprcop Conmaıcne, quıeuıc 1307.

Cpaob Ʒpellaın, eprcop Ʒpellan, pepc. 7.

Cpuaċan bpı éle. Mac Caılle, eprcop, aʒup ı ccpuacaın bpı éle ın ſb Paılʒe aca a ċell, 489.

Cúıl benbċaıp. eprcop Luʒaċ ı ccuıl benbċaıp, occ. 6.

Cúıl bpacaın. Mapcaın eprcop ı ccúıl bpacaın ın ıb Paılʒe .ı. ı ccuaıc ba ṁaıʒe.

Cuıl coppa. Senaċ mac eoın, aʒup Spapan, aʒup Senċell aʒup bpuıbıucʒın, u. eprcop aʒup Aıcecaenı aʒup eprcop mac Caıpcın, aʒup Conlaoʒ aʒup bpıʒıb ı cCuıl coppa.

Cuıl (cıll, no) cluaın poıcıpbe no poċaıpbe no puıcıpbe. Nacı eprcop, auʒ. 1; mac Senuıʒ.

---

[1] The same place as the preceding.

[2] Mart. Doneg. and Mart. Taml.

[3] Clonfad, bar. of Fartullagh, Co. Westmeath.

[4] *Senach.* His festival is set down in the Calendar at August 21.

[5] *Cluain-mor.* There are so many places of this name, that it would be useless, without further evidence, attempting to identify the one here referred to.

[6] Clonsost, King's County.

[7] Mart. Doneg.

[8] *Cluain-uais;* the same as Cluain-Eois, q. v.

[9] Four Mast.; Chron. Scot.; Ann. Ult.

[10] *Comann;* otherwise na cpı Comann, the Three Comanns; three septs anciently settled in the district comprising the southern part of the Queen's Co., and the northern part of Kilkenny.

[11] IV. M.

[12] *Conmaicne;* i. e. the bishoprick of Ardagh.

NOTE: Etchen, bishop of Cluain-fota-Baodan-abo, floruit circa annum 576.

CLUAIN-FODA-FERA-BILE.[1]—Etchen, bishop (of Cluain-foda-Fera-bile, in Meath). It was he that conferred the grade of priest on Colum Cille, Feb. 11.[2]

CLUAIN-FODA-FINE.[3]—Senach, bishop, from Cluain-foda-fine, in Fera-tulach, i. e., Cluain-foda-Librein. The comarb of Finnen of Clonard, and his disciple, was this bishop Senach.[4]

CLUAIN-MÓR.[5]—Bishop Colman of Clonmore.

CLUAIN-SOSTA.[6]—Berchan, bishop and prophet, from Cluain-sosta in Offaly, Dec. 4.[7]

CLUAIN-UAIS.[8]—Joseph, bishop of Cluain-uais, 839.[9]

COMANN.[10]—Cosgrach, son of Maolcairge, bishop of Tech-Mochua (Timohoe), and the Comanns, 951.[11]

CONMAICNE.[12]— Maelseachluin O'Ferrall, bishop of Conmaicne, quievit 1307.[13]

CRAOBH-GRELLAIN.[14]—Bishop Grellan, 7 September.[15]

CRUACHAN-BRI-ELE.[16]—Mac Caille, bishop, (and in Cruachan-Bri-Ele in Offaly his church is), 489.[17]

CUIL-BENDCHAIR.[18]—Bishop Lugach of Cuil-Bendchair, Oct. 6.

CUIL-BRACAIN.[19]—Martin, bishop of Cuil-Bracan in Offaly, i. e. in Tuath-da-mhaighe.[20]

CUIL-CORRA.[21]—Senach, son of Ecin, and Srafan, and Senchell, and Brodigan—five bishops[22]—and Aitecaem, and Bishop Mac Cairthin, and Conlaogh, and Brigid, in Cuil-Corra.

CUIL-(Cill, or Cluain)-FOITHIRBE (or Fothairbe, or Fuithirbe[23]).— Nathi, bishop, Aug. 1 ; the son of Senagh.

[13] Four Masters; Ann. Loch Ce.

[14] Craobh-Grellan ; probably Creeve, bar. of Ballymoe, Co. Roscommon.

[15] Sept. St. Grellan's festival is set down in Mart. Doneg. at Nov. 10.

[16] Croghan, in the bar. of Lower Philipstown, King's Co.

[17] IV. M. ; 487, Chron. Scot.

[18] Cuil-Bendchair. Probably Coolbanagher, in the barony of Portnahinch, and Queen's County. The Mart. Doneg. adds, that probably Lugach was either of this place or of another Coolbanaghar

"on the brink of Loch Erne."

[19] Coolbracken, King's Co.

[20] Tuath-da-mhaighe (Anglicè Tuomoy); i. e. "the district of the two plains." This district included the present barony of Warrenstown and a large portion of the adjoining district, in the north of the King's County.

[21] Coolarn, near Galtrim, Co. Meath.

[22] Five bishops. Only four are enumerated.

[23] See Cuil-Sacaille.

Cuil Ratain. Cairppe, eprcop, ó Cuil patain, Nou. 11.

Cuil racaille. Naṫi eprcop ċuile Poṫairbe, no cuile Sacaille, auᵹ. 1.

Daiṁinir. Siollan, eprcop Daiṁinri.

Daipinir. Paċtna, eprcop aᵹur ab Daipinri, auᵹ. 14.

Daipe ċalᵹaiᵹ. Caoncompac mac Maoluiṁir, eprcop aᵹur ab daipe Calᵹaiᵹ, 927.

Maolpinnen, rui eprcop daipe Calᵹaiᵹ, 948.

Daipe Lupain. Lupech (.i. Luipech), buanaipe ó daipe Lupain in Ulcaiḃ, eprcop, peb. 17.

Lupan, eprcop, ó daipe Lupain, occ. 24.

Daipe mop. Colman, eprcop, 20 maoi; July 31, Colman eprcop.

Daimliaᵹ. Cianan eprcop Daimliaᵹ i mḃreᵹaiḃ; ar do cuc Pacpaic a foircela; floruit, 488.

Perᵹur eprcop Daimliaᵹ, quieuic, 772.

Colmam eprcop Daimliaᵹ aᵹur Lupca, quieuic 902 (Colman rᵹriḃniṫ).

Caoncompac, eprcop Daimliaᵹ, 941.

Pionchap, eprcop Daiṁliaᵹ, 918.

Ᵹiolla Mochua, mac Camċuapta, eprcop Daiṁliaᵹ, quieuic 1117.

Cuaċal mac Oenecain, eprcop Daiṁliaᵹ, quieuic 927.

Ceċeċ eprcop (ó domnach Sairiᵹe aᵹ daiṁliaᵹ Ċianain), June 16.

Dapṁaᵹ. Copmac Ua Liaċain, ab Dapṁaiᵹe, aᵹur eprcop, anno Cpirci 868; June 21.

Dealᵹae. Occirir hEᵹnaiᵹi eprcoip dealᵹae, 837.

Derᵹept Epenn. Ᵹiolla na naeṁ Ua Muirċepcaiᵹ, uaral eprcop derᵹept Epenn, renoir oiᵹ cpaibbech eᵹne, deec 1149.

---

1 Coleraine, Co. Londonderry.
2 Mart. Doneg.
3 *Cuil-Sacaille ;* not identified.
4 Mart. Doneg. and Mart. Taml.
5 Devenish Island, in Loch Erne.
6 *Dairinis ;* Molana, Co. Waterford.
7 Mart. Doneg. and Mart. Taml.
8 Londonderry.
9 Four Masters.
10 Mart. Doneg. and Mart. Taml.
11 Oct. 28. Mart. Doneg.
12 Derrimore, in Eliogarty, Co. Tipperary.
13 Mart. Doneg. and Mart. Taml.
14 Duleek, Co. Meath.
15 Ob. 486 ; Chron. Scot.
16 Four Masters ; Ann. Ult. 782.
17 902, IV. M. ; 906, Chron. Scot.

Cuil-Rathain.[1]—Cairbre, bishop of Cuil-Rathain, Nov. 11.[2]

Cuil-Sacaille.[3]—Nathi, bishop of Cuil-Fothairbe, or Cuil-Sacaille, August 1.[4]

Daimhinis.[5]—Siollan, bishop of Daimhinis.

Dairinis.[6]—Fachtna, bishop and abbot of Dairinis, Aug. 14.[7]

Daire-Calgaigh.[8]—Caencomhrac, son of Maoluidhir, bishop and abbot of Daire-Calgaigh, 927.

Maolfinnen, distinguished bishop of Daire-Calgaigh, 948.[9]

Daire-Lurain.[10]—Lurech (i. e. Luirech), poet, from Daire-Lurain in Ulster, bishop, Feb. 17.[11]

Luran, bishop of Daire-Lurain, Oct. 24.

Doire-mor.[12]—Colman, bishop, 20 May ;[13] July 11, Colman, bishop.

Daimhliag.[14]—Cianan, bishop of Daimhliag in Bregia. It was to him Patrick gave his Gospel: floruit 488.[15]

Fergus, bishop of Daimhliag, quievit 772.[16]

Colman, bishop of Daimhliag, quievit 902.[17]	(Colman the scribe).

Caencomhrac, bishop of Daimhliag, 941.[18]

Fionnchar, bishop of Daimhliag, 918.[19]

Gilla-Mochua, son of Camchuairt, bishop of Daimhliag, quievit 1117.[20]

Tuathal, son of Aenacan,[21] bishop of Daimhliag, quievit 927.[22]

Cethech, bishop, (from Domnach-Sairighe[23] at Daimhliag-Cianain), June 16.[24]

Darmhagh.[25]—Cormac Ua Liathan, abbot of Darmhagh, bishop, anno Christi 865,[26] June 21.[27]

Delgae.[28]—The slaying of Egnach, bishop of Delga, 837.[29]

Desgert-Erenn.[30]—Giolla-na-naemh O'Muircheartaigh, the noble bishop of the south of Erinn, a virgin, pious, wise elder, died 1149.[31]

[18] Four Masters.

[19] 918, IV. M.; Chron. Scot.

[20] IV. M.

[21] Son of Aenacan. He is called O'Ene-cain in the Chron. Scot.

[22] IV. M., and Chron. Scot.

[23] Domhnach-Sairighe. Donaghseery, near Duleek, Co. Meath.

[24] Mart. Doneg. and Mart. Taml.

[25] Darmhagh. Durrow, King's Co.

[26] Four Masters. 867, Chron. Scot.

[27] June 21. Mart. Doneg, Taml., and Mar. Gor.

[28] Dealgae. Kildalkey, Co. Meath.

[29] IV. M.

[30] Desgert-Erenn. South of Erinn, i.e. the diocese of Cloyne.

[31] IV. M.

Oιριορτ Oιαρmαὸα. Oιαρmαιὸ αυα Ḋeὸα ροιη), eρρcορ o ὸιριορτ Oιαρmαὸα ιη Uιὸ Muιρeαὸαιᵹ, June 21.

Cumραὸ mαc Oeρeρο αᵹυρ Mαοηαch mαc Sοιτeὸαιᵹ, ὸα eρρcορ Oιριορτ Oιαρmαὸα, ὸο ecc 842.

Muιριᵹeρ eρρcορ ὸιριορτ Oιαρmαὸα, quιeuιτ 895.

Uα Ᵹαὸαιὸ, ρuι eρρcορ Oιριορτ Oιαρmαὸα, ὸο ecc 1038.

Oιριορτ Ƒυlαρταιᵹ.—Ƒυlαρταch mαc ὸριc, eρρcορ clυαηα hIραιρὸ ι Mιὸe, ιρ ό Oιριορτ Ƒυlαρταιᵹ ιη Iὸ Ƒαιlᵹe, anno 778, Marta 29.

Oιριορτ Cοlα.—Cοlα, eρρcορ ό Oιριορτ Cοlα ιη Uαċταρ Ὁαιl cCαιρ, Mαρ. 30.

Ὁοmηαċ mιc Lαιċὸe; .ι. Ὁοmηαc mόρ mιc Lαιċὸe; eρρcορ eċeρη. May 27.

Ὁοmηαὸ ρeὸe.—eρρcορ ταmlαchτα ιηὸοmηαċ ρeὸe.

Ὁοmηαċ mορ Mαιᵹe eρe.—Oιαηαch eρρcορ Ὁοmηαċ mόιρ Mαιᵹe eρe, Jan. 16.

Ὁοmηαċ mόρ Ɑοlmαιᵹe. Seċτ ηeρρcορ Ὁοmηαιċ mοιρ Ɑοl-mυιᵹe, Aug. 23.

Ὁοmηαċ mορ mυιᵹe Ὁαmαιρηe. eαρc eρρcορ Ὁοmηαιċ mοιρ Mαιᵹe Ὁαmαιρηe, ηο Mαιᵹe Cοbα, Sept. 17.

Ὁοmηαċ ηιόρ Seċηαιll.—Seαċηαll .ι. Secυηὸιηυρ, eρρcόρ, Nov. 27.

Ὁοmηαċ mορ mυιᵹe Lυαὸαὸ.—eαρc eρρcορ, Oct. 27.

Ὁ. Cαοιὸe.—Cαοτι eρρcορ, Oct. 24.

Ὁ. mυιᵹe Cοbα.—eαρc eρρcορ, Oct. 27.

Ὁ. Sαιριᵹe.—Ceτech eρρcορ, June 16.

Ὁρυιm αιρbeυlαιᵹ.—Uιι. Neρρcορ Ὁροmα αιρbeυlαιᵹ, Jan. 15.

[1] Castledermot, Co. Kildare.

[2] Mart. Doneg. and Mart. Taml.

[3] Four Masters ; Ann. Ult.

[4] IV. M.

[5] IV. M.

[6] *Disert-Fulartaigh.* Dysart, barony of Carbury, county of Kildare.

[7] 774; IV. M.

[8] Mart. Doneg. and Mart. Taml.

[9] *Disert-Tola.* Dysart O'Dea, county of Clare.

[10] Mart. Doneg. and Mart. Taml.

[11] *Domhnach-mic-Laithbhe.* In the Mart. Doneg. it is stated that this church was in Mughdborna, now the barony of Cremorne, county of Monaghan; but Dr. O'Donovan suggests (IV. M. 1150, note) that it may be the Donaghmore near Slane.

[12] Mart. Doneg. and Mart. Taml.

[13] *Domhnach-Febe.* Not identified. The entry seems defective.

[14] *Domhnach-mor of Magh Ere.* Not identified.

[15] Mart. Doneg. and Mart. Taml.

[16] *See* under Aolmagh.

DISERT-DIARMADA.[1]—Diarmuid (descendant of Aedh Ron), bishop of Disert-Diarmada in Hy-Muiredhaigh, June 21.[2]

Cumsadh, son of Derer, and Maonach, son of Soitedach, two bishops of Disert-Diarmada, died 842.[3]

Maurice, bishop of Disert-Diarmada, quievit 895.[4]

O'Gabhaidh, a distinguished bishop of Disert-Diarmada, died 1038.[5]

DISERT-FULARTAIGH.[6]—Fulartach, son of Brec, bishop of Clonard, in Meath, and from Disert-Fulartaigh in Offaly,778,[7] March 29.[8]

DISERT-TOLA.[9]—Tola, bishop, from Disert-Tola, in upper Dal-Cais, March 30.[10]

DOMHNACH-MIC-LAITHBHE,[11] i.e.Domnach-mor-mic-Laithbhe. Bishop Ethern, May 27.[12]

DOMHNACH-FEBE.[13]—The Bishop of Tamhlacht (sic), in Domhnach-Febe.

DOMHNACH-MÓR OF MAGH-ERE.[14]—Dianach, bishop of Domhnach-mor of Magh-Ere, January 16.[15]

DOMHNACH-MÓR-AOLMAIGHE.[16]—The seven bishops of Domhnach-mór-Aolmaighe, August 23.[17]

DOMHNACH-MOR OF MAGH-DAMAIRNE.[18]—Earc, bishop of Domhnach-mor of Magh-Damhairne, or of Magh-Cobha, September 17.[19]

DOMHNACH-MOR-SECHNAILL.[20]—Sechnall, i. e. Secundinus, bishop, Nov. 27.[21]

DOMHNACH-MÓR OF MAGH-LUADADH.[22]—Earc, bishop, Oct. 27.[23]

DOMHNACH-CAOIDE.[24]—Caoite, bishop, Oct. 24.[25]

DOMHNACH-MAIGHE-COBHA.[26]—Earc, bishop, Oct. 27.[27]

DOMHNACH-SAIRIGHE.[28]—Cethech, bishop, June 16.[29]

DRUIM-AIRBHELAIGH.[30]—The seven bishops of Druim-Airbhelaigh, Jan. 15.[31]

---

[17] Mart. Doneg. and Mart. Taml.

[18] *Domhnach-mor o Magh-Damairne.* Magh-Damairne is now Magheramorne, county of Antrim. *See* under Domhnach-Maighe-Cobha.

[19] Mart. Doneg. and Mart. Taml.

[20] *Donach-mor-Sechnall.* Dunshauglin, county of Meath.

[21] Mart. Doneg.

[22] Donaghmore, barony of Salt, county of Kildare.

[23] Mart. Doneg. and Mart. Taml.

[24] Donaghady, county of Tyrone.

[25] Mart. Doneg. and Mart. Taml.

[26] Donaghmore, barony of Upper Iveagh, county of Down.

[27] See under Domhnach-mor of Magh-Damhairne.

[28] Near Duleek, county of Meath.

[29] See under Daimhliag.

[30] Drumreilly, county of Leitrim.

[31] Mart. Doneg. and Mart. Taml.

Opuim beptach.—Nem eppcop Opoma beptaig, Feb. 18.
Aongup eppcop Opoma beptaig, Feb. 18.

O. Cuilinn.—baippionn eppcop, May 21.

O. Cpema.—Oupa (no Oupan) eppcop, Feb. 6.

O. ba letip.—Cuimin poba mac Fiaḃna, eppcop, Nou. 12.

O. Oallain.—Nem eppcop, May 3.

O. Eanuig.—Fionnḋan, eppcop May 17.

O. Fep, no Fepi.—Fionnḋan eppcop pempaite, May 17.

Opuim gobla.—Fiacc Slebte, eppcop.

Opuim Feaptain. — Captaḋ eppcop; lep Opuim Feaptain.
mapt. 5.

Opuim inepglain. Tigepnaḋ mac Muipebaig, eppcop Opoma
inepglain, quieuit 875.

Opuim Laigille.—Sanctan eppcop, Maoi. 9.

Opuim Letglaipi.—Fepgup eppcop Opoma Letglaipi, quieuit
583, Map. 30.

Opuim liap.—benen in abbaine i nOpuimliap, Nov. 9.

Opuim Tioil.—Uii. neppcoip Opoma Tioil, no cille Tíoil,
Nov. 1.

Opuim upḋaille.—Uii. neppcoip Opoma upḋaille.

Nota.—143 nuimip na cceall bḋ pelbaigtep peḋt neppcoip ba
gac cill (no ait) aca, gonab e a líon pin uile, ebon 1001 earpog mup
po in naoiṁ penḋap naoiṁ Epenn, topaigap lep in lan peḋt neppcoib
pin: peḋt nepbuicc Opoma upchoille, peḋt nepbuicc cille Oepc-
bain, 7 apaile.

Oán mbaile.—Caillin eppcop Fiobnaḋa, Nov. 13.

Eaḋopuim.—Aeliomapchaip, eppcop Eachpoma, quieuit 746.

<hr/>

[1] Burt, barony of Inishowen West,
county of Donegal.

[2] Mart. Doneg. and Mart. Taml.

[3] Drumcullen, barony of Eglish,
King's County.

[4] Mart. Doneg. and Mart. Taml.

[5] Not identified.

[6] Mart. Doneg. and Mart. Taml.

[7] Mart. Doneg.
Not known.

[9] Mart. Doneg. and Mart. Taml.

[10] Not known.

[11] Mart. Doneg. and Mart. Taml.

[12] Not known.

[13] Mart. Doneg. and Mart. Taml.

[14] *Drum-Gobhla.* Near Slatey, in the
present Queen's County.

[15] *Drum-Feartan.* In Carbury, county
of Kildare.

DRUIM-BERTACH.[1]— Nemh, bishop of Druim-Bertach, Feb. 18.[2] Aengus, bishop of Druim-Bertach, Feb. 18.

DRUIM-CUILINN.[3]—Bairrionn, bishop, May 21.[4]

DRUIM-CREMA.[5]—Dura, or Duran, bishop, Feb. 6.[6]

DRUIM-DA-LETHIR.[7]—Cumin Foda, son of Fiachna, bishop, Nov. 12.

DRUIM-DALLAIN.[8]—Nemh, bishop, May 3.[9]

DRUIM-EANUIGH.[10]—Fionnchan, bishop, May 17.[11]

DRUIM-FES, OR FESI.[12]—Fionnchan, bishop aforesaid, May 17.[13]

DRUIM-GOBHLA.[14]—Fiach of Sletty, bishop.

DRUIM-FEARTAN.[15]—Carthach, bishop (Drum-Feartan belongs to him); March 5.[16]

DRUIM-INESGLAIN.[17]—Tighernach, son of Muireadach, bishop of Druim-inesglain, quievit 875.[18]

DRUIM-LAIGHILLE.[19]—Sanctan, bishop, May 9.[20]

DRUIM-LETHGLAISI.[21]—Fergus, bishop of Druim-lethglaisi, quievit 583, Mar. 30.[22]

DRUIM-LIAS.[23]—Benen, in the abbacy of Druim-lias, Nov. 9.[24]

DRUIM-TIDIL.[25] — Seven bishops of Druim-Tidil, or Cill-Tidil, Nov. 1.[26]

DRUIM-URCHAILLE.[27]—The seven bishops of Druim-urchaille.

NOTE.—143 was the number of the churches that possessed VII. bishops to each church or place ; so that the full number of them all is, viz., 1001 bishops. Thus it is in the " History of the Saints of Erinn," which commences with this number of VII. bishops, viz., VII. bishops of Druim-urchaille; VII. bishops of Cill-Dercain, &c.

DUN-MBAILE.[28]—Caillin, bishop of Fiodnacha, Nov. 13.[29]

EACH-DRUIM.[30]—Aelimarchair,[31] bishop of Each-druim, quievit 746.[32]

---

[16] Mart. Doneg. and Mart. Taml.

[17] Drumiskin, county of Louth.

[18] 876; Four Masters.

[19] *Druim-laighille.* Not known.

[20] Mart. Doneg. and Mart. Taml.

[21] *Druim-lethglaisi.* Another name for Dun-lethghlaise, or Downpatrick.

[22] IV. M.; Chron. Scot.

[23] *Drum-leese.* County of Leitrim.

[24] Mart. Doneg.

[25] *See* under Cill-Tidil.

[26] Mart. Doneg.

[27] Drumurgill, county of Kildare ?

[28] Fenagh, county of Leitrim.

[29] Mart. Doneg.

[30] Aughrim, county of Galway.

[31] *Aelimarchair.* This name is written Maelimarchair by the Four Masters, which is probably the correct form.

[32] IV. M.

Eanac̉ ꝺuin.—Muiṗceṗcaċ O Ḟlaicḃéeṗcaiġ, eṗꞃcop Eanuiġ, quieuic 1242.

Comáꞃ O Meallaiġ, eṗꞃcop Eanuiġ, quieuic 1250.

Comáꞃ O Meallaiġ, eṗꞃcop Eanuiġ ꝺo ecc i ccuaiṗc an papa, 1328.

Eꝺnen.—Maelpoil mac Aililla, eṗꞃcop, ancoiṗe, aʓuꞃ ꞃʓꞃibniꝺ Lece Cuinn, aʓuꞃ aḃ in Eꝺnen, 920.

Ele.—Iꞃaac Ua Cuanain, eṗꞃcop Ele Roiꞃꞃ cꞃe, oʓ aʓuꞃ aꞃꝺ ꞃenoiꞃ ꝺomain, quieuic 1161.

Eꞃe beʓ .i. beʓ Eꞃe.—Eṗꞃcop Ibaꞃ.

Cꞃonnmaol. eṗꝺcop beʓ Eꞃe, eṗꞃcop aʓuꞃ ꝼeꞃ leʓinn Camlacca, 964.

Eꞃe.—Eoċaiꝺ Ua Cellaiʓ, aꞃꝺ cenn ꝼeꞃ Miꝺe, ꞃui eṗꞃcop na hEꞃenn uile, ꝺéʓ in ꝺeꞃmaʓ Coluim Cille, 1140.

Ꝼaꝺaꞃ.—Suaiꞃleċ, eṗꞃcop Ꝼaꝺaiꞃ, quieuic 745, Mart. 27.

Aeꝺʓin, eṗꞃcop iꞃ aḃ Ꝼaꝺaiꞃ, quieuic 766, Maoi 1.

Ꝼeꞃca Ceꞃbain.—Ceꞃban eṗꞃcop ó ꝼeꞃca Ceꞃbain, quieuic ciꞃca annum 500.

Ꝼeꞃca ꝼeꞃ ꝼeic.—Eṗꞃcop Eaꞃc Slaine.

Ꝼioꝺ cuilinn.—beoan mac Neꞃꞃain, eṗꞃcop, Auʓ. 6.

Ꝼioꝺ ꝺuín.—Colman eṗꞃcop iꞃ aḃ Ꝼeꝺa ꝺuín, 948.

Momaeꝺoʓ eṗꞃcop Ꝼeꝺa ꝺúin, Maoi 18.

Ꝼioꝺnacha.—Caillin eṗꞃcop, Nov. 13.

Ꝼionnabaiꞃ aḃa.—Ꝼeꞃʓil eṗꞃcop Ꝼinnabaiꞃ aḃa, aʓuꞃ aḃ inꝺ Eiꝺnen, 902.

Ꝼionnʓlaiꞃ.—Ꝼlann eṗꞃcop Ꝼionnʓlaiꞃe, Jan. 21.

Ꝼoꞃʓnaiꝺe.—Eṗꞃcop Muiniꞃ, ꝺecemb. 18.

Ɣael.—Ɣaiḃꞃinn eṗꞃcop, June 24.

---

1 Annaghdown, county of Galway.

2 1241; Ann. Loch-Cé, and Four Masters.

3 Ann. Loch-Cé, and Four Masters.

4 IV. M. and Ann. Loch-Cé.

5 Not identified.

6 IV. M.; 921 Chron. Scot.

7 Eliogarty, county of Tipperary.

8 IV. M.

9 *Ere-beg*, i. e. Beg-Ere. *See* Beg-Ere.

10 IV. M.

11 *Ere.* Ireland.

12 Four Masters.

13 *Fore*, county of Westmeath.

14 IV. M.; 749 Ann. Ult.

15 Mart. Doneg. and Mart. Taml.

16 IV. M.

17 Mart. Doneg. and Mart. Taml.

18 *Ferta-Cerbain.* Near Tara hill, in the county of Meath.

19 499, IV. M.; but 503–4 in the other annals.

EANACH-DUIN.[1]—Muirchertach O'Flaherty, bishop of Eanach-duin, quievit 1242.[2]

Thomas O'Mellaigh, bishop of Eanach-duin, quievit 1250.[3]

Thomas O'Mellaigh, bishop of Eanach-duin, died at the Papal court, 1328.[4]

EDHNEN.[5]—Maelpoil, son of Ailill, bishop, anchorite, and scribe of Leth-Chuinn, and abbot of the Edhnen, 920.[6]

ELE.[7]—Isaac O'Cuanain, bishop of Ele of Roscrea, virgin and chief elder of the world, quievit 1161.[8]

ERE-BEG, i. e. BEG-ERE.[9]—Bishop Ibar.

Cronmael, bishop of Beg-Ere, bishop and lector of Tallaght, 964.[10]

ERR.[11]—Eochaidh O'Cellaigh, chief head of the men of Meath, the eminent bishop of all Erinn, died in Dermagh of Colum-Cille, 1140.[12]

FABHAR.[13]—Suairlech, bishop of Fabhar, rested 745,[14] March 27.[15]

Aedgin, bishop and abbot of Fabhar, quievit 766,[16] May 1.[17]

FERTA-CERBAIN.[18] — Cerban, bishop, from Ferta-Cerbain, quievit circa annum 500.[19]

FERTA-FER-FEIC.[20]—Bishop Earc, of Slane.

FIODH-CUILINN.[21]—Beoan, son of Nessan, bishop, August 6.[22]

FIODH-DUIN.[23]—Colman, bishop and abbot of Fidh-duin, 948.[24]

Momhaedog, bishop of Fidh-duin, May 18.[25]

FIODHNACHA.[26]—Caillin, bishop, Nov. 13.

FIONNABAIR-ABHA.[27]—Fergil, bishop of Finnabhair-abha, and abbot of the Edhnen, 902.[28]

FINNGLAIS.[29]—Flann, bishop of Finnglais, January 21.[30]

FORGNAIDHE.[31]—Bishop Muinis, December 18.[32]

GAEL.[33] Gaibhrinn, bishop, June 24.[34]

[20] *Ferta-fer-Feic.* *See* under Baile-Slaine.

[21] Feighcullen, county of Kildare.

[22] August 8, Mart. Doneg. and Mart. Taml.

[23] *Fiodh-duin.* Fiddown, county of Kilkenny.

[24] Mart. Doneg. and Mart. Taml.

[25] Four Masters.

[26] *Fiodhnacha.* Fenagh, county of Leitrim. *See* under Dun-mbaile.

[27] Fennor, barony of Duleek, county of Meath.

[28] Four Masters; 906, Chron. Scot.

[29] Finglass, near Dublin.

[30] Mart. Doneg. and Mart. Taml.

[31] Forgney, county of Longford.

[32] Mart. Doneg.

[33] Gael. This place has not been identified.

[34] Mart. Doneg. and Mart. Taml.

Ʒlairꞇimber.—Paꝺraiʒ epꞃcop, Aug. 24.

Ʒlenn ꝺa lacha.—Caoimʒin Ʒlinne ꝺa lacha.

Ꝺairchill mac hⱯiriꞇa, epꞃcop Ʒlinne ꝺa lacha, quieuiꞇ 676, May 3.

Ꝺoirrʒel mac Ceallaiʒ, epꞃcop Ʒlinne ꝺa lacha, quieuiꞇ 809.

Ⱥmpuꝺan, no Ⱥmpaꝺan, epꞃcop ʒlinne ꝺa lacha, May 11.

Ⱥoꝺ Ó Moꝺain, epꞃcop Ʒlinne ꝺa lacha, quieuiꞇ 1126.

Cormac Ua Mail, epꞃcop Ʒlinne ꝺa lacha, quieuiꞇ 1101.

Ʒiolla na naem Laiʒen, uaral epꞃcop Ʒlinne ꝺa lacha, aʒur cenn manach iar rin in Uairirburʒ, ꝺo ꝺc an reaꞇꞇmaꝺ io Ⱥpril, 1085.

Maolbriʒꝺe Ua Maoilrinn, raʒarꞇ, ancoire, aʒur epꞃcop Ʒlinne ꝺa lacha, quieuiꞇ 1041.

Nuaꝺa epꞃcop Ʒlinne ꝺa lacha, 928.

Cionaoꞇh Ua Ronain, epꞃcop Ʒlinne ꝺa lacha aʒur cuairʒerꞇ Laiʒen, quieuiꞇ 1173.

Molioba mac Cholmaꝺa ó Ʒlenn ꝺa lacha, epꞃcop, Jan. 8.

Siollan epꞃcop Ʒlinne ꝺa lacha, Feb. 10.

Ruirin epꞃcop Ʒlinne ꝺa lacha aʒur bennchair, Apl. 22.

Ʒlenn uiren.—Ꝺiarmaiꝺ epꞃcop ʒlinne hUirren, July 8.

Ʒoꝺuil.—Ʒuaire epꞃcop in Ʒoꝺuil; Ⱥoꝺ epꞃcop ó Lior Ʒoꝺuil ar loꞇ Ꝺrne, 25 January.

Ʒranarꝺ.—Ʒuaraꞇꞇ epꞃcop, January 24.

Iae.—Coeꝺi epꞃcop Iae, quieuiꞇ 710.

Finʒin, ancoire ir epꞃcop Iae, 964.

Muʒron ab Iae, rʒribniꝺ aʒur epꞃcop aʒur rái na cꞃi rann, 978.

Ferʒna briꞇ, epꞃcop aʒur ab Iae Coluim cille, Marꞇa 2.

Imleꞇ broꞇaꝺa.—Ꝺpꞃcop brocaiꝺ, Iuil 9.

Inber Ꝺaoile.—Ꝺaʒꝺan epꞃcop, Marꞇa 12.

---

[1] Glastonbury, England.	[10] Four Masters.
[2] *Glenn-da-locha*; county of Wicklow.	[11] IV. M.; 929, Chron. Scot.
[3] Four Masters; 674, Chron. Scot.	[12] IV. M.
[4] Mart. Doneg. and Mart. Taml.	[13] Mart. Doneg. and Mart. Taml.
[5] IV. M.; 814, Chron. Scot.	[14] Mart. Doneg. and Mart. Taml.
[6] January 11, Mart. Doneg.	[15] Mart. Doneg.
[7] IV. M.	[16] Killeshin, barony of Slievemargy,
[8] IV. M.	Queen's County.
[9] IV. M.	[17] Mart. Doneg. and Mart. Taml.

Glaistimber.[1]—Patrick, bishop, August 24.

Glenn-da-lacha.[2]—Caoimhghin of Glenn-da-locha.

Dairchill, son of Haireta, bishop of Glenn-da-locha, quievit 676,[3] May 3.[4]

Edirsgel, son of Cellach, bishop of Glenn-da-locha, quievit 809.[5]

Ampudan (or Anpadan), bishop of Glenn-da-locha, May 11.[6]

Aedh O'Modhain, bishop of Glenn-da-locha, quievit 1126.[7]

Cormac O'Mail, bishop of Glenn-da-locha, quievit 1101.[8]

Giolla-na-naomh of Leinster, noble bishop of Glenn-da-locha, and chief monk afterwards in Uarisburgh (Wurtzburg), died on the seventh of the ides of April, 1085.[9]

Maelbrighde O'Maelfinn, priest, anchorite, and bishop of Glenn-da-locha, quievit 1041.[10]

Nuada, bishop of Glenn-da-locha, 928.[11]

Cinaeth O'Ronain, bishop of Glenn-da-locha, and of the north of Leinster, quievit 1173.[12]

Molioba, son of Colmadh, from Glenn-da-locha, January 8.[13]

Siollan, bishop of Glenn-da-locha, Feb. 10.[14]

Ruifin, bishop of Glenn-da-locha, and of Bangor, April 22.[15]

Glenn-Uissen.[16]—Diarmuid, bishop of Glenn-Uissen, July 8.[17]

Gobhuil.[18]—Guaire, bishop of the Gobhuil.[19]

Hugh, bishop of Lis-gabhuil on Loch-Erne, 25 January.[20]

Granard.[21]—Guasacht, bishop, January 24.[22]

Iae.[23]—Coedi, bishop of Ia, quievit 710.[24]

Finghin, anchorite and bishop of Ia, 964.[25]

Mughron, abbot of Ia, scribe and bishop, and sage in the 3 divisions [of knowledge], 978.[26]

Fergna Brit, bishop and abbot of Ia-Coluim-Cille, March 2.[27]

Imlech-Brochada.[28]—Bishop Brochad, July 9.[29]

Inver Daoile.[30]—Dagdan, bishop, March 12.

[18] *Gobhuil.* See Lis-Gobhuil.
[19] 25 January; Mart. Taml.
[20] Mart. Doneg. and Mart. Taml.
[21] *Granard.* County of Longford.
[22] Mart. Doneg. and Mart. Taml.
[23] *Iae.* Iona, or Hy-Coluim-Cille.
[24] Four Masters; 711, Ann. Ult.
[25] IV. M.; Chron. Scot.
[26] Four Masters and Chron. Scot.
[27] Mart. Doneg. and Mart. Taml.
[28] Emlech. Barony of Costello, county of Mayo.
[29] Mart. Doneg. and Mart. Taml.
[30] Enerreilly. Barony of Arklow, county of Wicklow.

Inip Alban.—Potað mac bpain, pgpíbnið ⁊ eppcop inpi Alban, 961.

Inip beg Epe.—Peð beg Epe.

Inip bo pinðe.—Nauigatio Colmani epipcop cum peliquip pco-copum að Inpolam uaccae albae, in qua punðabat ecclepiam, 667.

Columban epipcopup Inpulae uaccae albae, paupat 674; ı cConmacnaib mapa, Aug. 8.

baeðan eppcop Inpi bó pinði, quıeuıt 711.

Inip bpetan.—Pec bpitania, ıp Cill muine.

Inip Caoinðega.—Daig mac Caipill, tepba 586, Aug. 8.

Copgpað mac Ðunacaın, puı eppcop ıp aıpðınðeð Inpı Caoın bega, 961.

Inip Capðaıg.—Capðach eppcop, mac Aongupa, Mapta 5.

Inip Catarg.—Senan eppcop Inpı Catarg, Mart. 1.

Aoðan eppcop ó Inip Catarg, Aug. 31.

Aeð Ua bechaın, eppcop Inpı Catarg, 1188.

Inip Cealtpa.—Ðıapmaıð mac Caıchuıl eppcop inpı Cealtpa, 951.

Inip Clotpann.—Ðıapmaıð eppcop ó Inıp Clotpann ap loð Ríb, ðo píol Ðathı pı Epenn, agup Ðeðı ıngen Tpena mıc Ðubthaıg Ua Lugaıp, apð pıleð Epenn, mataıp Ðıapmaða, Enaıp 10.

Inip eunðaıṁ.—Caoncompac eppcop, Iuıl 23.

Inip Paıðlenn no Paıglenn.—Paıglenn ó Inıp Paıðlenn (no Paıglenn), mac Aeða baṁaın, no mac Aeða bennaın, ðo plíoðt Cuıpc mıc Luıgðech.

Inip maıc Eapca.—Ppaeðan eppcop, Nov. 20.

Inip muıge pam.—Ninnıð eppcop, Enaıp 18.

Inip maıc Ualaıng.—Mopıóce, eppcop Inpı Ualaıng, Aug. 1.

---

1 *Inis-Alban.* Scotland.

2 Four Masters.

3 Bophin Island, off the coast of Mayo.

4 IV. M.; 664, Chron. Scot.

5 IV. M.; Chron. Scot.

6 Mart. Doneg. and Mart. Taml.

7 IV. M.

8 Inishkeen, county of Louth.

9 Four Masters and Chron. Scot.

10 Mart. Doneg. and Mart. Taml.

11 IV. M.

12 *Inis-Carthaigh. See* Inis-Uachtar.

13 Mart. Doneg. and Mart. Taml.

14 Scattery Island, in the River Shannon.

15 Mart. Doneg. and Mart. Taml.

16 Mart. Doneg. and Mart. Taml.

Inis-Alban.[1]—Fothadh, son of Bran, scribe, and bishop of Inis-Alban, 961.[2]

Inis-Beg-Ere.—*See* Beg-Ere.

Inis-bo-finde.[3]—The navigation of Bishop Colman, with the remainder of the Scoti to Inis-bo-finde " the Isle of the White Cow," wherein he founded a church, 667.[4]

Columbanus, bishop of Insula-vaccæ-albæ, quievit 674 ;[5] in Con-maicne-mara, August 8.[6]

Baedan, bishop of Inis-bo-finne, quievit 711.[7]

Inis-Bretan. *See* Britannia, and Cill-Muine.

Inis-Caindegha.[8]—Daig, son of Cairell, died 586,[9] August 8.[10]

Cosgrach, son of Dunacan, eminent bishop, and herenach of Inis-Caindegha, 961.[11]

Inis-Carthaigh.[12]—Carthach, son of Aongus, bishop, March 5.[13]

Inis-Cathaigh.[14]—Senan, bishop, from Inis-Cathaigh, March 1.[15]

Aedhan, bishop, from Inis-Cathaigh, August 31.[16]

Aedh O'Bechain bishop of Inis-Cathaigh, 1188.[17]

Inis-Cealtra.[18]—Diarmaid, son of Caichel, bishop of Inis-Cealtra, 951.[19]

Inis-Clothrann.[20]—Diarmaid, bishop, from Inis-Clothrann in Loch-Ribh, of the race of Dathy, king of Erin ; and Dedi, daughter of Trian, son of Dubhthach Ua Lughair, chief bard of Erinn, was Diarmaid's mother; January 10.[21]

Inis-eundaimh.[22]—Caoncomrac, bishop, July 23.[23]

Inis-Faithlenn (or Faighlenn).[24]—Faighlen [or Faighlenn], from Inis-Faighlen, son of Aedh Damhan, or son of Aedh Bennan, of the race of Corc Mac Luigdech.

Inis-maic-Earca.[25]—Fraechan, bishop, Nov. 20.

Inis-Muighe-Samh.[26]—Ninnid, bishop, January 18.[27]

Inis-Maic-Ualaing.[28]—Moriocc, bishop of Inis-maic-Ualaing, Aug.1.[29]

[17] Four Masters.
[18] Iniscatha, in Lough Dergdeirc.
[19] IV. M.
[20] Iniscloghren, or Quaker's Island, in Lough-Ree.
[21] Mart. Doneg. and Mart. Taml.
[22] Inishenagh, in Lough-Ree.
[23] Mart. Doneg. and Mart. Taml.
[24] Inisfallen, Killarney.
[25] *Inis-maic-Earca.* *See* under Bochluain.
[26] *Inis-mac-Saint,* in Lough - Erne, county of Fermanagh.
[27] Mart. Doneg. and Mart. Taml.
[28] *Inis-Bofin* in Loch-Ree.
[29] Mart. Doneg. and Mart. Taml.

Inip mebċoiċ.—Aoḃan eprcop, Auᵹ. 31.

Inip moſp.—baoḃan eprcop, Enaip 14.

Inip uaċċaip.—Captaċ eprcop, Mapc. 5.

Ionnlaċa Ċineoil Luᵹaip.—Conlaeḃ aᵹup uii neprcoip, aᵹup un paᵹaipc, aᵹup uii mnᵹena oᵹa, in Ionnlaċa ċineoil Luᵹaip.

Laiᵹen.—Fiacc plebċa, ḃipciobal Paḃpaic, aipḃeprcop Laiᵹen 6, aᵹup a comapba ba ſp, Occob. 12.

Cele mac Donnacain, eprcop Laiᵹen, aᵹup apb ſenóip na nᵹaoiḃel, quieuic i nᵹlenn ba laċa, 1076.

Copmac Ua Caċapaiᵹ, apḃeprcop Laiᵹen, quieuic 1146.

Flaiċem Ua Duiḃiḃip, eprcop aip ċep Laiᵹen, quieuic 1104.

Ᵹpene, apḃeprcop Ᵹall aᵹup Laiᵹen, quieuic 1162. (Lopcan O Cuaċail, comapba Chaoimᵹin, bo oipbneb ina inab la comapba Paḃpaiᵹ.)

Ᵹiolla na naoim Ua Muipceptaiᵹ, uapal eprcop bepᵹept Epenn (paoilim ᵹop bon Mumain benup pe), quieuic 1149.

Lopcan O Cuaċaill (.i. Labpap), apḃeprcop Laiᵹen aᵹup leᵹaib na hEpenn, quieuic i Saxanaib 1180.

Lann Ᵹpeallain.—Ᵹpeallan eprcop ó Lainn, Sepc. 17.

Lann Lepe.—Ᵹopmᵹal mac Muipeaḃaiᵹ, eprcop Lainn Lépe, quieuic 843.

Maolciapain mac Foipccepn, eprcop Lainne, quieuic 900.

Laċpaċ bpiuin.—Copmac, eprcop Laċpaiᵹ bpſuin, quieuic 854.

Leacain Míbe.—Cpuimin eprcop, Iuin 28.

Leam ċoill.—Fionntan copaċ, Feb. 21.

Cuillenn, eprcop Leamċoille, Appil 22.

Moċonna eprcop ó Leamċoill, Enaſp 13.

<hr/>

[1] *Inis-Medcoit.* Either Farne, or Lindisfarne, in England.

[2] *See* under Inis-Cathaigh.

[3] *Baedan.* In the Mart. of Donegal it is added that this Baedan died A. D. 712.

[4] Mart. Doneg. and Mart. Taml.

[5] *Inis - uachtar.* In Loch-Sheelin, county of Cavan.

[6] Mart. Doneg. and Mart. Taml.

[7] Not identified.

[8] *Laighen.* Leinster.

[9] Mart. Doneg. and Mart. Taml.

[10] Four Masters.

[11] IV. M.

[12] IV. M.

[13] *Grene.* He is called Gregorius by Ware, and others. *See* Harris's edition of Ware's Works, vol. i., p. 311.

[14] IV. M.

[15] *Munster.* He was bishop of Cloyne.

Inis-Medcoit.[1]—Aedan, bishop, August 31.[2]

Inis-mor.—Baedan,[3] bishop, January 14.[4]

Inis-uachtar.[5]—Carthach, bishop, March 5.[6]

Ionnlatha-Cineoil-Lughair.[7]—Conlaed, and vii. bishops, and vii. priests, and vii. young virgins, in Innlatha-Cineoil-Lughair.

Laighen.[8]—Fiac of Sletty, disciple of Patrick; he was archbishop of Leinster, and his comarb after him. October 12.[9]

Cele, son of Donnacan, bishop of Laighen, and arch-elder of the Gaidhel, quievit in Glenn-da-locha, 1076.[10]

Cormac O'Cathasaigh, archbishop of Laighen, quievit 1146.[11]

Flaithemh O'Duibhidhir, bishop of East Laighen, quievit 1104.[12]

Grene,[13] archbishop of the Gaill, and of Laighen, quievit 1162.[14]

(Lorcan O'Tuathail, comarb of Caemhghin, was ordained in his place by the comarb of Patrick.)

Gilla-na-naomh O'Muirchertaigh, noble bishop of the South of Erinn. (I think he belongs to Munster),[15] quievit 1149.

Lorcan[16] O'Tuathail (i. e. Lawrence) archbishop of Laighen, and Legate of Erinn, quievit in England,[17] 1180.

Lann Grellain.[18]—Greallan, bishop, from Lann, September 17.[19]

Lann-Lere.[20]—Gormgal, son of Muireadach, bishop of Lann-Lere, quievit 843.[21]

Maol-Chiaran, son of Fortchern, bishop of Lann, quievit 900.[22]

Lathrach-Briuin.[23]—Cormac, bishop of Lathrach-Briuin, quievit 854.[24]

Leacan of Meath.[25]—Cruimin, bishop, June 28.[26]

Leamh-choill.[27]—Finntan Corach, February 21.[28]

Cuillenn, bishop of Leamh-choill, April 22.[29]

Mochonna, bishop of Leamh-choill, January 13.[30]

See Harris's "Ware," vol. i., p. 574.

[16] See note.

[17] England. Saxanaib. In the Annals of Boyle, Inisfallen, and Clonmacnoise, he is said to have died in France.

[18] Not identified.

[19] 18; Mart. Doneg. and Mart. Taml.

[20] Dunleer, county of Louth.

[21] Four Masters.

[22] IV. M.

[23] Laragh - Bryan, barony of North Salt, county of Kildare.

[24] Four Masters.

[25] Leckin, barony of Corkaree, county of Westmeath.

[26] Mart. Doneg. and Mart. Taml.

[27] Lowhill, Queen's County.

[28] Mart. Doneg. and Mart. Taml.

[29] Mart. Doneg. and Mart. Taml.

[30] Mart. Doneg. and Mart. Taml.

leaṫ Cuinn.—Maolpoíl mac Aillella, epſcop, ancoiſe, ẛgſíḃníḋ leiṫe Cuinn, aȝuſ ab inḋ Eḋnen, 920.

liaṫ ḋſuim.—Mac liaȝ, epſcop liaṫ ḋſoma, Ḟeb. 8.

liaṫ móſ (no leṫmóiſ).—Naȝaiſ, epſcop, Iuil. 12.

linn ḋuaċaill.—Comaſ epſcop aȝuſ ẛgſíḃ, ab linne ḋuaċaill, quieuit 803.

liolcaċ.—Eaſc Slaine, epſcop liolcaiȝ, Nov. 2 ; quieuit 512.

lioſ ȝoḃuil.—Aeḋ epſcop ó lioſ ȝoḃuil aſ loċ Eſne, Enaiſ 5.

lioſ móſ.—Moċuḋa epſcop, quieuit 636, Maoi 14.

Ronan epſcop lioſ móiſ Moċuḋa, Ḟeb. 9.

Caſṫaċ epſcop, Maſta 3.

loṫſa.—Ruaḋan epſcop loṫſa.

Colum mac Ḟaolȝuſa, epſcop loṫſa, quieuit 783.

Ḋineſtaċ epſcop loṫſa, quieuit 864.

loċ Con.—laoȝaiſe, epſcop ó loċ Con, Sept. 30.

luȝṁaḋ.—Moċta epſcop ó luȝṁaḋ, 300 bliaḋan a ſaeȝal, Maſta 20.

Eochaiḋ mac Cuaṫail, epſcop luȝṁaḋ, 820.

Maoltuile, epſcop luȝṁaḋ, 871.

Caoncompaċ epſcop luȝṁaḋ, 898.

Ḟionnaċta mac Ectiȝeſn epſcop, ẛgſíḃníḋ iſ ab luȝṁaḋ, 948.

Maolpatſaic mac ḋſoin, epſcop luȝṁaḋ, 936.

luiȝne, no tuaṫ luiȝne.—Maolḟinnia .i. Ua hAonuiȝ, ḟeſle-ȝinḋ Ḟaḃaiſ, aȝuſ epſcop tuaiṫ luiȝne, 992.

luſca.—Mac Cuilinn epſcop luſca. luacan mac Cuilinn

---

1 *Leath-Chuinn.* Ulster.

2 *Edhnen.* He died at Eu, in Normandy. *See* under Edhnen.

3 Leitrim.

4 Mart. Doneg. and Mart. Taml.

5 Leamakevoge, barony of Eliogarty, county of Tipperary.

6 Mart. Doneg. and Mart. Taml.

7 *Linn-duachaill.* Near Dundalk, county of Louth.

8 Four Masters.

9 Bective (?) county Meath.

10 *Eare of Slane. See* under Baile-Slaine.

11 Lisgoole, county Fermanagh.

12 25, Mart. Doneg.

13 Lismore, county Waterford.

14 Four Masters, and Chron. Scot. 637, Ann. Ult. Tig. and Clonmacnoise.

15 Mart. Doneg., and Mart. Taml.

16 *Carthach.* This is a mistake. The Carthach commemorated on March 5,

LEATH-CHUINN.[1]—Maelpoil, son of Ailill, bishop, anchorite, and scribe of Leth-Chuinn, and abbot of the Edhnen,[2] 920.

LIATH-DRUIM.[3]—Mac Liag, bishop of Liath-druim, Feb. 8.[4]

LIATH-MOR, OR LETH-MOR.[5]—Nazair, bishop, July 12.[6]

LINN-DUACHAILL.[7]—Thomas, bishop, scribe, and abbot of Linn-Duachaill, quievit 803.[8]

LIOLCACH.[9]—Earc of Slane,[10] bishop of Liolcagh, quievit 512. November 2.

LIS-GOBHUIL.[11]—Aedh, bishop, from Lis-Gobhuil on Loch-Erne, January 5.[12]

LIS-MOR.[13]—Mochuda, bishop, quievit 636,[14] May 14.

Ronan, bishop of Lis-mór-Mochuda, Feb. 9.[15]

Carthach,[16] bishop, March 3.

LOTHRA.[17]—Ruadhan, bishop of Lorrha.

Colum, son of Faolgus, bishop of Lorrha, quievit 783.[18]

Dinertach, bishop of Lorrha, quievit 864.[19]

LOCH-CONN.[20]—Laeghaire, bishop, from Loch-Conn, September 30.[21]

LUGHMHAGH.[22]—Mochta, bishop from Lughmhagh, 300 years was his age; March 20.[23]

Eochaidh, son of Tuathal, bishop of Lughmhagh, 820.[24]

Maoltuile, bishop of Lughmhagh, 871.[25]

Caencomrach, bishop of Lughmhagh, 898.[26]

Finnachta, son of Echtigern, bishop, scribe, and abbot of Lughmhagh, 948.[27]

Maolpatrick, son of Bran, bishop of Lughmhadh, 936.[28]

LUIGHNE.[29] Maelfinnia (i. e. O'hAenaigh), lector of Fabhar, and bishop of Tuath-Luighne, 992.[30]

LUSCA.[31]—Mac Cuilinn, bishop of Lusca. Luachan mac Cuilinn,

is the same whose name appears under Druim-fertain and Inis-Uachtar above.

[17] Lorrha, barony of Lower Ormond, county Tipperary.

[18] Four Masters.

[19] IV. M.

[20] i. e., Errew, near Loch-Conn, county Mayo.

[21] Mart. Doneg.

[22] Louth, county of Louth.

[23] March 20. Partly effaced. August 19, Mart. Doneg. and Mart. Taml.

[24] Four Masters; 822, Chron. Scot.

[25] IV. M.

[26] IV. M.; 903, Chron. Scot.

[27] IV. M.

[28] IV. M.; 737, Chron. Scot.

[29] Luighne, or Tuath-Luighne; the barony of Lune, county Meath.

[30] IV. M.

[31] Lusca. Lusk, county Louth.

a ainm biler, aɣur Cainniɣ, Cuinoiɣ no Cuinbeo a ceb ainm, quieuic 497.

Aréb aber Mac Firbiriɣ quier Cuinoeba maic Catbaba .ı. Mac Cuilinn, eprcop Lurca, et cetera, Sept. 6.

Ɣuin Colmain, eprcop Lurca, la .h. Cuirtre, 739.

Forbarat eprcop Lurca, 835.
Setnarat eprcop Lurcan quieuic 887.
Maolruanaıb eprcop Lurca, quieuic, 880.
Colman rɣribnıb, eprcop Oaimliaɣ aɣur Lurcain, quieuic 902.
Ailill mac Maonaıɣ, eprcop Suirb aɣur Lurcain, 965.
Ruaban eprcop Lurcan, 904.
Cuatal mac Oenacain, eprcop Oaimliaɣ aɣur Lurcca, maor muintire Pabraıɣ, 927.
Maɣ aı, no eó.—Fec Maɣeo.
Maɣ bile.—Finnian Muıɣe bile, eprcop, nó Finıa eprcop Maıɣe bile, Feb. 11.
Finnen eprcop Maıɣe bile.
Finnıa mac Uı Fıatat a ainm aile. aɣur Fionnbarr Maıɣe bile a ainm ele; ó Fıatat finb, rí Erenb, tainic ré. Sept. 10.
Sinell Maıɣe bile, eprcop, circa annum 600, no 602, quieuic.
brecan eprcop ır ab Maıɣe bile, April 24.
Maolaitɣin, eprcop Maıɣe bile, Sept. 9.
Siollan (mac Fionnchain), eprcop aɣur ab Maıɣe bile, anno bomini 618; Auɣ. 25.
Cairboe, eprcop Maıɣe bilc, Maoı 1.
Maɣ bolɣ. —Siric eprcop ó Maıɣ bolc, Nou. 26.
Maɣ breɣ.—Oubbabairenn mac Connuı, ruı eprcop Maıɣe breɣ, comarba buice aɣur eɣnuıb Laıɣen, 964.

1 544, Chron. Scot.
2 Mart. Doneg. and Mart. Taml.
3 Four Masters; and 743, Ann. Ult.
4 IV. M.
5 IV. M.
6 IV. M.; 883, Chron. Scot.
7 Lusca. The Four Masters, under 739, record the death of a Colman, scribe and bishop of Leassan, now the parish of Lissan, situated partly in the counties of Donegal and Londonderry, adjoining the territory of Hy-Tuirtre.
8 Four Masters; and Chron. Scot.
9 IV. M.
10 IV. M.; 928, Chron. Scot.
11 Magh-Ai. Mayo.
12 Movilla, barony of Lower Ards, county Down.
13 Mart. Doneg. and Mart. Taml.

was his proper name, and Cainnigh, Cuindigh, or Cuindedh, his first name.   He went to his rest in 497.[1]

What Mac Firbis says is "quies of Cuindid, son of Cathbadh, i. e. Mac Cuilind, bishop of Lusca, &c., September 6."[2]

The mortal wounding of Colman, bishop of Lusca, by the Hy-Tuirtre, 739.[3]

Forbasach, bishop of Lusca, 835.[4]

Sechnusach, bishop of Lusca, quievit 887.[5]

Maolruanaidh, bishop of Lusca, quievit 880.[6]

Colman, the scribe, bishop of Daimhliag and Lusca,[7] quievit 902.[8]

Ailill, son of Maenach, bishop of Sord and Lusca, 965.

Ruadan, bishop of Lusca, 904.[9]

Tuathal, son of Aenacan, bishop of Daimhliag and Lusca, steward of the people[10] of Patrick, 927.[11]

MAGH-AI (or Eo).—See Magh-Eo.

MAGH-BILE.[12]—Finnian of Magh-Bile; or Finnia, bishop of Magh-Bile, February 11.[13]

Finnen,[14] bishop of Magh-Bile.   Finnia Mac-Ui-Fiatach was his other name, and Fionnbar of Magh-Bile was another name of his. From Fiatach Finn, King of Erinn, he descended.   September 10.[15]

Sinell of Magh-Bile, bishop, circa annum 600, vel 602, quievit.[16]

Brecan, bishop and abbot of Magh-Bile, April 24.[17]

Maelaithghin, bishop of Magh-Bile, Sept. 9.[18]

Siollan, son of Fionchan, bishop and abbot of Magh-Bile, A°. D¹. 618,[19] August 25.[20]

Cairbre, bishop of Magh-Bile, May 1.[21]

MAGH-BOLG.[22]—Siric, bishop, from Magh-Bolc, November 26.[23]

MAGH-BREGH.[24]—Dubhdabhairen, son of Curoi, eminent bishop of Magh-Bregh, comarb of Bute,[25] and sage of Leinster, 964.[26]

---

[14] *Finnen.* The same as Finnian, or Finnia.

[15] Mart. Doneg.

[16] 602, Four M.; 603, Chron. Scot.

[17] 29 Mart. Doneg. and Mart. Taml.

[18] Mart. Doneg. and Mart. Taml.

[19] IV. M.; 619, Chron. Scot.

[20] Mart. Doneg. and Mart. Taml.

[21] 3, Mart. Doneg. and Mart. Taml.

[22] Moybolgue; partly situated in the counties of Cavan and Meath.

[23] Mart. Doneg.

[24] Bregia; a district comprising a large part of the counties of Dublin and Meath.

[25] *Bute.* Patron and founder of Mainister-Buite, or Monasterboice, county Louth.

[26] Ann. Ult. and Four Masters.

Maʒ cpeṁcoille.—Coʒan eppcop aʒup eʒnuiḋ Maiʒe cpeṁ-coille, Maoi 31.

Maʒ eó.—Ponṫipex Maiʒe eó Saxanum, Ʒapailt, obiiṫ 726; Mapṫa 13.

ḋpocaiḋ Imliʒ ḃpoċaḋa, i Muiʒ Co (no Aói), Iuil 9.

Aoḋan, eppcop Maiʒe eó, 768.

Mac an bpeṫemain, eppcop Maiʒe eó; biḃpip mac Uilliam bupc .i. anṫ ab caoċ ó.

Paṫpaic O hCliḋe, eppcop Maiʒe eó; ḋo bapuiʒeḋ ó i ccill Mocelloʒ, 1579, ap pon an cpeḋiṁ caṫoilcḋe.

Mainipṫip ḃhuiṫṫa.—ḃuiṫṫe .i. ḃoeṫíup, eppcop Mainipṫpeċ, quieuiṫ 521. ḋec. 7.

ḃuiṫṫe (.i. buaḃaċ mac ḃpónaiʒ).

Nṫ.—Ʒin ċaóin Choluim ap cclépiʒ,
Aniu óp Cpinḋ óluiʒ.
Pop aon líṫ ní páḋ nuaḃaip
báp báu ḃhuaḃaiʒ mec ḃpónaiʒ.

ḋomnall mac Máicniaḋa, aḃ mainipṫpeċ ḃuiṫṫe, eppcop aʒup penoip naoṁ, 1004.

Maicnia, eppcop aʒup comapba mainipṫpeċ ḃuiṫṫe, ḋo éc 1039.

Mainipṫip ṫuama.—Capṫaċ .i. an pen eppcop; pec Iiloċuba Maoi 14.

Meaṫhup ṫpuim.—Popannan, eppcop Meṫiup ṫpuim, 751.

Muʒna.—Maolpoil, eppcop Muʒna, 992.

Oipʒiall, no Aipʒiall.—Aoḋ ua hCoṫaiʒ eppcop Aipʒialla, quieuiṫ 1369.

Oppaiʒe.—ḋunċaḋ, ḃalṫa ḋiapmaḋa, eppcop 7 Saoi, aʒup ollaṁ Oppaiʒe, 9 * *

<hr>

1 *Magh-cremhchoille.* Not identified. The name Magh-cremhchoille signifies "the plain of the wild-garlic wood." Cremhchoill was the ancient name of the parish of Cranfield, barony of Upper Torme, county of Antrim. *See* Reeves' "Down and Connor," p. 8.

2 Mart. Doneg. and Mart. Taml.

3 Mayo, barony of Clanmorris, county Mayo.

4 Four M.; 781, Ann. Ult.; 731 Tig.

5 Mart. Doneg.

6 *See* under Imleach-Brochadha.

7 Ann. Ult., and IV. M.

8 Monasterboice, county Louth,

9 IV. M.; 518, Chron. Scot.

MAGH-CREMHCHOILLE.[1] — Eoghan, bishop and sage of Magh-Cremhchoille, May 31.[2]

MAGH-EO.[3]—The Pontiff of Magh-Eó of the Saxons, Gerald, obiit 726,[4] March 13.[5]

Brocaidh of Imlech-Brochada, in Magh-Eo (or Magh-Ai), July 9[6].

Aedhan, bishop of Magh-Eo, 768.[7]

Mac-an-Brehon, bishop of Magh-Eo; Mac William Burk, i. e. the Blind Abbot, expelled him.

Patrick O'Helidhe, bishop of Magh-Eo, who was put to death in Cill-Mochellog, 1579, for the Catholic faith.

MANISTER-BUITE.[8]—Bute, i. e. Boetius, bishop of Manister, quievit 521,[9] December 7.[10]

Buite (i. e. Buadach, son of Bronach).

NOTE.—" The gentle birth of Colum, our cleric,
          To-day over noble Erinn;
          On the same festival, it is no vaunting saying,
          [Is commemorated] the death of fair Buadach, son of
              Bronach."

Domhnall, son of Macniadh, abbot of Manister-Bute, a bishop and holy elder, 1004.[11]

Macnia, bishop and comarb of Manister-Buite, died 1039.

MANISTER-THUAMA.[12]—Carthach, i. e. the old bishop. See Mochuda, May 14.

MEATHUS-TRUIM.[13]—Forannan, bishop of Meathus-truim, 751.[14]

MUGHNA.[15]—Maolpoil, bishop of Mughna, 992.[16]

OIRGHIALL (or Airghiall).[17]—Aedh O'hEothaigh,[18] bishop of Airghiall, quievit 1369.[19]

OSRAIGHE.[20]—Dunchadh, foster-son of Diarmaid, bishop and sage, and ollave of Ossory, 9.[21]

---

[10] Mart. Mart.

[11] IV. M.; and Chron. Scot.

[12] *Manistir-Thuama.* Not identified. St. Carthach the Elder was the preceptor of St. Mochada, who is called Carthach Junior. *See* Lanigan's "Eccles. History," vol. 2., pp. 88, 9.

[13] *Meathus-truim.* Not identified.

[14] Four Masters.

[15] Dunnamanoge, county Kildare.

[16] Four Masters.

[17] Diocese of Clogher.

[18] *O'hEothaigh:* O'Hoey. The IV. M., and Ware call him Aedh O'Neill.

[19] IV. M.; Ann. Loch-Cé.

[20] Ossory.

[21] 971, IV. M.

Domnall Ua Fogaptaiʒ, epcop Oppaiʒe, quieuic 1178.

Raiɫ (no paɫ) aonaiʒ; Raiɫ muiʒe aonaiʒ (no eanaiʒ). bpuʒaḋ epcop, Nou. 1.

Raɫ ḃapɫaiʒe (no ḃepɫaiʒe).—Caɫhchan (no ʒomaḋ Caɫhǔu), epcop; Mapc. 20.

Raɫ Libɫen.—Iollaḃan ua Eachach, epcop, Iuin 10.

Raɫ muipbuilʒ.—Domanʒapc mac Eachaḋ, pui epcop, Mapɫa 24.

Raiɫ Oppain.—Oppan epcop. Feb. 17.

Raɫain.—Aeḃan Raɫain, [1] Aeḃan ua Concumba, epcopi, eɫ milicep Cpipci, in pace quieuepunc, aʒup Saepmuʒ Eanaiʒ buiḋ, 787.

Raɫ Colpa.—Epcop Cappach (a Raiɫ Colpa), ceḃ Paɫpaic; (ap 6 ɫuc comaoin ḃo Paɫpaic pe nécc); Appil 14.

Raɫ móp Muiʒe ɫuaipʒipɫ.—Luʒaiḋ epcop, Occob. 6.

Raɫ na neppcop.—Aoḃ ʒlap, Aonʒup. Feb. 16.

Raɫ Ronain.—Ronan, epcop i Raiɫ Ronain, in uiḃ Cellaiʒ Cualann.

Raɫ píche.—Eoʒan epcop Raɫha píche, quieuic cipca annum 615.

Reachpa.—Flann mac Ceallaiʒh, mic Cpunnḃmáil, epcop Rechpaiḃe, quieuic 734.

Roṁ.—Ʒpiʒoip Roṁa, Mapɫa 12.

Pupa Aipne po ʒab abḃaine Róma ɫapép Ʒpiʒóip, eɫ ceɫepa.

Rop-ailicpe.—Faɫɫna epcop, .i. mac Monʒaiʒ a Rop ailicpe. Auʒ. 14.

---

1 Four Masters.

2 Raymochy, barony of Raphoe, county of Donegal.

3 Not identified.

4 Mart. Doneg., and Mart. Taml.

5 Rathlihen, barony of Balliboy, King's County.

6 Mart. Doneg. and Mart, Taml.

7 Maghera, county Down.

8 Mart. Doneg. and Mart. Taml.

9 *Rath-Ossain.* *See* under Ath-Truim.

10 Rahin, King's County.

11 *Eanach-dubh,* i.e. "the black marsh," now Annagh-duff, near Drumana, county Leitrim.

12 Four Masters.

13 Raholp, barony of Lecale Lower, county Down.

Domhnall O'Fogarty, bishop of Ossory, quievit 1178.[1]

RAITH- (or Rath) -aenaigh ; Rath-Maighe-aenaigh, (or Eanaigh).[2]—Brugach, bishop. November 1.

RATH-DARTHAIGHE (or Derthaighe).[3]—Cathchan (or perhaps Cathchu), bishop ; March 20.[4]

RATH-LIBHTHEN.[5]—Iolladan, descendant of Eochaidh, bishop, June 10.[6]

RATH-MUIRBUILG.[7]—Domangart, son of Eochaidh, an eminent bishop, March 24.[8]

RATH-OSSAIN.[9]—Ossan, bishop, February 17.

RATHAIN.—[10]Aedhan of Rathain, [and] Aedhan, son of Cucumba, episcopi et milites Christi, quieverunt, and Saermugh of Eanach-dubh,[11] 787.[12]

RATH-COLPA.[13]—Bishop Tassach (in Rath-Colpa), Patrick's artist; (it was he that gave the communion to Patrick before his death); April 14.[14]

RATH-MOR-MUIGHE-TUAISCAIRT.[15]—Lughaidh, bishop, October 6.[16]

RATH-NA-NEPSCOB.[17]—Aodh Glas, and Aongus, February 16.[18]

RATH-RONAIN.[19]—Ronan, bishop, in Rath-Ronain in Ui-Cellaigh-Cualann.

RATH-SITHE.[20]—Eoghan, bishop of Rath-sithe, quievit circa annum 615.[21]

REACHRA.[22]—Flann, son of Cellach, son of Crundmael, bishop of Reachra, went to his rest 734.[23]

ROME.—Gregory of Rome, March 12.

The Pope of Ara[24] got the abbacy of Rome after Gregory, &c.

ROS-AILITRE.[25]—Fachtna, bishop, i. e. the son of Mongach, of Ros-Ailitre,[26] August 14.[27]

[14] Mart. Doneg. and Mart. Taml.

[15] Rattoo, county Kerry.

[16] Mart. Doneg. and Mart. Taml.

[17] Not known.

[18] Mart. Doneg. and Mart. Taml.

[19] *Rath-Ronain*, county Wicklow.

[20] Rashee, barony and county of Antrim.

[21] 617, Four Masters.

[22] Lambay, county Dublin.

[23] Four Masters.

[24] *Pope of Ara.* See under Ara- (Aelchu, son of Faelchu).

[25] *Ros-Ailitre.* Rosscarbery, county Cork.

[26] *Ros-Ailitre.* The Mart. Doneg. describes this Fachtna, whose festival occurs on the 14th of August, as of Dairinis-Maelanfaidh, countyWaterford.

[27] Mart. Doneg.

Roſ baiṗenn.—Cuiṗican (no) Ciṗiac epſcop aʒuſ ab Ruiſ menn, no Ruiſ baiṗenn. Maṗca 16.

Roſ menn.—ſeċ Roſ baiṗenn.

Roſ Comain.— Siabal epſcop iſ ab ſuiſ Comain, quieuic, 813.

Aeḃ mac Fianʒuſa, epſcop Ruiſ Comain, 872.

Roſ cſe.—Iſaac Ua Cuanain, epſcop Éle Ruiſ cſe, óʒ aʒuſ áṗo ſénóiſ aiṗċeṗ Muṁan, quieuic 1161.

Roſ ḃeala.—Sen Paċṗaic, epſcop iſ ab Ruiſ ḃeala i Muiʒ Lacha, Auʒ. 24.

Saiʒiſ.—Ciaṗan Saiʒſe, epſcop baoi in Eſinn ſia Paċṗaic, Maṗca 5.

Meḃṗan epſcop, Iuin 6.

Coſmac epſcop Saiʒſe, 907.

Saxan.—Aoḃan epſcop Saxan, quieuic ciſca annum 650.

Siḃ cſuim.—Epſcop Eaſc, Nou. 2.

Slaine.—Epſcop Eaſc, Nou. 2.

Niallan, epſcop Slaine quieuic 867.

Coſmac mac Elaḃaiʒ, epſcop Slaine, 867.

Maelbſiʒce, epſcop Slaine, 875.

Sleḃce.—Fiacc, epſcop Sleḃce, Occob. 12; ḃiſʒiobal Paċṗaic.

Aoḃ, epſcop Sleiḃce, 699; Feb. 7.

Sliab liaʒ.—Epſcop Aeḃ mac bſic ó ſliab Liaʒ; Nou. 10; quieuic 588.

Soṗḃ.—Maolmuiſe Ua Cainén, eʒnaiḃ aʒuſ epſcop Suiṗḃ Coluim .cille, quieuic 1023.

Siol Muiſeḃaiʒ.—Ʒaċ aic imbí epſcop ſíol Muiſeḃaiʒ (ḃó aſ mian ḃaſoile aſ) epſcop Oilepin; ʒiḃeḃ ni ſilimſi lan ḃileſ beſin in ʒaċ aen aimſiṗ.

---

1 *Ros-Bairenn.* Not identified.
2 Mart. Doneg. and Mart. Taml.
3 Roscommon.
4 813, Four Masters.
5 IV. M.; 873, Ann. Ult.
6 Roscrea, county Tipperary.
7 Aiṗċeṗ Muṁan, i. e. Ormond.
8 IV. M.
9 Rosdalla, county Westmeath.
10 Mart. Taml.
11 Seirkeeran, in the King's County.
12 Mart. Doneg. and Mart. Taml.
13 Mart. Doneg. and Mart. Taml.
14 Four Masters.
15 Saxan. England.
16 648 = 651, Chron. Scot.
17 Near Trim, county Meath.
18 *See* under Baile-Slaine.

Ros-Bairenn.[1]—Cuiritan, or Ciriac, bishop and abbot of Ros-menn, or Ros-Bairenn, March 16.[2]

Ros-menn. See Ros-Bairenn.

Ros-Comain.[3]—Siadhal, bishop and abbot of Ros-Comain, quievit 813.[4]

Aedh, son of Fiangus, bishop of Ros-Comain 872.[5]

Ros-cre.[6]—Isaac O'Cuanain, bishop of Ele of Ros-cre, virgin, and arch-elder of East Munster,[7] quievit 1161.[8]

Ros-dela.[9]—Old Patrick, bishop and abbot of Ros-dela, in Magh-Lacha, August 24.[10]

Saighir.[11]—Ciaran of Saighir, a bishop who was in Erinn before Patrick ; March 5.[12]

Medran, bishop, June 6.[13]

Cormac, bishop of Saighir 907.[14]

Saxan.[15]—Aedhan bishop of the Saxons, quievit circa annum 650.[16]

Sidh-truim.[17]—Bishop Erc, Nov. 2.[18]

Slaine.[19]—Bishop Erc, Nov. 2.

Niallan, bishop of Slane, quievit 867.[20]

Cormac, son of Eladach, bishop of Slane,[21] 867.

Maelbrighte, bishop of Slane, 875.[22]

Slebhte.[23]—Fiacc, bishop of Slebhte, October 12.[24]

Aedh, a disciple of Patrick, bishop of Slebhte, 699 ;[25] Feb. 7.

Sliabh-Liag.[26]—Bishop Aedh Mac Bric, from Sliabh-Liag, Nov. 10 ;[27] quievit 588.[28]

Sord.[29]—Maelmuire O'Cainén, sage and bishop of Sord-Coluim-Cille, quievit 1023.[30]

Siol-Muiredhaigh.[31]—Wherever a bishop of the Siol-Muiredhaigh may be, some are of opinion he is bishop of Elphin. However, I am not fully sure of this at all times.

[19] Slane, in the county Meath.

[20] Four Masters.

[21] Slane. The Ann. of the Four Mast. (867), and Ann. Ult. (861), state that Cormac, son of Eladach, was bishop and abbot of Saighir, or Seirkieran.

[22] 847, IV. M. ; 876, Ann. Ult.

[23] Slebhte. Slatey, in the Queen's County.

[24] Mart. Doneg. and Mart. Taml.

[25] 698, Four Masters ; 696 = 699 Chron. Scot.

[26] Slieve-League, county Donegal.

[27] Mart. Doneg.

[28] IV. M. ; and Chron. Scot.

[29] Swords, county of Dublin.

[30] IV. M. ; 1021, Chron. Scot.

[31] Diocese of Elphin.

Camlacca.—Maoilpuain eppcop Camlacca, 787: nír híteab peóil aʒup níp híbeb lionn aʒ mancaib Maoilpuain pe a pé pén; luil 7.

Eocaib eppcop Camlabca, quieuic 807.

Coppa eppcop Camlacca, quieuic 872.

Copmac eppcop Camlacca, 962.

Cponnmaol ab beʒ Epenn, aʒup eppcop aʒup penleʒinn Camlacca, 964.

Sʒanblain eppcop aʒup ab Camlacca, 913.

Iopep eppcop Camlacca Maoilpuain, Enaip 5.

Eocaib, eppcop aʒup ab Camlabca, Enaip 28.

Ainennán (no Enennán), eppcop Camlacca, peb. 10.

Camlacc Menainn. Cpiúp bo bpecnaib annpo .i. Napab, beoan eppcop, ip Meallan ó Camlacc Menain, aʒ loc bpicpenn in Uib Echac Ulab [n]ó o Camlacca Ui Mail.

Camnac buaba.—Uii neppcoip ó Camnac buaba, luil. 21.

Ceaʒ baoicin.—baoicin eppcop, peb. 19.

Ceaʒ Callain.—Cecepnac eppcop ó cíʒ Collain, quieuic in hI ina oilicpi, 1047.

Ceaʒ Connain.—Connan, eppcop o cíʒ Connain i cCpemcannuib, luin 29.

Ceaʒ bá bua.—Eppcop Cen mac Maine, a cciʒ báoua mic Nemain.

Ceaʒ Oioma.—Eppcop Oioma mac Senaiʒ, bo pocapcuib a cciʒ (no ó cíʒ) Oioma.

Ceac Mocua.—Copʒpac mac Maoilmoceipʒe, eppcop ciʒe Mobua aʒup na Comann, 931.

Ceac Molinʒ.—Molinʒ luacpa, eppcop, 696, luin 17:

1 Tallaght, county Dublin.
2 Four Masters.
3 Mart. Doneg. and Mart. Taml.
4 IV. M.
5 IV. M.; Ann. Ult.
6 IV. M.
7 IV. M.; 914, Chron. Scot.
8 Mart. Doneg. and Mart. Taml.
9 Mart. Doneg. and Mart. Taml.
10 Mart. Doneg. and Mart. Taml.

11 *Tamlacht-Menainn;* this was in the parish of Ahaderg, county Down, where there is a townland now called *Meenan. See* Reeves's " Down and Connor," p. 113.

12 *Loch-Bricrenn.* Lough Brickland, Co. Down.

13 *Ui-Echadh-Uladh.* Iveagh, county Down.

TAMLACHT.[1]—Maolruain, bishop of Tamlacht 789.[2]   Meat was not eaten, nor ale drunk, by Maelruain's monks during his own time: July 7.[3]

Eochaidh, bishop of Tamlacht, quievit 807.[4]

Torpa, bishop of Tamlacht, quievit 872.[5]

Cormac, bishop of Tamlacht, 962.[6]

Cronmael, abbot of Beg-Eri, and bishop and lector of Tamlacht, 964. *See* under Beg-Ere.

Sgandlan, bishop and abbot of Tamlacht, 913.[7]

Joseph, bishop of Tamlacht-Maolruain, Jan. 5.[8]

Eochaidh, bishop and abbot of Tamlacht, Jan. 28.[9]

Airennán, or Erennán, bishop of Tamlacht, Feb. 10.[10]

TAMHLACHT-MENAINN.[11]—Three of the Britons here, viz., Nasad, Beoan, a bishop, and Meallan, from Tamlacht-Menainn at Loch-Bric-renn,[12] in Ui-Echach-Uladh,[13] or from Tamlacht-Ui-Maille.

TAMHNACH-BUADHA.[14]—Seven bishops from Tamhnach-buadha, July 21.[15]

TEACH-BAITHIN.[16]—Baothin, bishop, February 19.[17]

TEACH-CALLAIN.[18]—Cethernach, bishop, from Tech-Collain, quievit at Hy, during his pilgrimage, 1047.[19]

TEACH-CONNAIN.[20]—Connan, bishop, from Tech-Connain in Crim-thann, June 29.[21]

TEACH-DACUA.[22]—Bishop Cén, son of Maine, from Tech-Dachua mic Nemain.

TEACH-DIOMA.—Bishop Dioma, son of Senach, of the Fotharta, in Tech-(or from Tech)-Dioma.

TEACH-MOCHUA.[23]—Cosgrach, son of Maelmocheirghe, bishop of Tech-Mochua and the Comauns, 931.[24]

TEACH-MOLING.[25]—Moling Luachra, bishop, 696,[26] June 17.[27]

---

[14] Not identified.

[15] Mart. Taml. and Mart. Doneg.

[16] Tibohine, county Roscommon.

[17] Mart. Doneg. and Mart. Taml.

[18] Stackallan, county Meath.

[19] Four Masters; 1045, Chron. Scot.

[20] *Teach-Connain.* Locality uncertain; but it was probably situated in *Crim-thann*, in Meath.

[21] Mart. Doneg. and Mart. Taml.

[22] Ticknevin, barony of Carbery, county Kildare.

[23] Timahoe, Queen's County.

[24] Four Masters.

[25] St. Mullin's, county Carlow.

[26] IV. M.; 693, Chron. Scot.

[27] Mart. Doneg. and Mart. Taml.

130   DE QUIBUSDAM EPISCOPIS.

Ceaċ na comairce.—Ull. neprcoip ó tiġ na comairce, Maoi 27.

Ceach Caláin.—Cillín, eprcop ó tiġ Caláin in Airġiall, Maoi 27.

Cír Ċonaill.—Eprcop tíre Chonuill .i. Maġ Ḋunġai(le), becc 1366.

Cír ba ġlar.—Aibbe, eprcop ir ab tíre ba ġlair, Maoi 24.

Ḋunċab mac Ceallaiġ, eprcop ir ab Círe ba ġlair, 963.

Cír Eoġain.—Ġiolla an coimbeb O Cearballain, eprcop tíre hEoġain, 1279.

Ḟliopint ó Cearballain, eprcop, tíre hEoġain, quieuit 1293.

Cír poir.—Caireall eprcop, i Cír poir, luin 13.

Cobar ḃhíín, i ttír Ḟiaccraċ Muaibe iar nIarġaiġ. birin eprcop, Ḋecem. 3.

Colan.—Ciaran, eprcop Colain, 919.

Creḃob.—Ḟonannan, rcriba, eprcop Créoib, quieuit 769.

Aob, ḟerleġinb aġur ab Creḃoibe, eprcop, eccnaiġ, aġur oiliċreċ, 1004.

Cuab Múṁa.—Cabġ ua Lonġarcain, eprcop Cuab Ṁúṁan, quieuit 1161.

Cuaim ba ualann.—Ḟerbomnaċ (.i. mac Caoṁain), eprcop Cuama ba ualann, anno Ḋomini 781; luin 10.

Cuaim Murġraiġe.—Ḋoṁainġin (no Ḋaṁainġin), eprcop, ó Cuaim Ṁurġraiġ, berbraċair brennuinn, April 29.

Cuairġirt Laiġen.—Cionaot Ua Ronain, eprcop Ġlinne ba lacha aġur cuairġirt Laiġen, quieuit 1173.

---

1 *Teach-na-comairce.* Parish of Clon-leigh, county Donegal.
2 Mart. Taml.; 28 March, Mart. Doneg.
3 Tyballen, county Monaghan.
4 Mart. Doneg. and Mart. Taml.
5 *Tir-Conaill;* i. e. the diocese of Raphoe.
6 Four Masters; Ware.
7 Terryglass, county Tipperary.
8 Mart. Doneg. and Mart. Taml.
9 Four Masters.
10 *Tir-Eoghain;* i. e. the diocese of Derry.
11 Ann. Loch-Cé; and IV. M.
12 Ann. Loch-Cé; and IV. M.
13 In the county Monaghan.
14 Mart. Doneg. and Mart. Taml.

Teach-na-Comairce.[1]—The seven bishops from Tech-na-comairce, May 28.[2]

Teach-Talain.[3]—Cillin, bishop, from Tech-Tallain in Airghiall, May 27.[4]

Tir-Conaill.[5]—The bishop of Tirconnell, i. e. Mac Dunghaile, died 1366.[6]

Tir-da-glas.[7]—Aidhbhe, bishop and abbot of Tir-da-glas, May 24.[8]

Dunchadh, son of Cellach, bishop and abbot of Tir-da-glas, 963.[9]

Tir-Eoghain.[10] — Gilla-an-Coimdedh O'Carolan, bishop of Tir-Eoghain, 1279.[11]

Florence O'Carolan, bishop of Tir-Eoghain, quievit 1293.[12]

Tir-Rois.[13]—Carell, bishop in Tir-Rois, June 13.[14]

Tobar-Birin, in Tir-Fiachrach of the Moy, behind Iaskagh (Easky, Co. Sligo). Birin, bishop, December 3.[15]

Tolan.[16]—Ciaran, bishop of Tolan, 919.[17]

Trefod.[18]—Forannan, scribe, bishop of Treoid, went to his rest 769.[19]

Aedh, lector and abbot of Treoid, a bishop and learned man, and pilgrim, 1004.[20]

Tuadh-Mumha.[21]—Tadhg O'Lonergan, bishop of Thomond, went to his rest 1161.

Tuaim-da-ualann.[22]—Ferdomhnach (i. e. son of Caomhan), bishop of Tuaim-da-ualann, anno Domini 781,[23] June 10.[24]

Tuaim-Muscraighe.[25]—Dombainghin, or Damhainghin, bishop of Tuaim-Muscraighe, brother of Brenainn, April 29.[26]

Tuaisgert-Laighen.[27]—Cionaoth O'Ronan, bishop of Glenn-da-locha, and of North Leinster, quievit 1173.[28]

[15] Mart. Doneg.

[16] Dulane, near Kells, county Meath.

[17] Four Masters; 920.

[18] Trevet, barony of Skreen, county Meath.

[19] IV. M.

[20] IV. M.; 1003, Chron. Scot.

[21] *Tuadh-Mumha*; i. e. the diocese of Kilfenora.

[22] Tuam, county Galway.

[23] Mart. Doneg.; 777, IV. M.

[24] Mart. Doneg. and Mart. Taml.

[25] Tomes, barony of West Muskerry, county Cork.

[26] Mart. Doneg. and Mart. Taml.

[27] North Leinster, i. e. the diocese of Glendalough.

[28] Four Masters.

Culuιʒ ċαρϐυιϐ.—Θρϲορ Cαlϐ, ó Culαιʒ ċαρϐυιϐ ι menna Cιρe ιn lϐ Mℓ́ℓ, Θnαιρ 26.

Uα ϐριυιn.—Cuαℓαl O Connαċℓαιʒ, eρϲορ Uα mϐριυιn, quιeυιℓ 1179.

Uα Cennρℓℓαιʒ.—Cln

Uα Cennρℓℓαιʒ.—Clnℓ eρϲορ Uα Cαℓℓαιn, .ι. αιρϐ eρϲορ Uα ϲCennριℓlαιʒ, quιeυιℓ 1135.

Uα ċonʒϐαιl.—Ϝαċℓnα eρϲορ on uα conʒϐαιl, Θnαιρ 19.

Uα ϝϜιαϲραċ.—lomαρ Uα Rυαϐαιn, eρϲορ ó ϝϜιαϲραċ, quιeυιℓ 1176.

Clnℓ eρϲορ O Ceαllαιʒ, .ι. eρϲορ O ϝϜιαϲραϐ, quιeυιℓ 1216.

Ꝫιollα ceαllαιʒ O Rυαιϐín, eρϲορ O ϝϜιαϲραϐ, quιeυιℓ 1254.

Mαolmαιρe O Conmαιo, eρϲορ O ϝϜιαϲραϐ ιρ ϲιneł Cleϐα, quιeυιℓ 1225.

Uα Mαιne.—Mαolιoρα mαϲ αn ϐαιρϐ, eρϲορ Uα Mαιne, quιeυιℓ 1174.

Uα Nell.—Moċℓα eρϲορ Uα Nell, αʒυρ ραʒαρℓ Clρϐα Mαϲhα, 924.

Ulαϐ.—Mαolιoρα mαϲ αn ϲłℓ́ριʒ ċυιρρ, eρϲορ Ulαϐ, quιeυιℓ 1175.

Ꝫιollα ϐomnαιʒ mαϲ Cormαιϲ, eρϲορ Ulαϐ, quιeυιℓ 1175.

---

1 Tullycorbet, county Monaghan.

2 Mart. Taml.

3 *Ui-Briuin ;* i. e. the diocese of Kilmore.

4 Four Masters.

5 Diocese of Ferns.

6 IV. M.; Ann. Loch-Cé.

7 Supposed by some to be Navan, county Meath.

8 Mart. Doneg. and Mart. Taml.

9 Diocese of Kilmacduagh.

10 Four Masters.

11 IV. M.

TULAGH-CARBUID.[1] — Bishop Calbh, from Tulach-Carbaid, in Menna-tire in Ui-Meith, January 26.[2]

UI-BRIUIN.[3]—Tuathal O'Connachty, bishop of the Hy-Briuin, went to his rest 1179.[4]

UI-CENNSELAIGH.[5]—The bishop O'Cattan, i. e. the arch-bishop of Ui-Cennselaigh, quievit 1135.[6]

UA-CONGBHAIL.[7]—Fachtna, bishop, from Ua-Congbhail, Jan. 19.[8]

UI-FIACHRACH.[9]—Iomhar O'Ruadhain, bishop of Ui-Fiachrach, quievit 1176.[10]

Bishop O'Cellaigh, i. e. bishop of the Ui-Fiachrach, quievit 1216.[11]

Gilla-Cellaigh O'Ruaidhin, bishop of the Ui-Fiachrach, quievit 1254.[12]

Maolmuire O'Conmaic, bishop of Ui-Fiachrach and Cenel-Aedha, quievit 1225.[13]

UA-MAINE.[14]—Mael-Isa Mac-a-Ward, bishop of Ui-Maine, quievit 1174.[15]

UA NEILL.[16]—Mochta, bishop of the O'Neills, and priest of Ard-Macha, 924[17].

ULADH.[18] — Maoliosa Mac-an-Clerigh-chuirr, bishop of Uladh quievit 1175.[19]

Gilla-domnaigh Mac Cormaic, bishop of Uladh, quievit 1175.[20]

[12] 1253, Four Masters.

[13] Ib.

[14] *Ua-Maine*; i. e. the diocese of Clon-fert.

[15] 1173, Four Masters.

[16] The O'Neills.

[17] Four Masters.

[18] Ulster, or the diocese of Down.

[19] Four Masters; Ann. Loch-Cé.

[20] Ib.

IV.—TAIN BO FRAICH.

From MS. H. 2, 18 (*fol.* 183, *et seqq.*), *in the Library of Trinity College, Dublin.*

TRANSLATED AND EDITED BY

J. O'BEIRNE CROWE, A. B.

THE following hitherto inedited romantic specimen of Irish life in the first century is taken from the oldest portion of the " Book of Leinster," a compilation of the twelfth. The subject is this :—

Froech, son of Idath (a chieftain of Eirros Domno, in the present county of Mayo), and of Befind, a *Sidè* lady, has come to learn that he is loved by Find-abair, daughter of Ailill and Medb, king and queen of the Connachta. He accordingly resolves to visit her parents in their palace of Cruachu, now Rathcroghan, in the county of Roscommon, and formally demand her hand in marriage. Before, however, proceeding on his journey, his friends say to him that, as Boand, the *Sidè* governess of the Boyne, was his mother's sister, it would be well for him to call on her at her palace in Mag Breg, and request her to fit him out suitably for the occasion. He does so, and, with his request fully granted, sets out for Cruachu.

The equipment of Froech's cavalcade was grand in the extreme. Gold and silver, carbuncle and other precious stones, glittered on man and horse; but the most curious beings in this train were the three *Sidè* harpers, the sons of Uaithne and Boand. Their origin, name, form, and dress are fully described, and in note (12) I have endeavoured to give an interpretation of this figurative description. The approach of Froech and his suite was duly announced by the watchman in Dun Cruachan; and as these visitors from the *Sidè* approached, such was the delicious odour which perfumed the air around, that several of the family of Cruachu died of the effect.

Among all nations, the presence of divinities was accompanied and attested by a supernatural perfume : and in our ancient tale, the *Sidè* are always thus introduced. In tropical lands, in India, for example, the deities when appearing to mortals exhibit also other characteristics, such as garlands of flowers, blooming and erect, as a symbol of immortality; this symbol with our *Sidè* is the never-fading, green tunic or head-dress.

Froech enjoyed the hospitality of his sovereigns for some weeks, and then preferred his suit in due form; the dowry, however, asked of him he deems too much, and so takes his leave abruptly. Meantime he had arranged everything with Find-abair; and though Ailill tried to have him drowned in the Brei, a river adjoining the palace, the kindness of his lady-love and the power of his divine mother saved him. The king and queen, finding him thus favoured, express regret for their conduct towards him, make their peace with him, and offer him their daughter, as soon as he should come back and join them in their intended spoil of the cows of Cualnge. He accepts the offer, and bids farewell.

On arriving at his mother's house, Froech learns that plunderers from the Alps had carried off his wife, his three sons, and his cows, and this is the origin of the title of our tale—"The Spoil of the Cows of Froech." The reader must not be surprised to find that our hero, though a suitor for the hand of Find-abair, had already a wife and family. To understand this, he must study life in ancient Eriu.

Froech consulted his mother in his present difficulty. She tried to dissuade him from the attempt to recover the stolen property, but he declined to take her advice. Accompanied, accordingly, by Conall Cernach, one of the three great champions of the Ulaid, he sets off for the Alps, brings back his wife, his children, and his cows; and then, agreeably to promise, joins in the Tain Bo Cualnge, in which expedition he perishes by the hands of his brother demigod, Cu Chulaind.

Τάιη bó ϝraich.

———

ϝroeċ mac Ιbaιċ το Chonnachtaιb—mac rιτe το béϝιητ a
Sϝοιb: τerb-ϝιur rιτe το τοιητ. Ιr hé laeċ ιr άιlτem
rοbάι το ϝeraιb hΕrento ⁊ Οlban, aċt nι ba ruċaιn.
Dobert a maċaιr τί ba τéc τó arr ιnτ Sίτ: ιτ é ϝιnτa, όι-berʒa.
bόι τrebat maιċ οca co cent οċṁ blιaτna cen τabaιrτ mna
ċuca. Cόιca maιc rίʒ ϝor é lίn a τeʒlaιċ: comάιr, comcuτ-
rumma ϝrιr ule eτer όruch ⁊ όorc. Captċaι ϝιnτ-abaιr, ιnʒen
Οιlella ⁊ Μeτba, ar a ιrcélaιb. Οτϝιaτar τorum oc a ċaιʒ.
Ropu lάn hΕrιu ⁊ Οlbu τι a allut ⁊ τι a rcélaιb.

Ιar ruιτιu tocorartar ϝaιr τul το acallaιm na hιnʒιne: ιm-
maroraιτ ϝrι a muntιr anί rιn. "Τιaʒar uaιτ τιn co rιaιr τo
maċaτ co τucċaτ nί τo éτυċ ιnʒantaċ ⁊ τe arcetaιb Sίτe τuιτ
uaτι." Luιτ ιarum co ϝιaιr .ι. co τόιnt, com τύι ιm Μaʒ breʒ,
⁊ τobert τοιcaιcṁ bratċι ʒorm ⁊ ba cormaιl ceċ ae ϝrι ϝιn-
τruιṁeη τόιle, ⁊ ceċeora oa τub-ʒlarra ϝor ceċ bruτ, ⁊ mιleċ
τerʒʒ-όιr la ceċṁ bratċ: ⁊ lénτι bάn-ʒela co τuaʒ-mίlaιb όιr
ιmpu. Ocur cόιca rcίaċn anʒτιτe con ίmlιb, eτ caιnτel rίʒ-
ċhιʒι ιl laιm ceċ ae: ⁊ cοίca ϝemmanτ ϝιn-τruιne ar ceċn ae.
Cοίca τopaċτ τι όr ϝorloιrċhι ιn ceċn ae: ermιτιuba τι chapp-
mocul ϝοιb anίr, ⁊ ιr τι lecaιb loʒmaιrιb an aιrϝarn: nolartaιr
ιn aιτche amaιl beτίr ruιċnι ʒϝénι.

Ocur cοίca claιτebn όr-τuιrn leo, ⁊ ʒabar boc-ʒlar ϝό ϝuιτι
ceċ ϝιr, ⁊ beιlʒe όιr ϝrιu; maellanτ arʒʒaιτ co clucιnιu όιr ϝo
braʒιτ ceċ eιch. Cόιca acrann concra co rnaċιb arʒaιτ erτιb,
co rίblaιb όιr ⁊ arʒaιτ ⁊ co cent-mίlaιb. Cόιca eċlarc ϝιn-
τruιne com baccάn orba ϝor cιnn ceċ ae. Ocur reċτ mιl-ċοιn ι
ϝlabraτaιb arʒaιτ, ⁊ ubullη όιr eτer ceċn ae. broca creτumaι

THE SPOIL OF THE COWS OF FROECH.

F ROECH[1], son of Idath of the Connachta—a son he to Befind from the
Sidè[2]: a sister she to Boand[3]. He is the hero, who is the most
beautiful that was of the men of Eriu and of Alba, but he was not long-
lived. His mother gave him twelve cows out of the Sid : they are white-
eared. He had a good residence till the end of eight years without the
bringing of a woman to him. Fifty sons of kings—it was the number of his household, co-aged, cosimilar to him all between form and
dress. Find-abair[4], daughter of Ailill and Medb, loves him for the
great stories about him. It is declared to him at his house. Eriu
and Alba were full of his renown and of stories about him.

After this going to a dialogue with the daughter fell upon
him : he discussed that matter with his people. "Let there be a
message then sent to thy mother's sister, so that a portion of wondrous
robing and of gifts of *Sidè* be given thee from her." He goes accordingly to sister, that is, to Boand, until he was in Mag Breg[5], and he
carried away fifty blue cloaks, and each of them was like to the
findruiné[6] of a work of art, and four black-grey ears on each cloak,
and a brooch of red gold with each cloak ; and pale-white shirts with
loop-animals of gold around them. And fifty silver shields with
edges, and a candle of a king-house in the hand of each of them
[the men] : and fifty studs of *findruiné* on each of them [the shields] :
fifty knobs of thoroughly burned gold in each of them : pins of carbuncle under them from beneath, and their point of precious stones.
They used to light the night as if they were sun's rays.

And fifty swords of gold-hilt with them, and a soft-grey mare under
the seat of each man, and bits of gold to them : bands of silver with a
little bell of gold around the throat of each horse. Fifty horse-robes
of purple with threads of silver out of them, with drops of gold and
of silver, and with head-animals. Fifty whips of *findruiné*, with
a golden hook on the end of each of them. And seven chase-hounds in

---

[1] This and the subsequent figures refer to the appended notes.

impu : no co pabi bać nab bech incib. Moppeppep copnaipe leo
co copnaib ópbaib ⁊ apzbibib, con ecaizib il-bachaćaib, co mon-
zaib ópbáib, píobubib, co lennaib ecpaćcaib.

baćip cpi bpúich pemib co minbaib apzbibib po bióp. Sceić
co pechul ćonbuala la cećn ae, co cíp-bachlaib con epnabaib
cpebumai iapn a coebaib. Cpiap cpuiccipe con écopc piz im
cećn ae. Documláć app bo Chpuaćnaib copp inb ecupc pin leu.

Dopnbéccai in bepccaib bi'n bún in can bobećacap im Maz
Cpuaćan. "Dipimm aććiu-pa," ol pe, "bo'n bún inn a lín. O
zabpac Ailell ⁊ Mebb plaić, ni copcánic piam ⁊ ni copcicpa bí-
pimm bap chóimiu, na bep páiniu. Ip cumma lemm beb i caul-
chubu pina nobech mo ćenb lap in zaéch bochaec caippiu. A
bpap ⁊ abaipc bozní inc óc-láeć pil anb, no ćonacca-pa piam a
bućpumma. Poćeipb a bunpaiz poucn aupchopa uab : piu
cocpí pi calmain, nopzaibec na pećc mil-ćoin con a pećc plabpa-
bib apzbibib."

La pobain bochiazac inc pluaiz a Dún Chpúaćan bi án bécpin.
Immupmućac in bóini ipp in Dún con apćacap pé pip béc oc on
beicpin. Caiplenzaic in bopup in búine. Scoipic an eoću ⁊ lécic
a míl-ćona. Dopennac na pećcn aize bo Ráich Chpuaćan, ⁊
pećc pinću ⁊ pećc mila maize, ⁊ pećc copcu alca, conbapubacap
inb óic ipp inb auplainb in búine. Iap pain pocherbac in mil-
ćoin bebz im bpei : zabaic pećcn bobop-ćona. Dopbepcacap
boćum na apbba in bopup na ppím-pácha. Deippicep ip puibiu.

Docciazap o'nb píz bi an acallaim. Imchomappap cia bu ćan
bóib : nobaploinbec iapum iapn a plonccib pípaib : "Ppóeć Mac
Ibaich inpo," ol peac. Ráice in pećcaipe ppip in píz ⁊ in píznai
(recte pízain). "Pochen bóib," ol Ailell ⁊ Mebb. "Ip óćláć án pil
anb," ol Ailell : "caéc ipp in lepp." Dolleicchep bóib cećpamchu
in caize. Eb a écopc in caize—pećc-opbb anb ; pechcn imbái
o chein co ppaiz ip in caiz immecuaipb. Aipineć bi ćpebumu pop
ceć imbái : auppcapcab bepzz-ibaip pó mpećc-puncain uile.
Cpí pcéill ćpebumai in aulaich ceća imbai. Sećc pcialla umai

chains of silver, and an apple of gold between each of them. Greaves of bronze about them : by no means was there any colour which was not in them.   Seven trumpeters with them with golden and silver trumpets, with many-coloured garments, with golden, silken heads of hair, with shining cloaks.

There were three jesters' before them with silver diadems under gilding. Shields with a cover of embroidery with each of them, with black staffs with filigrees of bronze along their sides. Three harpers with a king's appearance about each of them. They depart for Cruachna⁸ with that appearance with them.

The watchman sees them from the dun when they had come into the Plain of Cruachu. "A multitude I see," he says, "towards the dun in their fulness.   Since Ailill and Medb assumed sovereignty, there came not to them before, and there shall come not to them a multitude, which is more beautiful or which is more distinguished. It is the same with me that it were in a vat of wine my head should be, with the breeze that goes over them. The activity and play the young hero who is in it makes—I have not before seen its likeness. He shoots his pole a shot's discharge from him : before it reaches to earth the seven chase-hounds with their seven silver chains catch it.

At this the hosts come from the dun of Cruachu to view them. The people in the dun hide themselves, so that sixteen men die while viewing them. They alight in the door of the dun. They tent their steeds and they loose the chase-hounds. They (the hounds) chase the seven deer to Rath Cruachan, and seven foxes, and seven hares, and seven wild boars, until the youths kill them in the lawn of the dun. After that the chase-hounds dart a leap into Brei⁹; they catch seven water-dogs. They brought them to the elevation in the door of the chief-rath. They (Froech and his suite) sit down there.

A message comes from the king for a parley with them. It is asked what was their whence : they name themselves then according to their true names : "Froech, son of Idath, this," say they. The steward tells it to the king and to the queen. "Welcome to them," say Ailill and Medb; "It is a noble youth who is in it," says Ailill; "let him come into the *Less*¹⁰. The fourth of the house is allowed to them¹⁰. It is the array of the house¹⁰—a septi-range in it; seven apartments from fire to side-wall in the house all round. A rail of bronze to each apartment; a partitioning of red yew under variegated planeing all.

o 'n vambavaiᵈ co cleite iꞃꞃ in cig. De ᵹúꞃ voᵹnich a
ceᵈ: ba cuᵹa ꞃlinneᵈ bói ꝼaiꞃ vianeccaiꞃ. bacaꞃ ꞃé ꞃeniꞃcꞃi
véc iꞃꞃ in cig, ec camlae humae aꞃ ceón ái: cuiñᵹ umai vaꝼꞃ a
ꝼoꞃlér. Cecheoꞃ occᵹa humai ꝼoꞃ imbái Ailella ꞇ Mevva,
immveꞃnive ve chꞃevumu uili, iꞃꞃ ꝼi cepc-mevón in caiᵹe. Da
auꞃaineᵈ aꞃᵹᵹaic impe ꝼo vióꞃ. ꝼleꞃc aꞃᵹaic iꞃ inv aiꞃinniuc
ꞃoꞃaiᵹeᵈ miv-liꞃꝼiu in caiᵹa. Cimᵈellav a ceᵈ immecuaiꞃv o'n
voꞃuꞃ vi alailiu. Aꞃꞃocbac an ᵹaiꞃceva iꞃꞃ in caiᵹ ꞃin ec
revaic, ꞇ ꞃeꞃchaiꞃ ꝼailce ꝼiu.

"ꝼoᵈen vuiv," ol Ailell ꞇ Mevv. "Iꞃꞃ ev voꞃoaccamaꞃ," ol
ꝼꞃóeᵈ. "Ni ba vuꝼaiꞃ aꞃ aꞃᵹ-baiᵹ on," ol Mevv, ꞇ ecꞃaic Mevv
ꞇ Ailell ꝼiochell iaꞃ ꞃin. Ᵹaiviv ꝼꞃoeᵈh iaꞃum imbeꞃc ꝼiochille
ꞃi ꝼeꞃ vi a munciꞃ. ba cáinve ꝼiᵈᵈella. Clár ꝼinv-ꞃuine anv
co cecheoꞃaiv awaiv ꞇ uilneiv ꝼoꞃꞃi. Cainvel ve líc loᵹmaiꞃ oc
ꝼuꞃꞃannuv voiv. O'ꞃ ꞇ aꞃᵹᵹac inv ꝼuiꞃenv boi ꝼoꞃꞃ in chlár.
"Auꞃᵹnaiv biav vo naiv ocaiv," ol Ailell. "Ní hev iꞃ accoboꞃ
limm," ol Mevv, "acc vul vo imbeꞃc na ꝼiochille chall ꝼꞃi
ꝼꞃoeᵈ." "Eiꞃᵹ vó: iꞃ maic lim-ꞃa," ol Ailill. Imbeꞃac in
ꝼiochill iaꞃum ꞇ ꝼꞃóeᵈ.

bói a muinceꞃ colléic oc ꝼuiniu na ꝼiav-mfl. "Sennac
vo cꞃuicciꞃi vún," ol Ailill ꞃi ꝼꞃaéc. "Sennac ém," ol ꝼꞃáeᵈ.
Cꞃocc-bolᵹ vi cꞃocniv vovoꞃ-ᵈon impu, con an imvenam vo
ꝼaꞃcaiñᵹ ꝼo an imvenam vi óꞃ ꞇ aꞃᵹᵹac. biann-neꞃbbav
impu ammevón: ba ᵹiliviꞃ ꞃnecca: ꞃella vuv-ᵹlaꞃꞃa inn
am mevonaive. vꞃuic lín ᵹiliviꞃ ꝼuanñ ᵹeꞃꞃa im na céca ꞃin.
Imꝼeichicíꞃ na velva ꞃin iaꞃum inna ꝼiꞃu immecuaiꞃv.
Sennaic vóiv iaꞃum, conив aꞃcacaꞃ va ꝼeꞃ véc vi a munciꞃ la cói
ꞇ coꞃꞃi. ba cáin ꞇ ba binv in cꞃiaꞃ-ꞃa, ꞇ bacaꞃ Cáini U'aiéni
inꞃein. Iꞃ hé in cꞃiaꞃ iꞃvaiꞃcc cꞃi veꞃbꞃachiꞃ .i. Ᵹol-cꞃaiᵹeꞃ, Ᵹen-
cꞃaiᵹeꞃ ꞇ Suan-cꞃaiᵹeꞃ. boinv aꞃ Síviv am machaiꞃ a cꞃiuꞃ.
Iꞃ vi'n ᵈeol ꞃeꝼhainn Uáiéne cꞃuicc in Daᵹvai, ainmniᵹcheꞃ a
cꞃiuꞃ. In can bóe in ben oc lamnav, ba ᵹol maiꞃᵹᵹ lee la ᵹúꞃi
nan ивan i coꞃꞃuᵈ, ba ᵹen ꞇ ꝼáilce aꞃbíc aꞃmevón aꞃ imcholcain
in va mac; ba ꞃúan alᵹine aꞃabeicce in mac vevenaᵈ aꞃ cꞃumme
inna bꞃiche; coniv ve ꞃoainmniᵹeᵈ cꞃian in chiúil. Doꞃiúꞃꞃiᵹ

Three plates of bronze in the skirting of each apartment. Seven plates of brass from the ceiling to the roof-tree in the house. Of deal the house was made; it is a covering of shingle it had externally. There were sixteen windows in the house and a shutting of brass to each of them; a tie of brass across the roof-light. Four tester-poles of brass on the apartment of Ailill and of Medb, adorned all with bronze, and it in the exact centre of the house. Two rails of silver around it under gilding. In the front a wand of silver that reached the girders of the house. The house was encircled all round from the door to the other. They hang up their arms in that house, and they sit, and welcome is given to them.

"Welcome to you," say Ailill and Medb. "It is it we have come for," says Froech. "It shall not be a habitation for begging contention[11] this," says Medb, and Medb and Ailill arrange the chess-board after that. Froech then takes to the playing of chess with a man of their people. It was a beauty of a chess-board. A board of *fidruine* in it, with four ears and elbows on it. A candle of precious stone at illuminating for them. Gold and silver the party that were on the table. "Prepare ye food for the youths," says Ailill. "Not it is my desire," says Medb, "but to go to play the chess yonder against Froech." "Get to it; I am pleased," says Ailill. They play the chess then and Froech[12].

His people were all at cooking of the wild animals. "Let thy harpers play for us," says Ailill to Froech. "Let them play indeed," says Froech. A harp-bag of the skins of water-dogs about them with their adornment of ruby beneath their adornment of gold and silver. The skin of a roe about them in the middle; it was whiter than snow; black-grey eyes in their centre. Cloaks of linen whiter than a swan's tunic around these ties. These figures accordingly used to run about the men all round. They play for them then, so that twelve men of their family die with weeping and sadness. Gentle were and melodious were this triad; and they were the Chants of Uaithne[13]. The illustrious triad are three brothers, namely, *Gol-traiges*, and *Gen-traiges* and *Suan-traiges*. Boand from the *Side* is the mother of the triad. It is from the music which Uaithne, the Dagda's harp played, the triad are named. The time the woman was at parturition, it had a cry of sorrow with the soreness of the pangs at first: it was smile and joy it played in the middle for the

ⲓⳑⲣⲩⲙ ⲁⲣⲣ ⲓⲛⲧ ⲫⲩ́ⲁⲛ ⲓⲛ ⲃⲟⲓⲛⲃ. "ⲁⲩⲣⲫⲟⲓⲙ-ⲣⲓⲩ," ⲟⳑ ⲣⲓ, "ⲃⲟ ⳓⲏⲣⲓ maccu,ⲁ ⲩⲁⳅⲏⲛⲓ ⳑⲁⲛ-ⲃⲣⲟⳅⲁ: ⲣⲟⲃⲓⳓⲏ ⲣⲓⳑⲉ ⲣⲩⲁⲛ-ⳓⲣⲁⲓⲃⲉ ⳋ ⳓⲉⲛ-ⳓⲣⲁⲓⲃⲉ ⳋ ⳓⲟⳑ-ⳓⲣⲁⲓⲃⲉ ⲁⲣ ⲃⲩⲁ́ⲓⲃ ⲣⲥⲉⲟ ⲙⲛⲁ́ⲓⲃ ⲃⲟⳓⲟⲉⳅⲣⲁⳓ ⳑⲁ ⳟⲉⲓⲟⲃ ⳋ ⲁⲓⳑⲓⳑⳑ, ⲁⳓⲃⲉⳑⲁⳓ ⲣⲓⲣ ⳑⲁ ⳑⳑⲩⲁ́ⲓⲣⲣⳋ ⳓⳑⲉ́ⲣⲣⲁ ⲃⲟ́ⲓⲃ."

ⲁⲛⲁⲓⳓ ⲃ'ⲓⲛⳓ ⲫⲉⲛⲙⲁⲓⲙ ⲓⲁⲣ ⲣⲁⲓⲛ ⲓⲣⲣ ⲓⲛⲃ ⲣⲓ́ⳓ-ⳓⲁⲓⳓ. "ⲓⲣ ⲣⲉ́ⳓⲟⲛⲃ ⲃⲟⲫⲁⲛⲓⳓ," ⲟⳑ ⲫⲉⲣⳓⲩⲣ. "ⲫⲟⲃⳑⲓⲃ ⲃⲩ́ⲛ," ⲟⳑ ⲫⲣⲟ́ⲉⳓ ⲫⲣⲓ ⲁ ⲙⲩⲛⳓⲓⲣ, "ⲁⲙ ⲃⲓⲁⲃ: ⳓⲩⳓⲁⲓⲃ ⲓⲣ ⲁ ⳓⲉⳓ." ⲃⲟⳓⲓⲛⳓⳓ ⳑⲟⳓⲩⲣ ⲫⲟⲣ ⳑⲁ́ⲣ ⲓⲛ ⳓⲁⲓⳓⲉ: ⲣⲟⲃⲁ́ⲓⳑⲉ ⲃⲟⲓⲃ ⲁⲙ ⲃⲓⲁⲃ: ⲫⲟⲣ ⲁ ⲃⲉⲣⲛⲁⲓⲛⲃ ⲛⲟⲣⲁⲛⲛⲁⲃ ⳓⲉⳓⲛ ⲁ́ⳓⲉ ⳓⲟⲛ ⲁ ⳓⳑⲁⲓⲛⲛⲓⲩⲃ ⳋ ⲛⲓ ⲁⲓⲃⳑⲉⳓⲏ ⳓⲟⲙⲁⲓⳑⳓ ⲛⲁ ⲣⲉⲟ́ⳑ (recte ⲣⲉⲟ́ⳑⲁ): ⲟ ⳓⲁⲃⲁⲓⲣ ⲣⲁⲛⲛⲁⲓⲣⲉⳓⳓ ⲛⲓ ⲁⲣⳓⲏⲓⳋⲓⲣ ⲃⳑⲁⲃ ⲫⲟ ⲁ ⳑⲁ́ⲓⲙ ⲣⲓⲁⲙ.

ⲃⲁⳓⲁⲣ ⳓⲣⲓ ⳑⲁⲁ ⳋ ⳓⲉⲟⲣⲁ ⲁⲓⲃⳓⲏⲉ ⲟⳓ ⲓⲙⲃⲉⲣⳓ ⲛⲁ ⲫⲓⲃⳓⲏⲓⳑⳑⲉ ⳑⲁ ⲓⲙⲙⲉⲃ ⲛⲁⳑ ⳑⲓⲁⳓ ⳑⲟⳓⲙⲁⲣ ⲓ ⳓⲉ̄ⳑⲩⲃ ⲫⲣⲟ́ⲓⳓ. ⲓⲁⲣ ⲣⲓⲛ ⲁⲃⳓⳑⲁⲃⲁⲣ ⲫⲣⲟ́ⲉⳓ ⳟⲉⲓⲟⳓ: "ⲓⲣ ⲙⲁⲓⳓⲏ ⲣⲟⲛⳓⲁⲃⲩⲣ ⲫⲣⲓⳓⳓ," ⲟⳑ ⲣⲉ: "ⲛⲓ́ ⲃⲓⲩⲣ ⲃⲟ ⳓⲟⳓⲁⲓⳑⳑ ⲃⲓ'ⲛⲃ ⲫⲓⳓⲏⳓ⳿ⲓⳑⳑ, ⲛⲁ ⲣⲁⲓⲃ ⲙⲉⳓⲏⲛ ⲉⲓⲛⲓⳓ ⲃⲉⲓⳓ ⲁⲛⲃ." "ⲟ ⳓⲩ́-ⲣⲁ ⲓⲣⲣ ⲓⲛ ⲃⲩ́ⲛ-ⲣⲁ, ⲓⲣⲣ ⲉⲃ ⳑⲁⲓⳓⲏⲉ ⲓⲛⲣⲟ ⲁⲣ ⲣⲁⲙ ⳑⲓⲙⲙ," ⲟⳑ ⳟⲉⲃⲃ. "ⲃⲉⲓⲃⳓⲏⲓⲣ ⲟ́ⲛ," ⲟⳑ ⲫⲣⲁⲉⳓ: "ⲁⳓⲁⲁⳓ ⳓⲣⲓ ⳑⲁⲁ ⳋ ⳓⲉⲟⲣⲁ ⲁⲓⲃⳓⲏⲓ ⲁⲛⲃ." ⳑⲁ ⲣⲟⲃⲁⲓⲛ ⲁⳓⲣⲁⲓⳓ ⳟⲉⲃⲃ. ⲃⲁ ⲙⲙⲉⲃⲩⳑ ⳑⲉⲉ ⲃⲩⲓⳓⲏ ⲃⲟ ⲛⲁⲓⲃ ⲟ́ⳓⲁⲓⲃ ⳓⲉⲛ ⲃⲓⲁⲃ. ⳑⲩⲓⲃ ⳓⲟ ⲁⲓⳑⲓⳑⳑ: ⲣⲁⲓⲃⳓⲓ ⲫⲣⲓⲣⲣ: "ⳟⲟ́ⲣ-ⳓ⳿ⲛⲓ́ⲙ ⲃⲟⲣⲓⳓⲏⳓⲉⲛⲣⲁⲙ," ⲟⳑ ⲣⲓ, "ⲓⲛⲃ ⲟ́ⲓⳓ ⲁⲛⲛⲉⳓⳓⲁⲓⲣ ⲃⲟⲛⲛⲁ́ⲛⲥⲁⳓⲁⲣ ⲃⲟ ⲃⲓⳓ ⳓⲉⲛ ⲃⲓⲁⲃ." "ⲃⲓⳑⲓⲩ ⲃⲩⲓⳓ ⲓⲙ-ⲃⲉⲓⲣⳓ ⲫⲓⲃⳓⲏⲓⳑⳑⲉ," ⲟⳑ ⲁⲓⳑⲓⳑⳑ. "ⲛⲓ ⲃⲉⲣⲃⲁⲛ ⲓⲛ ⲣⲟⲃⲁⲓⳑ ⲃⲓ ⲁ ⲙⲩⲛⳓⲓⲣ ⲣⲉⲟⲙ ⲣⲉⳓⲛⲩ ⲓⲛ ⳓⲁⲓⳓⲉ. ⲁⳓⲁⲁⳓ ⳓⲣⲓ ⳑⲁⲁ ⳋ ⳓⲉⲟⲣⲁ ⲁⲓⲃⳓⲏ ⲁⲛⲃ," ⲟⳑ ⲣⲓⲣⲓ, "ⲁⳓⳓ ⲛⲁⲃⲁ́ⲛⲁⲓⲣⲓⳓⲙⲉⲣ ⲓⲛⲛ ⲁⲓⲃⳓⲏⲓ ⳑⲁ ⲃⲁ́ⲛ-ⲣⲩⲓⳑⲣⲓ ⲓⲛⲃ ⳑⲓⲁⳓ ⳑⲟⳓⲙⲁⲣ ⲓⲣⲣ ⲓⲛ ⳓⲓⳓ." "ⲁⲣⲣⲁⲓⲃ ⲣⲓⲩ," ⲟⳑ ⲁⲓⳑⲓⳑⳑ, "ⲁⲛⲁⳓ ⲃⲓ ⲛⲁ ⳓⲩ́ⲙⲓⲃ ⳓⲟ ⲣⲟⲃⲁⲓⳑⳓⲉⲣ ⲃⲟ́ⲓⲃ." ⲫⲟⲃⲁⲓⳑⳓⲉⲣ ⲃⲟ́ⲓⲃ ⲓⲁⲣⲩⲙ ⳋ ⲃⲁ ⲙⲁⲓⳓ ⲣⲟⲙⲃⲟⳓ ⲫⲣⲓⲩ, ⳋ ⲁⲛⲣⲁⲓⳓ ⳓⲣⲓ ⳑⲁⲁ ⳋ ⳓⲉⲟⲣⲁ ⲁⲓⲃⳓⲏⲉ ⲁⲛⲃ ⲓⲁⲣ ⲣⲓⲛ ⲫⲟⲣⲣ ⲓⲛ ⲣⳑⲉⲃⲩⳓⲩⲃ.

ⲓⲣ ⲓⲁⲣⲩⲙ ⳓⲟⲛⲁⳓⲣⲁⲃ ⲫⲣⲁ́ⲉⳓⲏ ⲓⲣⲣ ⲁ ⳓⲉⳓⲏ ⲓⲙⲙⲁⳓⲁⳑⳑⲁⲙⲁⲉ, ⳋ ⲓⲙⳓⲏⲟⲟⲙⲣⲁⲣ ⲃⲟ́ ⳓ⳿ⲃ ⲃⲟⲃⲛⲩⳓⲁⲓ. "ⲓⲣ ⲙⲁⲓⳓⲏ," ⲟⳑ ⲣⲉ, "ⳑⲓⲙⲙ ⳓⲉ́ⳑⲓⲃⲉ ⳑⲓⲃ-ⲣⲓ." "ⲛⲓ ⲏⲟⳑⳓ ⲟ́ⲙ ⳑⲁⲣⲣ ⲁ ⳓⲉⳓⳑⲁⳓ ⲣⲟⲣⳋ ⳓⲛⲁ́ⲣ, ⲟⳑ ⲁⲓⳑⲓⳑⳑ: "ⲓⲣ ⲫⲉⲣⲣ ⲫⲟⲣ ⳓⲟⲣⲙⲁⲃ ⲟⳑⲃⲁ́ⲣ ⲫⲟⲣ ⲃⲓⳓⲃⲁ́ⲓⳑ." "ⲁⲛⲣⲓⲙ-ⲛⲓ ⲃⲓⲛ," ⲟⳑ ⲫⲣⲁⲉⳓⲏ "ⲛⲁⳓ ⲣⲉⳓⲏⳓⲙⲁⲓⲛ." ⲁⲛⲁⲓⳓ ⲓⲁⲣ ⲣⲓⲛ ⳓⲟ ⳓⲉⲛⲃ ⳓⲟⲓⳓⳓⲓⳓⲓⲣ ⲓⲣⲣ ⲓⲛ ⲃⲩ́ⲛ, ⳋ

pleasure of the two sons : a sleep of soothingness which it played was
the last son, on account of the heaviness of the birth; so that it is from it
the third of the music has been named. The Boand awoke afterwards
out of the sleep. "I accept," she says, "thy three sons, O Uaithne,
of full ardour: since there is *Suan-traide*, and *Gen-traide*, and *Gol-
traide* on cows and women, who shall fall by Medb and Ailill, men
shall perish by the hearing of art from them."

They cease from the playing after that in the palace. "It is
rushing it has come," says Fergus. "Divide ye to us," says Froech
to his people, "the food: bring ye it into the house." Lothar went
upon the floor of the house: he divides to them the food. On his
haunches he used to divide each joint with his cleaver, and he used
not touch the eating of the meats: since he assumed dividing, food
never failed beneath his hand.

They were three days and three nights at playing of the chess, on
account of the abundance of precious stones in the household of
Froech. After that Froech addresses Medb : "It is well we have
been entertained with thee," he says: "I take not away thy stake from
the chess-board that there be not a decay of hospitality for thee in it."
"Since I am in this dun, this is the day which I deem quiet,"
says Medb. "This is reasonable," says Froech: "they are three
days and three nights" in it." At this Medb starts up. It was a
shame with her that the youths were without food. She goes to
Ailill: she tells it to him. "A great deed we have done," she says;
"the extern youths who have come to us, to be without food."
"Dearer to thee is playing of chess," says Ailill. "It hinders not
the distribution to his suite throughout the house. They are three
days and three nights in it," she says, "but that we perceived not the
night with the white light of the precious stones in the house." "Tell
them," says Ailill, "to cease from the chanting until distribution is made to them." Distribution is then made to them, and things
are pleasing to them; and they stayed three days and three nights in it
after that over the feasting.

It is after that Froech was called into the house of conversation,
and it is asked of him what had brought him. "A visit with you," he
says, "is pleasing to me." "Your company indeed is not displeasing
with the household," says Ailill: "your addition is better than your
diminution." "We shall stay then," says Froech, "another week."

coppunꝺ ꝺóib ceċ oen-lá ꝺoċum ın ꝺúıne. Ꝺopaıʒcıp Connaċᴄa ꝺı an ꝺécpın. ba ımneꝺ la Ꝼpaeċ cen acallaım na ınʒıne, peċ ba hé lepp noᴄṁbepᴄ.

Laıchen anꝺ acpaıʒ ꝺeuꝺ aıꝺċe ꝺo ınluᴄ ꝺo'nꝺ abaınꝺ. Ir hé ᴄan ꝺolluıꝺ pón ⁊ a hınaıle ꝺo ınꝺluᴄ. Ʒaıbıꝺ-pom al láım-pı. "Ɑn pı m'acallaım," ol pe: "ır ᴄú ꝺo poaċᴄamap." "Ir poċen limpa ém," ol ınꝺ ınʒen : "ma ċocírpınꝺ, nı ċumʒaım ní ꝺuıᴄᴄ." Ceıpᴄ, ın elápa lım?" ol pe. " Nı élub," ol pı, " op ıpam ınʒen pıʒ ⁊ píʒna. Nı ꝼıl ꝺo ᴄ'ꝺaıꝺbpı-pıu naċ ımmeᴄà·pa o m' muncıp; ⁊ bıꝺ hé mo choʒa-pa ꝺan ꝺul ċucuᴄ-pa: ır ᴄu pochapup. Ocup beıp-pıu laᴄ ınꝺ op-naıpc·pe," ol ınꝺ ınʒen, "⁊ bıꝺ eᴄponꝺ ꝺo ċomapchu. Ꝺoppaᴄ mo machaıp bam-pa," ol pı, "ꝺı a ᴄaıpcıꝺ, ⁊ apbeıp ır coppoꝺalláup ım muꝺu." Ceıᴄ ꝺan ceċᴄap ꝺe aleċ ıap paın.

"Ɑᴄᴄaʒup-pa," ol Ɑılıll, "eluꝺ ınna hınʒıne ucuᴄ la Ꝼpóeċ, ce ꝺobepchá ꝺó 'n ınmaıꝺe ⁊ ꝺo ᴄáıpeꝺ apṁ ꝺoċum con a ċeċpaı ꝺo ꝺoꝺaıp ꝺún oc on Ćaín." Ꝺoċaeᴄ Ꝼpoeċ cuccu ıꝼr a ᴄeċn ımmacalꝺmae. " In cocup ꝼıl lıb ?" ol Ꝼpaeċ. "Ꝺoᴄallpa-pu ınꝺı," ol Ɑılıll. " In ᴄıbepaıꝺ bam-pa ꝼopn ınʒın ?" ol Ꝼpaeċ. " Immanaıcceᴄ ınᴄ ꝼlúaıʒ ꝺobepchap," ol Ɑılıll, "ꝺıa ᴄuca ᴄınnpcpa amaıl apbepchap." "Roᴄbıa," ol Ꝼpáeċ, "Ćpí pıchıᴄ eċṅ ꝺub-ʒlapp bam-pa," ol Ɑılıll " con am beılʒıb óıp ꝼpıu, ⁊ ꝺı laulʒaıċ ꝺeec cummbleʒıcap óln aıpp o ceċ ae, ⁊ laéʒ ꝼınꝺ, óı-ꝺepʒ la ceċn ae ; ⁊ ᴄuıꝺeċᴄ ꝺuıᴄ lımm co ᴄ'lín uıle ⁊ co ᴄ' aep chıúıl ꝺo chabaıp ınnam bó a Cuaılnʒıu; ⁊ ꝺobepchap mo ınʒen-pa ꝺuıᴄ ꝺcᴄ cocíp." " Ꝺochoṅʒu-pa ᴄap mo pcıach ⁊ ᴄap mo claıꝺeb ⁊ oap m' épelam, nı chıbpınꝺ ı ᴄınꝺpcpa cıꝺ Meıꝺbı ınpın." Ꝺoċınʒ uaꝺaıb ap a ᴄaıʒ ıapum. Immopnacaılleᴄ ıapum Ɑılıll ⁊ Meꝺb. "Ꝼoapbbıba poċaıꝺen ımmunꝺ ꝺe pıʒaıꝺ hꝪpenꝺ ꝺıa puca pom ınn ınʒın. Ɑní ır maıᴄ—puaıppem ınn a ꝺeʒaıꝺ ⁊ mapbam poċeᴄoıp pepıu poppuma bıne popnn." " Ir lıaċ ón," ol Meꝺb ⁊ ır mechn eıníċ ꝺúnn." " Nı ba meċn eınıʒ ꝺúnn : nı ba meċn enıċ ꝺún," ol Ɑılıll, "ᴄuċᴄ apanꝺalpap-pa."

They stay after that till the end of a fortnight in the dun, and they have a hunt every single day towards the dun. The Connachta used to come to view them. It was a trouble with Froech not to have a conversation with the daughter: besides, it was the benefit which brought him.

A certain day he starts up at the end of night for washing to the river[15]. It is the time she had gone and her maid for washing. He takes her hand. "Stay for my conversing," he says : "it is thou we have come for." "I am delighted truly," says the daughter: "if I were to come, I can do nothing for thee." "Query, would'st thou elope with me?" he says. "I will not elope," she says, "for I am a king and a queen's daughter. There is nothing of thy display that I have not learned from my family : and it shall be my choice accordingly to go to thee : it is thou I have loved. And take thou with thee this ring," says the daughter, "and it shall be between us for a token. My mother gave it to me to put it by, and I shall say it is that I put it astray." Each of them accordingly goes apart after that.

"I very much fear," says Ailill, "the eloping of yon daughter with Froech, though she would be given to him on solemn pledge that he would come towards us with his cattle for aid to us at the Spoil.[16]" Froech goes to them into the house of conversation. "Is it a whisper ye have?" says Froech. "Thou would'st fit in it," says Ailill. "Will ye give me your daughter?" says Froech. "The hosts will clearly see she shall be given," says Ailill, "if thou would'st give a dowry as shall be named." "Thou shalt have it," says Froech. "Sixty black-grey steeds to me, with their bits of gold to them, and twelve milch cows, so that there be milked liquor of milk from each of them, and an ear-red, white calf with each of them : and thou to come with me with all thy force and with thy musicians for bringing of the cows from Cuailnge : and my daughter shall be given thee provided thou shouldst come." "I swear by my shield and by my sword, and by my accoutrement, I would not give that in dowry even of Medb." He went from them out of the house then. Ailill and Medb then hold a conversation. "It shall drive at us several of the kings of Eriu around us if he should carry off the daughter. What is good—let us dash after him, and let us slay him forthwith, before he may inflict destruction upon us." "It is a pity this," says Medb, "and it is a decay of hospitality for us." "It shall not be a decay of hospitality for us, it shall not be a decay of hospitality for us, the way that I shall prepare it."

Doċaeᵵ Ailill ⁊ Meḋb is aᵲ ᵱiᵹ-ṫeḋ. "Ciaᵹam aᵲᵲ," ol Ailill, "con accamaᵲ na mmil-ċona oc ᵵoᵲᵲunḋ, com meḋón lái ⁊ comḃᵵaᵲ ᵲeíċa. Ciaᵹaiᵵ aᵲᵲ uili iaᵲum ḋo'nḋ aḃainn bi a poċᵲucuḋ. "Aḋᵲiaḋaᵲ ḋam," ol Ailill, "aᵵ maiċ in uᵲciu. Caiᵲ iᵲᵲ inḋ linn iᵲea, con accamaᵲ ḋo ᵱnám." "C'inḋaᵲ na linḋi-ᵲe?" ol ᵲe. "Ni ᵱeᵵamaᵲ naċn ḋoḃainᵹ inᵵi," ol Ailill, "⁊ iᵲ comᵵiᵹ poᵵᵲucuḋ inᵵi." Ᵹaᵵaiḋ a éᵵaċ ḋe iaᵲum ⁊ ᵵeiᵵ inᵵi, ⁊ ᵲacḃaiḋ a cᵲiᵲᵲ ᵵúaᵲ. Oᵲlaiᵹiḋ Ailill iaᵲum a boᵲᵲán bi a éiᵲ, ⁊ bói inḋ oᵲḋ-naᵲc anḋ. Aᵵaᵹeuin Ailill iaᵲum. "Caiᵲċi, a Meḋb," ol Ailill. Doċáeᵵ Meḋb iaᵲum. "Inn aiċċein ᵲin?" ol Ailill. "Aiᵵᵹen," ol ᵲi. Poᵲceiᵲḋ Ailill iᵲᵲ inn aḃainḋ ᵲíᵲ. Roaiᵲiᵹeᵲᵵaᵲ Fᵲáeċ aniᵲ ᵲin. Conaccai ní ḋolleḃlainᵹ inᵵ écne aᵲ a ċenḋ ⁊ ᵹaḃᵲuᵲ inn a ḃeulu. Poċeiᵲḋ beḋᵹ cucai ⁊ ᵹaiḃiḋ a óileċ, ⁊ ḋoċáeᵵ ḋoċum ᵵíᵲi, ⁊ ḋomḃeiᵲ im maᵹin ḋiamaiᵲ im ḃᵲúᵵ na haḃanḋ. Doċáeᵵ ḋo ᵵuiḋeᵵᵵ aᵲᵲ inḋ uᵲci iaᵲum. "Na ᵵaiᵲ," ol Ailill, "co ᵵuca ċᵲóᵲḃ ḋam bi'n ċaiᵲᵵenḋ ᵵall ᵱil im ḃᵲuuċ na haḃanḋ: iᵵ ailḃi lim a ċaeᵲa." Ceiᵵ ᵲium aᵲᵲ iaᵲum, ⁊ ḃᵲiᵲᵲiᵲ ᵹeᵲca bi'n ċᵲunḋ ⁊ ḋamḃeiᵲ ᵲi a aiᵲᵲ ᵵaᵲᵲ inn uᵲci. Ba heḋ iaᵲum aᵵeᵲc Finḋ-aḃᵲaċ: "Naċ álainḋ aᵵċiḋ?" Ba hailḋiu lee Fᵲóeċ ḋo acᵲin ᵵaᵲ ḋuḃ-linḋ: in coᵲᵲ ḋo ᵲoᵹili, ⁊ in ᵱolc ḋo ᵲoḋilli, inḋ aiᵹeḋ ḋo ċumᵵaċᵵai, inᵵ ᵱúil ḋo ᵲoᵹlaᵲᵲi: iᵲ he móeᵵ-óclaċ cen loċᵵ, cen anim, con aᵹaiḋ ᵱoċael, ᵱoᵲleċain: iᵲ hé ḋiᵲiuċ, ḋianim: in ċᵲaeb coᵲ na caeᵲaiḃ ḋeᵲᵹaiḃ eᵵeᵲ inṁ ḃᵲaᵹiᵵ ⁊ inn aᵹiḃñ ᵹil. Iᵲᵲ eḋ aᵵḃeᵲeḋ Finḋ-aḃaiᵲ no conᵲacca ni ᵲoᵲaiᵲᵲeḋ leᵵ ná ᵵᵲian ḋo cᵲuᵵ.

Iaᵲ ᵲain ḋocuiᵲeᵵaᵲ na cᵲaeba ḋóiḃ aᵲᵲ inḋ uᵲciu. "Iᵵ ᵲéᵹḋái ⁊ iᵵ áilḋi na caeᵲa: ᵵuc ᵵóᵲmaċ ḋún ḋíḃ." Céiᵵ aᵲᵲ aᵵeᵲᵲuċ comḃúi im meḋón inḋ uᵲci. Ᵹaiḃéi in beiᵲᵵ aᵲᵲ inḋ uᵲci. "Domiceḋ claiḋeb uaiḃ," ol ᵲe, ⁊ ní ᵲaḃai ᵱoᵲᵲ in ᵵíᵲ ᵱeᵲ nolamaḋ a ᵵaḃaiᵲᵵ ḋó aᵲ omun Ailella ⁊ Meḋḃa. Iaᵲ ᵲin ᵹaᵵaiḋ Finḋ-aḃaiᵲ a heᵵaċ, ⁊ ᵲoċeiᵲḋ beḋᵹ iᵲᵲ inn uᵲce coᵲᵲ in ċlaiḋiub. Dolleici a haᵵaiᵲ ᵱleiᵹ cóic-ᵲinḋ bi anuaᵲ ᵲouen auᵲċoᵲa, col luiḋ ᵵᵲe ḋá ᵵᵲiliᵲᵲ ⁊ con ḋoᵲaᵹaiḃ Fᵲóeċ inn a láim in ᵲḃᵹ. Poᵲceiᵲḋ ᵲiḃe iᵲᵲ a ᵵíᵲ ᵲúaᵲ in'ᵲḃᵹ, ⁊ am miᵱl in a

Ailill and Medb go into the palace. "Let us go away," says Ailill, "that we may see the chase-hounds at hunting till the middle of the day, and until they are tired." They all go off afterwards to the river to bathe themselves. "It is declared to me," says Ailill, "that thou art good in water[17]. Come into this flood, that we may see thy swimming." "What is the quality of this flood?" he says. "We know not anything dangerous in it," says Ailill, "and bathing in it is frequent." He strips his clothes off him then, and goes into it, and he leaves his girdle above. Ailill then opens his purse behind him, and the ring was in it. Ailill recognises it then. "Come here, O Medb," says Ailill. Medb goes then. "Dost thou recognise that?" says Ailill. "I do recognise," she says. Ailill flings it into the river down. Froech perceived that matter. He sees something—the salmon leaped to meet it, and caught it into its mouth. He (Froech) gives a bound to it, and he catches its jole, and he goes to land, and he brings it to a lonely spot on the brink of the river. He proceeds to come out of the water then. "Do not come," says Ailill, "until thou shalt bring me a branch of the rowan-tree yonder, which is on the brink of the river: beautiful I deem its berries." He then goes away and breaks a branch off the tree and brings it at his back over the water. The remark of Find-abair then was: "Is it not beautiful he looks?" Exceedingly beautiful she thought it to see Froech over a black pool: the body of great whiteness, and the hair of great loveliness, the face of beauty, the eye of great greyness: and he a soft youth without fault, without blemish, with a below-narrow, above-broad face: and he straight, blemishless: the branch with the red berries between the throat and the white face. It is what Find-abair used to say, that by no means had she seen any thing that could come up to him half or third for beauty.

After that he throws the branches to them out of the water. "The berries are mellow and are beautiful; bring us an addition of them." He goes off again until he was in the middle of the water. The serpent catches him out of the water. "Let a sword come to me from you," he says; and there was not on the land a man who would dare to give it to him through fear of Ailill and of Medb. After that Find-abair strips off her clothes, and gives a leap into the water with the sword. Her father lets fly a sharp-point spear at her from above, a shot's throw, so that it passes through her two tresses, and that Froech

cháeb. Lecuiꝺ ón co ꝼoꞃᵹaᴃail cenelen imbeꞃᴄa ᵹaiꞃciꝺ, col
luiꝺ ᴄaꞃꞃ in claċᴄ coꞃcꞃa ⁊ ᴄꞃeꞃ in léine ᴃái im Cilill. Laꞃꞃin
coᴄeiꞃᵹeᴄ inꝺ óic la Cilill. Ꝺoċꝺeᴄ ꝼinꝺ-aᴃaiꞃ aꞃꞃ inꝺ uiꞃciu, eᴄ
ꞃacᴃaiꝺ in claiꝺeᴃ il láim ꝼꞃaeċ ; ⁊ comben a chenꝺ ꝺe'n mil com
bai ꝼoꞃ a chóieᴃ, ⁊ ꝺobeꞃᴄ am mil leiꞃꞃ ꝺoċum ᴄíꞃe. Iꞃ ꝺe aᴄá
Ꝺub-linꝺ ꝼꞃaeċ im ᴃꞃeiᴃ, i ᴄíꞃiᴃ Connaċᴄ. Ceiᴄ Cilill ⁊ Meꝺb
in an ᴃún iaꞃum.

"Móꞃ ᵹním ꝺoꞃinᵹenꞃam," ol Meꝺb. "Iꞃꞃ innaiċꞃeċ," ol
Cilill, "an ꝺoꞃinᵹenꞃam ꞃiꞃ in ꝼeꞃ : inꝺ inᵹen, immoꞃo," ol ꞃe,
"aᴄᴃélaᴄ a ᴃéoil ꞃiꝺe im baꞃaċ ꝺaᴃaiᵹ, ⁊ ni ba cinṁ ᴃꞃeiċe in
chlaiꝺiᴃ beiċhiꞃ ꝺi. Ꝺenᴄaꞃ ꝼoᴄꞃucuꝺ liᴃ ꝺo'nꝺ [ꝼ]iꞃ-ꞃa .i. en-
bꞃuiċen úꞃꝼaille ⁊ cáꞃna ꞃamaiꞃci ꝺo inꝺaꞃᵹᵹain ꝼo ᴄál ⁊ beúil
⁊ a ᴄhabaiꞃᴄ iꞃꞃ in ꝼoᴄhꞃucuꝺ." Ꝺoᵹníᴄ uile aní ꞃin amail
aꞃbeꞃᴄ ꞃom. C choꞃnaiꞃi iaꞃum ꞃemi ꞃium ꝺochum in ᴃúine.
Sennaiᴄ ꝺi[n] coniꝺ abbaꝺ ᴄꞃꞃcha ꝼeꞃ ꝺi ꝼain-chaemaiᴃ Cilella aꞃ
ꝼíꞃeċᴄai. Ꝺoᴄaeᴄ iaꞃum iꞃ in ᴃún ⁊ ᴄeiᴄ iꞃꞃ in ꝼoᴄꞃucuꝺ. Cone-
ꞃaiᵹ in ban-ċuiꞃe imbi oc on ꝺaᴃaiᵹ ꝺi amblich ⁊ ꝺia ꝼolcuꝺ a
chinꝺ. Ꝺobꞃech aꞃꞃ iaꞃum ⁊ ꝺoᵹníᴄ ꝺeꞃᵹuċ.

Cocualaᴄaꞃ ní an ᵹol-ᵹaiꞃe ꝼoꞃ Cꞃuaċnaiᴃ. Conaccaꞃ na ᴄꞃí
cóicaiᴄ ban con inaꞃaiᴃ coꞃcꞃaiᴃ, co cenbaꞃꞃaiᴃ uaniꝺiᴃ, co
milechaiᴃ aꞃᵹᵹaiᴄ ꝼoꞃ an ꝺóiciᴃ. Ciaᵹaiꞃ ꝺuccu ꝺo ꝼiꞃ-ꞃcél
ꝺúꞃ ciꝺ ꞃoċꝺinꞃeᴄ. "ꝼꞃaeċ mac Iꝺaiᴄh," ol in ben, "mac-
ꝺꞃeiᴄᴄel ꞃiᵹ Sꝼoeñ hEꞃenꝺ." La ꞃin ꞃoċluineᴄaꞃ ꝼꞃaech añ
ᵹol-ᵹaiꞃe. "Ꝺomᴄóċbaiꝺ aꞃꞃ," ol ꞃe, ꞃi a munᴄiꞃ. "ᵹol mo
maċaꞃ-ꞃa inꞃo ⁊ banᴄꞃochᴄa ꝺoinni." Cocabaiꞃ immiaċ la
ꞃoꝺain ⁊ beꞃaiꞃ cucu. Ꝺoᴄiaᵹaiᴄ na mnꝺ immi ⁊ beꞃꝺaiᴄ uaꝺiᴃ
iꞃ Sꝼꝺ Cꞃuaċan.

Conaccaᴄaꞃ ní in ᴄꞃách nóna aꞃꞃ a bꝺꞃaċh ; ꝺochꝺeᴄ ⁊
coica ban imme, iꞃꞃ é uꝺᵹ-ꝼlán cen ón, cen anim ; comaeꞃa,
comᴃelba, comaillɪ, coinċꝺini, comchóꞃai, coinċꞃocha, con ecoꞃc
ban Sꝼꝺ impu, con na ᴃái aiᴄhᵹne neiċ ꞃeċ alaile ꝺíᴃ.
ᴃec naꝺ muċċiꝺ ꝺóine impu. Scaꞃꞃaᴄ in ꝺoꞃuꞃ inꝺ liꞃꞃ. Cᴄna-
ᵹaᴄ añ ᵹol oc ꝺul úaꝺ, co coꞃaꞃᴄaꞃ na ᴃáini baᴄaꞃ iꞃ inꝺ liꞃꞃ
ᴄaꞃ cenꝺ. Iꞃ ꝺe aᴄá ᵹol-ᵹaiꞃe ban Sꝼꝺ la aéꞃ cíuil hEꞃenꝺ.

caught the spear in his hand. He shoots the spear into the land up, and the monster in his side. He lets it fly with a charge of the methods of playing of championship, so that it goes over the purple robe and through the shirt that was about Ailill. At this the youths who were with Ailill rise to him. Findabair goes out of the water and leaves the sword in Froech's hand; and he cuts his head of the monster, so that it was on its side, and he brought the monster with him to land. It is from it is Dub-lind Froech in Brei, in the lands of the Connachta. Ailill and Medb go into their dun afterwards.

"A great deed is what we have done," says Medb. "It is lamentable," says Ailill, "what we have done to the man; the daughter, however, he says—her flesh shall perish to-morrow at once, and it shall not be the guilt of bringing of the sword that shall be for her. Let a bath be made by you for this man, namely, broth of fresh bacon and the flesh of a heifer[18] to be minced in it, under adze and axe, and he to be brought into the bath." All that thing was done as he said. His trumpeters then before him to the dun. They play then until thirty men of the special friends of Ailill die for pleasureableness. He goes then into the dun and he goes into the bath. The female company rise around him at the vat for ablution and for washing of his head. He was brought out of it then and a bed was made.

They heard something—the lament-cry on Cruachu. There were seen the three fifty women with purple tunics, with green head-dresses, with pins of silver on their wrists. A messenger is sent to them to learn to know what they had bewailed. "Froech, son of Idath," says the woman, "boy-pet of the king of the *Sidè* of Eriu." At this Froech heard their lament-cry. "Lift me out of it," he says to his people. "This is the cry of my mother and of the women of Boand." He is lifted out at this, and he is brought to them. The women come around him and bring him from them into the Sid of Cruachu[19].

They saw something—the time of none on the morrow he comes and fifty women around him, and he quite whole, without stain and without blemish; of equal age (the women), of equal figure, of equal beauty, of equal fairness, of equal symmetry, of equal form, with the dress of women of the *Sidè* about them, so that there was no knowing of one beyond the other of them. Little but persons were suffocated around them. They separate in the door of the *Less*. They give forth their lament on going from him, so that they moved the persons who were in the *Less* excessively. It is from it is the lament-cry of the women of the *Sidè*[20] with the musicians of Eriu.

Ceic ꝼeom iapum iꝽ in bún. Acapeʒac inc ꝼludiʒ húili aꝼ a
chenb ⁊ ꝼepaic ꝼailci ꝼꝽiꝽꝽ, amail bab a bomun aile chiꝽꝽab.
AcꝽaiʒ Cilill ⁊ Mebb ⁊ boʒniac aichꝽiʒin bó bo'nb eꝽ boꝽinʒenꝽac
ꝼꝽiꝽ, ⁊ boʒniac choꝽi. ƷaibchiꝽ ꝼlebuʒub leu babaiʒ. ConʒaiꝽ
FꝽáeċ ʒilla bi a muncip: "AiꝽʒ aꝽꝽ," ol Ᵹe, "coꝽ in maʒin in
beoċab-Ᵹa iꝽꝽ in uiꝽce. eícne ꝼoꝽacbaꝽa anb—bonuc bo Finb-
abaiꝽ, ⁊ iꝽbbab ꝼeꝽꝽin ꝼaiꝽ: ⁊ ꝼonaiċeꝽ inc écne lee commaich,
⁊ aca inb oꝽb-naꝽc im mebón inb éicni. Iꝼ boíʒ lim con beꝽꝽaꝽ
ċucann innoċc." ƷabchuꝽ meꝽca ⁊ aꝽuꝽꝼeiccec céola ⁊ aꝽꝼici.
AꝽbeꝽc Cilill iaꝽum: "Cucaib mo ꝼéocu bam-Ᵹa huili," ol Ᵹe.
DobꝽecha bó iaꝽum com bacaꝽ aꝽ a belaib. "AmꝽa, amꝽa," ol
cáċ. "ƷaiꝽib bam-Ᵹa Finb-abaiꝽ," ol Ᵹe. Doċaec Finb-abaiꝽ
cucai ⁊ coíca inʒen imꝽe. "A inʒen," ol Cilill, "inb oꝽb-naꝽc bo
Ᵹacu Ᵹ-[Ᵹ]a buic-Ᵹiu inuꝽaib—in maiꝽ lacc? Cuc bam conbacca-
caꝽ inb óic. Rocbia-Ᵹu iaꝽum." "Ní ꝼecaꝽ," ol Ᵹi, "cib beꝽnab
be." Finca-Ᵹu ém," ol Cilill: "iꝼ eiceñ a cunʒib, no chanim bo
bul aꝽ bo ċuꝽꝼ." "Ní conꝼiu," ol inb óic; "acá moꝽ bi maich
anb chena." "Ní ꝼail ní bo'm ꝼécaib-Ᵹe nab cei baꝽ cenb na
hinʒine," ol FꝽaeċ, "baiʒ Ᵹuc in claibeb bam bo ʒiull bo'm an-
main." "Ní ꝼuil lac bo ꝼécaib ní noboccain mani aiꝽce úaibi
inb oꝽb-naꝽc," ol Cilill. "Ní comchá-Ᵹa cumanʒ bi a cabaiꝽ,"
ol inb inʒen: "an ꝽoċaꝽa baʒne bim-Ᵹa." Cuñʒu bia conʒeꝽ mo
ċúaiċ, acbelac bo beóil, meni aiꝽce uaic," ol Cilill. "Iꝼ aiꝽe
conbeʒaꝽ ċucuc uaiꝽ iꝼ becmaiʒ, aꝽ ꝽoꝼecaꝽ-Ᵹa co ciꝽac na
boíni acbachacaꝽ o choꝽꝽuch bomuin, ni chic aꝽꝽ in maʒin in
Ᵹoláb." "Ní concicꝽa Ᵹi món na ablaic chꝽa," ol inb inʒen:
" in Ᵹec conneʒaꝽ anb—ciaʒ-Ᵹa conbacuc-Ᵹa, uaiꝽ iꝼ cꝽicc conbeʒaꝽ." "Ní Ᵹeʒa-Ᵹu," ol Cilill: " caéc neċ úaic immoꝽo bi
a cabaiꝽc."

FóibiꝽ inb inʒen a inailc bi a cabaiꝽc, "Conʒu-Ᵹa bo bia ċoñ-
ʒeꝽ mo ċúaċ, bia ꝼaiʒbicheꝽ ní conbeó-Ᵹa ꝼo c' ċumaċca-Ᵹu ba
ꝽíꝽe, bian bumꝽoib ꝼoꝽ ꝽaꝽ-ol moʒꝽeiꝽ. "Ní conʒeb-Ᵹa ón
bíc-Ᵹu ón cib coꝽꝽ inn eċaiꝽe cheiꝽi, ma ꝽoʒabċaꝽ inb oꝽb-naꝽc,"
ol Cilill. DobeꝽc iaꝽum inb inailc in meiꝽ iꝼꝽ a Ᵹiʒ-ċeċ ⁊ inc

He then goes into the dun. All the hosts rise before him, and bid welcome to him, as if it were from another world he were coming. Ailill and Medb arise and do penance to him for the attack²¹ they had made at him, and they make peace. Feasting commences with them at once. Froech calls a servant of his suite: " Go off," he says, " to the spot in which I went into the water. A salmon I left there— bring it to Find-abair, and let herself take charge over it; and let the salmon be well broiled by her, and the ring is in the centre of the salmon. I expect it will be set to us²² to-night." Inebriety seizes them, and music and amusement delight them. Ailill then said: " Bring ye all my gems to me," he says. They were brought to him then, so that they were before him. " Wonderful, wonderful," says every one. " Call ye Find-abair to me," he says. Find-abair goes to him, and fifty daughters around her. " O daughter," says Ailill, " the ring I gave to thee last year—does it exist with thee? Bring it to me that the youths may see it. Thou shalt have it afterwards." " I do not know," she says, " what has been done about it." " Ascertain then," says Ailill: " it must be sought, or thy soul must depart thy body." " It is by no means worth," say the youths: " there is much of value there without it." " There is nought of my gems that will not go for the daughter," says Froech, " because she brought me the sword for pledge of my soul." " There is not with thee of gems anything that should aid thee unless she returns the ring from her," says Ailill. " I have by no means the power to give it," says the daughter; " what thou mayest like do it in regard to me." " I swear²³ the oath my territory swears, thy flesh shall perish unless thou returnest it from thee," says Ailill. " It is why it is asked of thee, because it is difficult, for I know until the persons who have died from the beginning of the world come, it comes not out of the spot in which it was flung." " Now it shall not come with gift or liking," says the daughter: " the gem which is asked in the case—I go that I may bring it to thee, since it is keenly it is asked." " Thou shalt not go," says Ailill; " but let one go from thee to bring it."

The daughter sends her maid to bring it. " I swear as an oath the oath of my territories, if it shall be found, I shall by no means be under thy power any longer, though I should be at great drinking con- tinually." " I shall by no means bring it as a fault against thee, namely— that it were to the groom thou should'st go, if the ring is found," says

éicne ꝼonaiᴛe ꝼuiꝿꝿe, iꝛ é ꝼuilleᴄᴛa ꝼo mil ꝺoᵹnıch Laꝛꝛ ınn ınᵹın
co maıch ⁊ ʙóı ınꝺ oꝛʙ-naꝛᴄ óıꝛ ꝼoꝛꝛ ınꝺ eıcnı anuaꝛ. Ꝺoꝛ-
ꝼeᴄᴄaı Aılıll ⁊ Meꝺʙ. Ꝺa leı conꝺeꝛᴄaꝛ aꝛ Ꝼꝛaeᴄ ⁊ ꝺoéᴄᴄaı a ʙoꝛꝛán. "Inꝺaꝛ lemm ıꝛ la ᴄeıꝛᴄ ꝼoꝛaᴄʙuꝛ mo ᴄꝛıꝛꝛ," ol Ꝼꝛᴅeᴄ.
"Ꝼoꝛ ꝼíꝛ ꝺo ꝼlaᴄa," ol Ꝼꝛaeᴄ, "aꝛaıꝛ cıꝺ ꝺeꝛnaıꝛ ꝺ' ınꝺ oꝛʙ-
naıꝛᴄ." "Nı ᴄelᴄaꝛ oꝛuᴄ ón," ol Aılıll: "lemꝛa ınꝺ oꝛʙ-naꝛᴄ
ꝛoʙaı ıᴄ' ʙoꝛꝛan, ⁊ ꝼoꝼeᴄaꝛ ıꝛ Ꝼınꝺ-aʙaıꝛ ꝺoꝛaᴄ ꝺuıᴄ. Iꝛ ıaꝛum
ꝛolaꝛa ıꝛꝛ ın Ꝺuıʙ-lınnı. Ꝼoꝛ ꝼíꝛ ᴄhaınıᴄ ⁊ ᴄ'anma, a Ꝼꝛoeıᴄ,
aꝛnꝺıch cıa ᴄꝛuᴄh aꝛꝛalaꝺ a ᴄaʙaıꝛᴄ aꝛꝛ." "Nı ᴄelᴄaꝛ ꝼoꝛᴄ-
ꝛu," ol Ꝼꝛaéch. "A ᴄeᴄ la ꝼoꝛꝼuaꝛ-ꝛa ınꝺ oꝛʙ-naıꝛᴄ ın ꝺoꝛuꝛ
ınꝺ lıꝛꝛ, ꝼoꝼeᴄaꝛ ꝼoꝼu ꝛéᴄ cáeım. Iꝛ aıꝛı ꝺoꝛꝛoıꝛeᴄᴄ-ꝛa colleıꝛ
ı m' ʙoꝛꝛán. Roᴄᴄualaꝛ-[ꝛ]a al laa ꝺoᴄoaꝺ ꝺo'nꝺ uıꝛcıu ınꝺ ınᵹen
ꝛoꝺlaa ımmaᴄ oc a ıaꝛmoꝛaᴄᴄ. Aꝛʙeꝛᴄ-ꝛa ꝼꝛıe: "cıa lóᵹ
ꝛomʙıa laᴄᴄ aꝛ a ꝼaᵹʙaıl ?" Aꝛ-ʙeꝛᴄ-ꝛı ꝼꝛım-ꝛa ꝺomʙéꝛaꝺ
ꝛeıꝛeṁ ʙlıaꝺna ꝺam-ꝛa. Ecmaınᵹ nıꝛꝛaᵹʙuꝛ-[ꝛ]a ımmım : ꝼoꝛ-
ꝛáᴄʙuꝛ ı m' ᴄhaıᵹ ꝺı m' eíꝛ. Nı comaıꝛnecmaꝛ·nı co comaıꝛnec-
maꝛ oc ᴄaʙaıꝛᴄ ın ᴄlaıꝺıʙ ıꝛꝛ ınꝺ aʙaınꝺ ı m' láım-ꝛe. Iaꝛ ꝛın
aᴄᴄonꝺaꝛᴄ-ꝛa ın ᴄan ꝛaoꝛlaıcı-ꝛıu ınṁ ʙoꝛꝛan ⁊ ꝼollaıꝛ ınꝺ oꝛʙ-
naıꝛᴄ ıꝛꝛ ın uıꝛᴄe, aᴄᴄonnaıꝛᴄ ınn eícne ꝺoꝛꝛoeʙlaınᵹ aꝛ a ᴄınꝺ,
conıꝺᵹaꝺ ınn a ʙeolu. Ronᵹaʙuꝛ-[ꝛ]a ınn eícnı ıaꝛum, caᴄnócaıꝺ
ıꝛꝛ ınṁ ʙꝛaᴄ, ꝺaꝛoluꝛ ıl láım na hınᵹıne. Iꝛ hé ınᴄ eıcne ꝛın
ıaꝛum ꝼıl ꝼoꝛꝛ ın méıꝛ."

Ᵹaıʙᴄhıꝛ aꝺmıllıuꝺ ⁊ aꝺamꝼuᵹuꝺ na ꝛᴄel-ꝛa ıꝛ ᴄeᵹluꝺ. "Nı
ꝼᵹıᴄuꝛ-ꝛa mo menmaın ꝼoꝛ óᴄlaᴄn aıle ın hEꝛınn ꝺıaıꝺ-ꝛıu," ol
Ꝼınꝺ-aʙaıꝛ. "Aꝛoᴄnaıꝛᴄ ꝺó," ol Aılıll ⁊ Meꝺʙ, "⁊ ᴄaıꝛ ᴄuᴄunnı
co ᴄ'ʙúaıʙ ꝺo Ᏽhaın nam ʙó a Cuaılnᵹıu; ⁊ ın ᴄan ꝺoꝛeᵹa-ꝛu co
ᴄ'ʙúaıʙ anaıꝛ ꝺoꝛıꝺıꝛı, ꝼíʙaıꝺ ꝛınꝺ [recte ꝛunꝺ?] ınn aıꝺᴄı ꝛın ꝺaʙaıᵹ
⁊ Ꝼınꝺ-aʙaıꝛ." Ꝺaᵹén-ꝛa aní ꝛıu," ol Ꝼꝛᴅech. bııᴄ anꝺ ıaꝛum
co aꝛn a ʙaꝛaᴄ. Ᵹaʙaıꝛ Ꝼꝛaeᴄ ımmı con a munᴄıꝛ. Cele-
ʙꝛaıꝺ ıaꝛum ꝺo Aılıll ⁊ Meıꝺʙ. Ꝺocumláᴄ ꝺ'a cꝛíchaıʙ ıaꝛum.

ᴇcmonᵹ ꝛoᵹaᴄá a ʙaé calleíc. Ꝯanıc a maᴄaıꝛ ᴄuᴄe. "Nı
ʙéoꝺa ꝺo ꝼeᴄᴄaꝛ ꝺoᴄoaꝛ: ꝼoꝼıꝛꝼe móꝛn ımnıꝺ ꝺuıᴄ," aꝛ ꝛı
"Roᵹaᴄᴄa ⁊ ꝺo baı ⁊ ꝺo ᴄꝛı meıcc ⁊ ꝺo ʙen conꝺaꝛaıl oc Sléıʙ
ᴇlꝼae. Aᴄaaᴄ ᴄeoꝛa ʙae ꝺíʙ ın Alʙaın ᴄuaꝛcıꝛᴄ la Cꝛuᴄhneᴄu."
"Ceꝛᴄ, cıꝺꝺoᵹen-ꝛa?" ol ꝛe ꝛı a máᴄhaıꝛ. "Ꝺoᵹena nephᴄheᴄᴄ

Ailill. The maid then brought the dish into the palace, and the broiled salmon on it, and it dressed under honey which was well made by the daughter : and the ring of gold was on the salmon from above. Ailill and Medb view it. After that Froech looks at it, and looks at his purse. "It seems to me it was for proof I left my girdle," says Froech. "On the truth of the sovereignty," says Froech, "say what thou did'st about the ring." "This shall not be concealed on thee," says Ailill ; "mine is the ring which was in thy purse, and I knew it is Find-abair gave it to thee. It is therefore I flung it into the Duib-linne. On the truth of thy hospitality and of thy soul, O Froech, declare thou what way the bringing of it out happened." "It shall not be concealed on thee," says Froech. "The first day I found the ring in the door of the *Less*, I knew it was a lovely gem. It is for this reason I put it up industriously in my purse. I heard, the day I went to the water, the daughter who put it out a-looking for it. I said to her—'What reward shall I have at thy hands for the finding of it ?' She said to me that she would give a year's love to me. It happened I did not leave it about me; I had left it in my house behind me. We met not until we met at the giving of the sword into my hand in the river. After that I saw the time thou opened'st the purse and flungest the ring into the water—I saw the salmon, which leaped for it, so that it took it into its mouth. I then caught the salmon, took it up in the cloak, put it into the hand of the daughter. It is that salmon accordingly which is on the dish."

The criticizing and the wondering at these stories begin in the household. "I shall not throw my mind on another youth in Eriu after thee," says Find-abair. "Bind thyself for it," say Ailill and Medb, "and come thou to us with thy cows to the Spoil of the Cows from Cuailnge; and when thou shalt come with thy cows from the East back, ye shall wed here that night at once and Find-abair." "I shall do that thing," says Froech. They are in it then until the morrow. Froech sets about himself with his suite. He then bids farewell to Ailill and Medb. They depart to their territories then.

It happened his cows were all stolen. His mother came to him. "Not active of journey hast thou gone; it shall cause much of trouble to thee," she says. "Thy cows have been stolen, and thy three sons, and thy wife²⁴, so that they are at the mountain of Elpa. Three cows of them are in Alba of the North with the Cruthnechi."

ꝺι α cunᵹιꝺ: nι chaιbꝶea τ'α[n]maιn ꝼoꝶꝶu," ol ꝶι. "Roτbιατ
bαι lem-ꝶα chena," ol ꝶι. "Nιmcha ꝶon," ol ꝶe; "ꝺoċoιꝺ ꝼoꝶ
m'eιneċ ⁊ ꝼoꝶ m'anmaιn aιꝶec co Aιlιll ⁊ co Meιꝺb co m' búaιb
ꝺo chάιn nam báu a Cúalnᵹιu." "Nι ꝼoċebτaꝶ," ol a mάchaιꝶ,
"a conꝺaιᵹι." Ceιτι úaꝺ ιaꝶum la ꝶobaιn.

Ꝺoċumlάι ꝶom aꝶꝶ ιaꝶum τꝶíb nonbaꝶaιb ⁊ ꝼιꝺ-ċuaċ ⁊ cú
lomna leu, col luιꝺ hι cꝶíċn Ulaꝺ, co comaꝶnaιc ꝶι Conall
Ceꝶnaċ oc bennaιb baιꝶċι. Ráꝺιꝺ a ċeιꝶτ ꝼꝶι ꝶιꝺe. "Nι bu
ꝶιꝶꝶan ꝺuιτ," ol ꝶe ꝶιꝺe, "aní aꝶꝺoττά. Aꝶꝺoττά móꝶn
ιmnιꝺ," ol ꝶe, "cιꝺ anꝺ ꝺobeτ ꝺo menma." "Ꝺommάιꝶ-ꝶe,"
ol Ꝼꝶaeċ ꝶι Conall, "con ꝺιchιꝶ lemm naċ ꝶé conaꝶnecmaꝶ."
"Raᵹaꝺ-ꝶa ém," ol Conall Ceꝶnach. Ꝺocumlaτ aꝶꝶ a τꝶιuꝶ τaꝶ
muιꝶ, τaꝶ Saxoιn τuaꝶcιꝶτ, τaꝶ muιꝶn hlċτ, co τuaꝶceꝶτ
Lanᵹbaꝶꝺ, coꝶ ꝶancaτaꝶ ꝶleιbτe Elꝼae. Conaccaτaꝶ ꝶꝶacc na
τaιn oc ιnᵹaꝶιu ċaéꝶeċ aꝶ a cιnꝺ. "Cιaᵹam anꝺeꝶꝶ," ol Conall,
"a Ꝼꝶóιch, con acalꝺam ιn mnaι chall, eτ anaτ aꝶn oιc ꝶunꝺ."
Loταꝶ ιaꝶum ꝺι acalꝺaιm. Aꝶbeꝶτ-ꝶι : "Can ꝺuιb?" Ꝺι ꝼeꝶaιb
hEꝶenn," ol Conall. "Nι bu ꝼιꝶꝶan ꝺo ꝼeꝶaιb hEꝶenn ém,
τíchτaιn ιn τíꝶι-ꝶe. Ꝺo ꝼeꝶaιb hEꝶenꝺ ém mo machaιꝶ-ꝶe.
Ꝺomꝼaιꝶ aꝶ conꝺaιlbι." "Aꝶnιꝺ ní ꝺún ꝺι aꝶn ιmcheċταιb.
C'ιnnaꝶ ιn τιꝶe ꝺonancamaꝶ?" "Cíꝶn ꝺuaιᵹn, uachmaꝶ con
ócaιb anꝶιb, ꝶeᵹaιτ ꝼoꝶ cech leτh ꝺo chabaιꝶτ bó ⁊ ban ⁊ bꝶaτ,"
ol ꝶι. "Cιꝺ aꝶ nuιꝺem τucꝶaτ?" ol Ꝼꝶáeċ. "baι Ꝼꝶáeċ
meιcc Ioaιch a ιaꝶchuꝶ hEꝶenꝺ, ⁊ a ben ⁊ a τꝶι meιcc. Unꝶe
a ben laꝶ ιn ꝶιᵹ ; onꝺaτ a baι ιꝶꝶ ιn τíꝶ aꝶ ꝼaꝶm belaιb."
"Ꝺonꝼaιꝶ-nι ꝺo ċobaιꝶ," ol Conall. "Iꝶ bec mo ċumaṅᵹ aċτ
eolaꝶ namma." "Iꝶ ꝶe Ꝼꝶáeċ ιnꝶo," ol Conall, "⁊ ιτ é a baι
τucέa." "In τaιꝶιꝶι lιb-ꝶι ιn ben?" ol ꝶι. "Cιꝺ τaιꝶιꝶꝶι lιnꝺ
ιn τan ꝺolluιꝺ, beꝶ nι τaιꝶιꝶꝶι ιaꝶ τιaċταιn." "ben τaιċιᵹι nam
báu—aιꝶᵹιꝺ aꝺoċum: eꝶꝶιꝺ ꝼꝶιe ꝼoꝶ τoιꝶc : ꝺι ꝼeꝶaιb hEꝶenꝺ
a cenel: ꝺι Ulcaιb ιnτꝼaιnꝶιuέ."

Cιaᵹαιτ co ꝶuιꝺιu: aꝶꝺaᵹaιbeτ ⁊ noꝶlaιnꝺeτ ꝺι, ⁊ ꝶeꝶaιꝶ

"Query, what shall I do?" he says to his mother. "Thou shalt do a non-going for seeking of them; thou would'st not give thy soul for them," she says. "Thou shalt have cows at my hands besides them." "Not so this," he says: "I have pledged my hospitality and my soul to go to Ailill and to Medb with my cows to the Spoil of the Cows from Cuailnge." "What thou seekest shall not be attained," says his mother. At this she goes from him then.

He then sets off with three enneads [nines] and a wood-cuckoo (hawk), and a hound of tie with them, until he goes to the territory of the Ulaid, so that he meets with Conall Cernach²⁸ at Benna Bairchi. He tells his quest to him. "What awaits thee," says the latter, "shall not be lucky for thee. Much of trouble awaits thee," he says, "though in it thy mind should be." "It occurred to me," says Froech to Conall, "that thou would'st come with me any time we might meet." "I shall go truly," says Conall Cernach. They set off the three [that is, the three nines] over sea, over Saxony of the North, over the Sea of Icht, to the north of the Longbards, until they reached the mountains of Elpa. They saw the woman of the herd at tending of sheep before them. "Let us go south," says Conall, "O Froech, that we may address the woman yonder, and let our youths stay here." They went then to a conversation. She said, "Whence are ye?" "Of the men of Eriu," says Conall. "It shall not be lucky for the men of Eriu truly—the coming to this country. From the men of Eriu too is my mother. Aid thou me on account of relationship." "Tell us something about our movements. What is the quality of the land we have come to?" "A grim, hateful land with troublesome youths, who go on every side for carrying off cows and women and captives," she says. "What is the latest thing they have carried off?" says Froech. "The cows of Froech, son of Idath, from the west of Eriu, and his wife and his three sons. Here is his wife with the king; here are his cows in the country in front of you." "Let thy aid come to us," says Conall. "Little is my power, save guidance only." "This is Froech," says Conall, "and they are his cows that have been carried off." "Is the woman constant in your estimation?" she says. "Though constant in our estimation the time she went, perchance she is not constant after coming." "The woman who frequents the cows—go ye to her; tell ye her your errand; of the men of Eriu her race; of the Ulaid exactly."

They come to her; they receive her, and they name themselves to

ραιlατ ϝριu. "Cιch ιbϝοριunech?" ol ρι. "Ϝοnροιρeτ ιmneb,"
ol Conαll : "lειn nα bαι, ⁊ ιn ben ϝιl ιρ ιnb lιρρ." "Νι bu ριρραn
bύιb óm," ol ρι, "bul ϝο bιριmm ιnnα mnα: αnbρu bύιb ceċ ρéτ"
ol ρι, "ιnb nαιchιρ ϝαιl οc ιmbeζαιl ιnb lιρρ." "Νι mchíρ-αιnm,"
ol Ϝnαeċ: "nι ταιριρρι lιmm, ατ αριρι-ριu lιmm : ροϝeταmαρ n' ιn-
meρα, uαιρe ιρ bι Ulταιb buιτ." "Cαn bι Ulταιb bύιb?" ol ρι.
"huιnρe Conαll Ceρnαch ρunb, lαeċ αρ beċ lα Ulτu," ol Ϝnαeċ.
Ϝocheιρb ρι bι lάιm ιm bραζιτ Conαιll Ceρnαιch. "Reιρρ ιnb ορζαιn
hι ϝechτ-ρα," ol ρι, "uαιρe bοnbαnιc ριbe; uαιρ ιρ bo ρuιbe
bοραιρñζeρeb ορζαιn ιn buιnι-ρeα. Cιαζ-ρα αρρ," ol ριρρι : "nι
beo ϝριñ bleζοn nαm bó. Ϝαιceb ιn leρρn οιbelα: ιρ me
nonϝαbα. Αρbéρ ιρ be ól ροbιneταρ ιnb lóιζ. Cιρται-ρι ιρρ ιn
bun, αċτ comταlατ: ιρρ αnbρu bύιb ιnb nαιτιρ ϝαιl οc on bύn :
bolleιceταρ ιl-τuαċα bι." "Reζmαι, αmιn," ol Conαll.
Ϝuαbbραιτ ιn leρρ : ϝocheιρbb ιnb nαιchιρ bebζ ι cριρρ Conαιll
Ceρnαιζ, eτ ορζαιτ ιn bun ϝoċeτóιρ. Ceρραιρζιτ ιαρum ιn mnάι
⁊ nα τρι mαccu, ⁊ bobeρατ αn αρ beċ ρéτ ιn bύιne, ⁊ leιcιb Conαll
ιn nαchιρ αρρ α chριρρ, eτ nί beρζenι neċταρbe olc ϝρι α ċéιle.
Eτ bochιαζατ ι cρích Cρuιchen-τuαche, co ϝαcα τeoρα bú bι αm
buαιb αρραιbe. Conτullαταρ bo Dύn Ollαιċ meιc bριuιn ϝριu,
com bαταρ ιn Αιρb hUαñ Echαch. Ιρ αnb ατbαch ζιllα Chonαιll
οc τιmmαιn nαm bó .ι. bιcne mαc Lαeζαιρe. Ιρ be ατα Ιnbeρñ
bιcne οc benchuρ. Coτucρατ αm bu ταριρ ιlleι. Ιρ αnb
ροlαρατ αn αbαρcα bíb conιb be ατα Cραchñ benċoιρ. Luιb
Ϝnαeċ αρρ ιαρum bι α ċρíċ ιαρum, ⁊ α ben ⁊ α meιcc, ⁊ α bαι
lαιρρ, conluιb lα Αιlιll ⁊ Meιbb bo Chαιn nαm bó α Cuαlñζιu.

her, and she bids welcome to them. "What has led you forth?" she says. "Trouble has led us forth," says Conall : "ours are the cows and the woman that are in the *Less*." " It shall not be lucky for you truly," she says, " the going up to the multitude of the woman ; more troublesome to you than every thing," she says, " is the serpent which is at guarding of the *Less*." " She is not my country-name," says Froech ; " she is not constant in my estimation ; thou art constant in my estimation ; we know thou wilt not lead us astray, since thou art of the Ulaid." " Whence of the Ulaid are ye ?" she says. " This is Conall Cernach here, the bravest hero with the Ulaid," says Froech. She flings two hands around the throat of Conall Cernach. " The destruction has come in this expedition," she says, " since he has come to us ; for it is to him the destruction of this dun has been prophesied. I shall go out of it," she says ; " I shall not be at the milking of the cows. I shall leave the *Less* opened ; it is I who close it. I shall say it is for drink the calves were sucking. Come thou into the dun, when they are sleeping ; more troublesome to you is the serpent[26] which is at the dun ; several tribes are let loose from it." " We shall go truly," says Conall. They attack the *Less;* the serpent darts a leap into the girdle of Conall Cearnach, and they plunder the dun at once. They save off then the woman and the three sons, and they carry away whatever was best of the gems of the dun, and Conall lets the serpent out of his girdle, and neither of them did harm to the other. And they come to the territory of the Cruithen-tuath, until they saw three cows of their cows in it. They drove off to Dun Ollaich[27] Meic Briuin with them, until they were in Ard hUan Echach. It is there Conall's gilla died at driving of the cows, that is, Biene son of Loegaire ; it is from it is Inber Bicne at Benchor. They brought their cows over it thither. It is there they flung their horns off them, so that it is from it is Trachm Benchoir. Froech goes away then to his territory after, and his wife, and his sons, and his cows with him, until he goes with Ailill and Medb for the Spoil of the Cows from Cualnge.

TAIN BO FRAICH.

NOTES.

[1] Froeċ. In the Tain Bo Cuailngi, Leb. na hUidre, Froech's father is called Idad (= our Idath), but in later writings he is called Fidach. Some have supposed that it is from our Froech "Carn Froich" beside Rath Cruachan has been named. This, however, is a mistake, for the Carn has been called after Froech, son of Conall of Cruachu, as we learn from the Dind-senchus, "Book of Lecan," fol. 243, b. From the same account, as well as from the "Tain," Leb. na hUidre, we learn that our hero was drowned in a ford at Sliab Fuait, a mountain in the county of Armagh, the highest of the "Fews" mountains, by his brother demigod Cu Chulaind; and, being a demigod, that immediately after he was carried off by the *Sidè* into an adjoining hill, which, from that circumstance, has been called "Sid Fraich."

[2] a Síoıb: That is, from the "*Sidè* immortals," not from the "Sid hills," which would be a Síoaıb. There are in Irish two words, which must not be confounded; namely, Síð, an artificial structure, within which has been laid, that is to say, dwells a deified mortal; the other, Síðe, which means that deity himself. The former is the Lat. *situs*, a substantive, gunated *sétu;* the latter is *situs*, an adjective, gunated, and with -*ya* termination, *sétya*. The verbal root is *si* -, " to enclose," " to mound." For the former compare Hor. lib. 3, Od. 30:— " Regalique situ pyramidum altius ;" and for the latter, Cic. de Leg. lib. 2, cap. 22 :—" Declarat Ennius de Africano : Hic est ille *situs*. Vere : Nam *siti* dicuntur ii qui mortui sunt." The two forms occur in the following passage at the close of the *Serg-ligi:*—coniò ḟpıᚱ na caıobı ᚱın acbeṗac na haıneolaıᵹ Síðe ꝛ ᵭeᚱ Síðe : so that it is to those apparitions the unlearned give the name *Sidè* and the class of *Sid.* That the ancient Irish held this *rationale* of the word ᚱíð, " a residence for the immortals," (knowing nothing of the mythic ᚱíðe, a blast of wind), is clear from the following, the most ancient Irish passage on the subject : — Síð móᚱ hıcaam, coniò ᵬeᚱuıoıb non-

naınmnıȝċe�024ᵖ deᵖ Sfoe : "it is a large *Sid* (structure) in which we
are, so that it is from it that we are called the class of sɪᴅ." This is the
explanation of the *Sidè* goddess to Condla Ruad, when inviting him
away to the "Lands of the Living" (Leb. na hUidre). I may observe
that the *Sidè* government in ancient Erin was of the same federal form
as that of the secular government; that is, a presidential king with
provincial and sub-kings. This is evident from several passages.

³ Ꝺo boınꝺ. Boand, who gave her name to the Boyne, was the
daughter of Delbaeth, a chieftain of the mythological Tuatha de Danann, and wife of Nechtan. See her story, "Battle of Magh Lena,"
p. 90, note p., ed. O Curry.

⁴ Fınꝺ-abaıᵖ. That is, "Bright-beam," not "bright-brow," as
hitherto interpreted. The gen. of abaıᵖ, "eye-lash," not "eye-brow,"
is abᵖaċ, while that of abaıᵖ in Fınꝺ-abaıᵖ is abᵖach, as will be
seen further on. This abaıᵖ is declined like naċhıᵖ, a serpent (gen.
naċhᵖach); comp. the Lat. *apricum*. Find-abair appears conspicuous
in our great Irish Wiliad, "The Spoil of the Cows of Cualnge,"
which gives a graphic account of her warlike mother's seven years'
raiding in the lands of Ulster.

⁵ Maȝ bᵖeȝ. That is, "Campus Bregum," not "Planities
amœna." bᵖeȝ is gen. pl., the nom. sing. of which would be in Gaul-
ish *Brex*, like *rix* (Ir. ᵖíȝ), a *g*-stem. This plain extends from the
Liffey to the Boyne. See O'Donovan's supplement to O'Reilly.

⁶ Fınꝺ-ᵖuını. What this highly prized metal or metallic compound was, has not yet been determined. In the "Feast of Bricriu,"
Leb. na hUidre, Medb says: "The difference between bronze and findruine is between Loegaire and Conall Cernach, and the difference
again between findruine and red gold is between Conall Cernach and
Cu Chulaind." For works of art, then, it stands in value between
bronze and red gold.

⁷ Ꝺᵖúıċh. This word is a masc. *a*-stem = *druta*, and means a
"buffoon," a "satirist," while the word for druid is bᵖuí, gen. bᵖuaꝺ,
a *d*-stem. See my "Faeth Fiada" (Journal of the Hist. and Archæol.
Association of Ireland, April, 1869, p. 305, note *v*).

⁸ Ꝺo Chᵖuchnaıb. This dat. plur. may be from either Cᵖuachu
or Cᵖuachan, both of which forms occur as nom. sing., the former an
n-stem, and the latter an *a*-stem. We may, then, here write the
English form Cruachan, or Cruachna.

* ḃṗeı. Accus. Plural; see further on.

¹⁰ ın ċaıᵹe. In the "Feast of Bricriu," Leb. na hUidre, this palace is thus described:—Seċt cuaṗḋa anḃ ⁊ ṗeċtn ımḃaḃa o ᴛꝏm co ꝼṗaıᵹ. Aıṗınıċ cṗeḃuma ⁊ auṗꝼcaṗcaḃ ḃeṗᵹ-ıḃaıṗ. Cṗı ṗceıll cṗeḃuma ı caulaıċ ın caıᵹe. Ċeċ ḃaṗaċ co cuıᵹı ṗlınneḃ. Ꝺı ṗenıṗcıṗ ḃec anḃ co comlaċaıḃ ᵹlaınıḃıḃ ꝼṗıu. Imḃuı Aılella ⁊ Meḃḃa ım meḃon ın caᵹe; aıṗınıᵹ aıṗᵹḃıḃı ımṗe ⁊ ṗceıll ċṗeḃuma ⁊ ꝼleṗc aıṗᵹıc oc onḃ aıṗınuċ aṗ belaıḃ Aılella, aḃcomceḃ mıḃ-lıṗṗe ın caᵹe, ⁊ṗ. . . . . "Seven circles in it and seven apartments from fire to side-wall. Rails of bronze and a partitioning of red yew. Three plates of brass in the plinth of the house. A house of oak, with a roof of shingle. Twelve windows in it, with glass shuttings to them. Ailill and Medb's apartment in the middle of the house; silver rails around it, and a strip of bronze and a wand of silver at the rail in front of Ailill, which used to touch the girders of the house," &c.

In the "Tochmarc Emire," Leb. na hUidre, one of the palaces of Emain is thus described:—"Iṗ amlaıḃ ıaṗum ḃáı a ceċ ṗın .ı. ın Cṗaeḃ Ruaḃ Con-choḃuıṗ, ꝼo ınc [ꝼ]amaıl Cıᵹe Mıḃ-ċuaṗḋa .ı. noın ımḃa ó ċenıḃ co ꝼṗaıᵹıḃ anḃ; xxx. cṗaıᵹeḃ ın aṗḃaı ceċ aıṗınıᵹ cṗeḃuma boı ıṗ cıᵹ. Eṗṗcaṗ ḃe ḃeṗᵹ-ıḃaṗ anḃ. Scıall aṗċaṗúṗ hé ıaṗn ꝼóċoṗ, ⁊ cuᵹı ṗlınḃeḃ ıaṗn úaċcoṗ. Imḃoí Con-ċoḃuıṗ ın aıṗenuċ ın cıᵹı co ṗcıallaıḃ aıṗᵹıc, con úacnıḃ cṗéḃu-maıḃ, co lıᵹṗaḃ óıṗ ꝼoṗ a cenḃaıḃ, con ᵹemmaıḃ caṗṗmocuıl ıncıḃ, combá comṗoluṗ lá ⁊ aḃaıᵹ ıncı, con a ṗceıll aıṗᵹıc uaṗ ınḃ ṗıᵹ co aṗḃ-lıṗṗ ınḃ ṗıᵹ-ċıᵹı. In um noḃúaleḃ Con-choḃuṗ co ꝼleıṗc ṗíᵹḃa ın ṗceıll, concóıcıṗ Ulaıḃ ulı ꝼṗıṗ. Ꝺa ımḃaı ḃec ın ḃa eṗṗeḃ ḃeac. ımmon ımḃaı ṗın ımmacuaıṗḃ." "It is how accordingly that house was, that is, the Craeb Ruad of Con-chobur, under the likeness of Tech Mid-chuarta, that is, nine apartments from fire to side-wall in it; thirty feet in the height of each rail of bronze that was in the house. A partitioning of red yew in it. A jointed stripe is it according to base, and a cover of shingle on it according to top. The apartment of Con-chobar in the centre of the house with stripes of silver, with bronze pillars, with adornments of gold on their heads, with gems of carbuncle in them, so that co-bright were day and night in it, with its strip of silver above the king to the girder of the palace. The time Con-chobur used to strike the strip with a royal wand, the Ulaid all used to turn to him. The twelve apartments of the twelve champions about that apartment all round."

The Croeb Ruad is thus described in H. 2, 18 :—"Sciall apċopup do beppɜɜ-ıbup a ceɜ ⁊ na ımḃaḃa. Imḃa Con-choḃuıp pop láp ın caıɜe. Aıpınıɜ cpeḃuma ımpe com bappıḃaıḃ apɜıc, ⁊ eóın óıp popp na haıpenċaıḃ, ⁊ ɜemma do ḃıc loɜmaıp—ıc ó púlı no-bıcíp ın a cennaıḃ. Slacc apɜaıc uap Chon-ċoḃup ⁊ ceopa uḃla óıp ḟuppı, ḟpı ċınċopc ınc ḟlúaıɜ : ⁊ ın can nocpoıċeḃ, no copchaḃ pon a ɜoċa ḟeppın, no ċóaḃ ın ḟluaɜ : ⁊ ce ḃopaıḃpaḃ pnaċac pop láp ın caıɜe, po cluınpıḃe lap ın cuı bıcíp ap aıpmıcın pom."
" A jointed plate of red yew the house and the apartments. The apartment of Con-chobur on the centre of the house. Rails of bronze about it with tops of silver, and birds of gold on the rails; and gems of precious stone—they are the eyes that used to be in their heads. A rod of silver above Con-chobur and three apples of gold on it, for check-ing of the host; and the time he used to shake it, or used to raise the sound of his own voice, the host would become silent: and though a needle should fall on the floor of the house, it would be heard with the silence in which they used to be for reverence to him."

As the Tech Mid-chuarta of Temair, and its copy, ʿthe Croeb Ruad, were oblongs, lying north and south, it is probable the palace of Cruachu was of the same form. For the compound peċc-apḃḃ, " seven-rank," of our text, the " Feast of Bricriu" has peċc cuapḃa, " seven circuits;" and for our *sixteen* windows with *brass shuttings* it has got *twelve* with *glass.* These apparent discrepancies, however, might be reconciled. As both accounts give only seven apartments, I take the opḃḃ of one and the cuaıpḃ of the other to denote the space occupied by each apartment. These apartments were three on one side, three on the other, and one at the end; and this constituted a fourth part of the house from one door to another; that is, from the western to the eastern.

The royal *imdai* was always in the centre of the house, as we see from the preceding extracts. This location is sometimes expressed by ın aıpenuch, where the word aıpenech is different from aıpıneċ, a rail. O'Clery, in his Glossary, explains it by "the principal place;" and so in the Prologue to the Felire of Oengus :—Ppım-puıḃe do Ne-paınn ın aıpenach peíne : "a chief seat for Nero in the centre of pain." The auppcapcuḃ, or eppcap, I take to mean the *wood-par-titioning* within the house, or perhaps the *grand hall.* It cannot mean area, or any place external to the house, for it is said to be " in it." In H. 2, 18, the word is thus used as a verbal noun :—Do uppcapcaḃ na ꞅlóꝣ ꝺı Maıꝣ Muꞃṫemne: "for the separating (expelling) of the hosts from the Plain of Murthemne." In the phrase ın aulaıꞇh ceċa ımꝺaı, the aulaꞇh bears the same relation to the ımꝺaı that ꞇaulach, in the first extract, does to the whole house. Aulaꝺ = ꞅaulaꝺ (English, vault?) is the name given to a warrior's tomb or *bed* of stone. The ꞅoꞃleꞃ, of which we sometimes find several on one house, was our *sky-light*. On a certain occasion Mider Bri Leith puts Etain under his right arm, and flies off with her by the ꞅoꞃleꞃ of the palace of Tara, (Leb. na hUidre).

[11] Nı ba ꝺuꞃaıꞃ, ⁊c. This phrase seems to be an old proverb; the translation is conjectural.

[13] Cáını. In this paragraph the three harpers are called the Chants and sons of Uaithne, the Dagda's harp, and their mother is said to be Boand from the *Sidè*. When this lady was in the pangs of triple child-birth, Uaithne played her a *Sorrow-strain*, at the commencement; a *Joy-strain*, towards the middle; and a *Sleep-strain* towards the close. When she awoke from her sleep, she addressed Uaithne, and accepted the three sons: and in anticipation of the future Spoil of the Cows of Cualnge, which formed a portion of her own Mag Breg, she predicted that as *sorrow*, *joy*, and *sleep* were to be the lot of the women and cows that were to fall by Ailill and Medb, so men should die by the hearing of the music of these three. This prediction was now being fulfilled.

Uaithne properly means *child-birth*, *puerperium*. "Puerperius," then, is the player on the harp, and this harp is Boand herself; and thus she is the mother of these *Sidè* strains, while "Puerperius" is the father. In the original it is hard to decide whether we have cꞃuıꞇꞇ, a harp, or cꞃuıꞇꞇıꞃe, a harper; the sense, however, is the same whether we take the *harp* or the *harper* of the Dagda. Meantime it must be stated that cꞃuıꞇꞇ is written in full in the original with a sort of mark of contraction over it, and that Uaithne is the traditional harper of the Dagda. If then we take the "harper," we must give the translation somewhat thus; "she (Boand) had a cry of sorrow: *he* played: . . . which *he* played."

The reader will, no doubt, note the peculiar dress of these Chants of Uaithne. Born of a harp, they are, of course, of the form of harps, and consequently dressed as harps; and so the writer says:—"those forms used to run about the men all round." This is the old Iberno-Celtic method of representing spiritual beings under the embodiment

of their functions. Thus in the "Vision of Adamnan," Leb. na
hUidre :—Seċc míle ainꝩel ın ꝺelbaıꝺ ꝑꝑım-caınnel oc ꝑoılꝛıꝩuꝺ
ocuꝛ oo ınoꝛċuꝩuꝺ na caċꝛaċ mácuaıꝺ: " seven thousand angels
in the *forms* of chief-candles at lighting and illuminating of the city
(the celestial) all round."

The following is the dress of the ancient Irish harper, as given in
the "Brudin da Derga," Leb. na hUidre :—Ꝺcconꝺaꝛc nonbuꝛn aıle
ꝑꝑıu. Ꞃoı monꝩae cꝛaeꝺaċa, caꝛꝛa ꝑoꝛaıꝺ: noım ꝺꝛoıc ꝩlaꝛꝛa,
luaꝛcaıꝩ ımꝑu: noın ꝺelce óıꝛ ın am ꝺꝛacaıꝺ: noí ꝑaılꝩe ꝩlano
ım á láma. Oꝛꝺ-naꝛc óıꝛ ım oꝛꝺaın cáċ ae: au-ċumꝑıuċn óıꝛ
'm ó ċaċ ꝑ-ıꝛ : muınce aıꝛcıc ım ꝺꝛáꝩıc caċ ae. Ꞃoım buılc con
ınċaıꝺ óꝛꝺaıꝺ hı ꝑꝑaıꝩ: noı ꝑleꝛca ꝑınꝺ-aꝛcıc ınn a lamaıꝺ:
" I saw another ennead [nine] by them. Nine branching, curling heads
of hair on them : nine grey winding cloaks about them : nine brooches
of gold in their cloaks: nine rings of pearl around their hands.
A ring of gold around the thumb of each of them: an ear-tie of gold
around the ear of each man : a torque of silver about the throat of each
of them. Nine bags with golden faces in the side-wall : nine wands
of white silver in their hands.

¹²Imbeꝛac ın ꝑıꝺchıll, ꝛc. That is, "Medb and Froech then play
the chess." So further on : ꝑıꝺbaıꝺ ꝛunꝺ ınn aıꝺċı ꝛın ꝺaꝺaıꝩ ꝛ
Ꝑınꝺ-aꝺaıꝛ : " Ye shall unite here that night at once and Find-abair:"
that is, thou and Find-abair. This is a form of expression occasionally met with in Irish; that is, an assertion, direct or dependent, is
made in the plural of two subjects in the singular coupled by ocuꝛ
(and), but with the first, or principal subject omitted. In the present
case the principal subject, *Medb*, is omitted. The following are other
examples: Ꝺolluıꝺ Ꝑácꝛıcc ó chemaıꝛ hı cꝛıch Laıꝩen : con-
ꝛancacaꝛ ꝛ Ꝺubchach macc U Luꝩıꝛ : " Patric went from Temair
into the territory of the Laigne : they met and Dubthach Mac U Lugir:"
that is, Patric and Dubthach . . . . met (Book of Armagh). Roꝩell-
ꝛom ꝛ ın ꝑılı ucuc ım Ꝺıꝺıꝺ Ꝑoċaıꝺ Ꝺıꝛꝩcıꝩ. "We held a wager
and yon poet about the destruction of Fothad Airgtech ;" that is,
myself and yon poet ; (Stories of Mongan, Leb. na hUidre). It will be
observed that the omitted subject here is a person of distinction as
compared with the second and expressed subject, and this may be the
true origin of the construction. In the following passage in the Tain
Bo Cúailnge Fergus addresses Medb in the second person plural :—

Inṁnaiḃiṁ ꝼunṁ co ꞇíꞅa aꞃ inṁ ꝑiṁ, ocuꞃ níꞅ maċḃaṁ liḃ ciṁ cꞁan oo ꞇꞁꞃoꞃ : "Wait *ye* here until I come out of the wood, and let there be no wondering with *you*, though it be long until I come."

[14] Cꞃi laa ꞁ ꞇeoꞃa aiḃċi. This is the accus. of time, the only case of time in Irish. All our apparent genitives of time are simply ordinary dependents, though of course expressing *time ;* and accordingly the governing substantive always accompanies them. The example Ḃommaꞃꞁ Ϝiaḃo caċ ꞇꞃaċha : "May God at every hour come to me," quoted by Dr. W. Stokes, Goidilica, p. 94, as a case of time, is in construction, "the God of every hour;" and this is the construction of all his other examples. When there is no governing substantive we have the accus. ; as, maꞇain (not maꞁcne) ꞇancaꞇaꞃ a ꞇech : "in the morning they came home" (Brocan's Hymn) : Cocumlai aꞃꞃ maꞇ-ꞇain muich : "he goes off at early morn :" (Tain Bo Cuailnge, Leb. na hUidre). ḃa anṁ conꞇuileṁ caċn aiḃċi : "it was in it she used to sleep every night :" (Tochmarc Etaine, Ib.). The use of the genitive is very extended in Irish; the following are two examples,—ocuꞃ máṁ uꞃċuꞃ, maiꞃꝼiṁ nónboꞃ caċa uꞃċaꞃa : "and if it is a shot, it will kill an ennead of each shot;" that is, each shot will kill nine, (Brudin da Derga, Leb. na hUidre) ; ocuꞃ ḃobeꞃaꞇ cloiċ caċ ꝑiꞃ leó ḃo ċuꞃ ċaiꞃnṁ : "and they bring a stone of each man with them to set up a cairn;" that is, each man brings a stone with him to set up a cairn, (Ib.). In accordance with this peculiar construction, we have generally a dependent genitive where we should otherwise have an accusative of time.

[15] Ḃo'nṁ abainṁ. This river of Cruachu is the *Brei,* mentioned above, and that in which Froech bathes, a few lines further on. It must be the stream from the fountain *Clebach,* at which the two daughters of king Loegaire met St. Patric. These, like Find-abair and her maid, came at early morn to the fountain to wash. The Irish Tripartite (Royal Irish Academy), introduces this meeting as follows :—Ḃoluiṁ Ꝑaꞇꞃic iaꞃ ꞃin Ḃo'n ꞇoꞃuꞃ .ꞁ. Cliḃech ꞁ ꞃleꞃaiḃ Cꞃuachan ꝼꞃi ꞇuꞃcubailn ꞅꞃeine. Ḃeꞃꞇiꞇaꞃ in chleꞃiꞅ ic on ꞇiꞃꞃaiꞇ. Ḃolo-ꞇaꞃ ḃe inꞅin Loiꞅaiꞃi maic Neill com moch ḃo'n ꞇiꞃꞃaiꞇ, ḃo niꞅi al láim [*sic*] amail ha beꞃ ḃoiḃ .ꞁ. Giċne Ϝinṁ ꞁ Ϝeḃelm Ḃeꞃcc. Con-naiꞃneċꞇaꞇaꞃ ꞃenaṁ inna cleiꞃeċ ic on ꞇiꞃꞃaiꞇ con heꞇaiꞅiḃ ꞅelaiḃ ꞁ al liḃaiꞃ aꞃ a [*sic*] belaiḃ. Roinꞅanꞇaiꞅꞃeꞇ ḃeilḃ inna cleiꞃech: ḃoꞃuimenaꞇaꞃ ḃauꞃ ꝼiꞃ Siche, no ꝼanꞇaiꞃi : "Patric

after that went to the well .ı. Clibech in the sides of Cruachu with the rising of the sun. The clerics sat down at the fountain. Two daughters of Loigare mac Neill came early to the fountain for the washing of their hands, as was their custom; that is, Eithne the White and Fedelm the Red. They found a synod of the clerics at the fountain with white garments, and their books before them. They wondered at the form of the clerics; they imagined them to be men of the *Side*, or a phantasy."

From this ancient authority we learn that the Lat. *lavare* of the Book of Armagh means "*washing* of hands," &c., not washing of *clothes;* and from it we learn also that in the celebrated passage " viros *Sidè* aut deorum terrenorum, aut phantassiam," "men of the *Sidè* or of terrene gods, or a phantasy," the words " deorum terrenorum " are merely explanatory of *Sidè*. See my " Daim Liacc," p. 8, where this passage has been for the first time so translated and explained. In our tract Froech goes to the river ɖo ınɫuᴄ, and so do Find-abair and her maid, and this ınɫuᴄ is the proper term for " washing of hands," &c. Thus in the *Serg-lige*: Ɖo ᴄaéᴄ Eoᴄaıɖ ɪuıɫ ıaᴘom ɖo ınɫuᴄ a ɫám ɖo'n ᴄıᴘᴘaıᴄ: " Eochaid Iuil goes afterwards for the washing of his hands to the fountatn." The term for washing the head is ᴘoɫᴄaɖ and for bathing the whole person, ᴘoɫᴘaᴄaɖ.

I may remark that the phrase ᴘᴘı ᴄuᴘᴄubaıɫn ᴣᴘéıne, which Colgan, Fifth Life of St. Patric, lib. 2, cap. 14, renders, contra ortum solis— " opposite the rising of the sun," means, in my opinion, *time*, not *locality*. The Book of Armagh, Betham's text, (I cannot get a sight of the Original) has a double phrase : " contra ortum solis, ante ortum solis," a confusion which goes to confirm my interpretation. The present phrase is ɫᴁ eıᴘᴣhı na ᴣᴘeıne; the ancient ᴘᴘı, *ad*, is always ɫᴁ in modern Irish. Compare ɫa ᴄoᴘᴄbáıɫ ᴘoᴘᴄeɫa (Vis. of Adamnan), " cum ortu evangelii :" " with the rising of the Gospel."

It would seem, then, that it is not necessary to go to the east of Rathcroghan to look for the fountain *Clebach*, or the *Sen-domnach* (Oldchurch) which St. Patric founded beside it. At the same time it is as likely that both are to the east as to the west of the palace. It is impossible, however, that this fountain could have been three miles from the palace, as Dr. O'Donovan, in his Roscommon Ordnance Survey Letters, supposes : but it is not impossible, that the *palace* may have been two miles away from the spot now called Rathcroghan. He says nothing of the Brei, which must have been a considerable river, abounding in otters, and in that spot where Froech bathed so dark and deep as to merit the name Ꝺub-linꝺ, Black-pool. With the data developed in this note I think it would not be difficult to identify the fountain, river, and church of Cruachu.

¹⁶ Oc on ᴄain : That is, at the "Tain Bo Cuailngi."

¹⁷ Ꝺc maich in uᴘoiu. Ailill induces Froech to get into the Brei, with the hope of his being drowned, for he was well aware of the prophecy that drowning was to be the ultimate fate of the son of Befind. His aunt Boand frequently cautioned his mother against allowing her heroic son to indulge in bathing; or by any chance to come in contact with Cu Chulaind. Thus in the Book of Fermoy, Boand says:—

Ꝺ bhebínn, bean aᴘ ꝺo mac
Ᵹan ṁnꝺi cᴘiallꝼuᴘ bó cóómaᴘc,
Uaiᴘ an bliaꝺain ꝺobeᴘa
Iᴘ anꝺ céilᵹꝼiꝺ-ᴘa béᴘa.

Na caóaiᴘ ᴘe Coin na cleᴘ,
Uaiᴘ noóan anꝺ acꝺ ꝺo leᴘ :
Iᴘ e ꝺoᴘaᵹa ᴘe ᴘé—
Macaṁ Ṁhuiᵹi Múᴘᴄeiᴘṁne.

Na ꝺena ᴘnaṁ ꝺobúiᴘ ꝺúiꝺ
Uaiᴘ iᴘ ann ꝼéᴘᴘaᴘ a ꝼuil :
Na bíꝺ a ᵹaiᴘciꝺ an ᵹll,
Ꝺbaiᴘ ᴘe Ꝼᴘoeó, a bébinn.

TRANSLATION.

O Befind, impress on thy son
Not to court a woman who shall come to him,
For the year he shall bring her—
It is in it thou shalt shed tears.

Contend not thou with Cu of the feats,
Since it is not in it thy advantage is :
It is he who shall come by time—
The youth of Mag Murthemne.

Let him not make the swimming of black water.
For it is in it he shall shed his blood :
Let not his armour be in pledge,
    Tell to Froech, O Befind.

[18] Capna pamaipci. A bath of this nature was made for Cethern Mac Fintain, who attacked Medb's camp single-handed, and as the result received innumerable wounds: Ip anopin conaccacc Pinʒin Pachac pmip-ammaip pop Coin Culaino bo íc ꝛ bo leiʒip Chechipn meic pincain. Canic Cu Chulaino peme in bunuo ꝛ il lonʒpopc pepn hEpeno, ꝛ na puaip b' almaib ꝛ b' éicib ꝛ b' inbilib ano—cuc leipp app íac: ꝛ boʒni pmip-ammaip bíb, ecip peoil ꝛ cnamaib ꝛ lechap. Ocup cucab Cechepn mac Pincain ip in pmip-ammaip co cenb ceopa lá ꝛ ceopan aioche, ꝛ paʒab ac ól na pmip-ampac imme. Ocup paluib in pmip-ammaip ano ecip a cnebaib ꝛ ecip a cpeccaib, bap a alcaib ꝛ bap a il-ʒonaib. Anopin acpacc pom app in pmip-ammaip i cinb ceopa lá ꝛ ceopan aioóe, see 160. " It is then Fingin Fathach (the physician) asked Cu Chulaind for a *smir-ammair* for the saving and for the healing of Cethern mac Fintain. Cu Chulaind went forward to the fortress and to the encampment of the men of Eriu, and of what he found of flocks, and of herds, and of cattle there—he brought them with him out of it: and he makes a *smir-ammair* of them, between flesh and bones and hide. And Cethern mac Fintain was brought into the *smir-ammair* till the end of three days and three nights, and he set to at the drinking of the *smir-ammair* around him. And the *smir-ammair* went into him between his sores and between his scars, over his cuts and his many wounds. Then he arose out of the *smir-ammair* at the end of three days and three nights, and so forth." The word pmip-ammaip is a compound, of which the first member means "marrow;" what the second means I cannot say at present. In our tract, the phrase po chal ꝛ beuil is, I think, correctly rendered, beuil being = biail. The cál and bial are frequently associated; thus—" aep cáil ocup beli, adze—and axe-men" (O'Donovan's Supp. to O'Reilly). The *adze* to cut the flesh ; the axe to chop up the bones.

[19] Sio Cpuachan. This *Sid*, the temple and burial vault of the royal family and clan, was, as we see, at some distance from the piʒcec, palace, but probably within the *raths* or enclosures. Of these there were several, as we find the *chief-rath* spoken of, p. 138. The whole place was called *Cruachu*, or *Cruachan*, in the singular; or, *Cruachan* or *Cruachna*, in the plural. It was also called *Dun Cruachan*, and *Rath Cruachan*. In the History of the Cemeteries, Leb. na hUidre, it is called *Cathair Cruachan*. Every royal residence con-

sisted of three principal parts within the circumvallations; namely, the
pṁ-ċeċ, palace; the *dun*, or fortified part, appropriated to visitors: and
the *less*, which comprised the whole space within the enclosure, save
what was occupied by the *palace* and *dun*. In this *less* were the stables,
cow-houses, and the houses of all the menial retainers of the king. On
coming up, Froech and his suite sat at the door of the *first-rath.*
Ailill orders them to be admitted into the *less*, p. 138. The fourth
part of the palace is then allowed them. Every *imdai* or apartment, with its occupants, was called the ceᵹlaċ, or household of
the chief person in it. Thus ceᵹlaċ Ḟṗaɩċ p. 142. Then there was
a ceċ ḟmacallmae, " house of conversation ;" and this was outside
the palace, though, perhaps, communicating with it; for Ailill and
Medb go out of the "house of conversation" into the palace, p. 144. I
have said above that the *dun* was the residence of visitors. This is
evident from the " Stories of Mongan," Leb. na hUidre, where we find
the poet Forgall and his company residing in it. This will explain
the use of the word *dun*, not *palace*, where it is stated, p. 142, that
Froech and his suite " stayed till the end of a fortnight in the *dun*."

⁲⁰ Ꙅol-ᵹaɩṗe ban Sɩ̇oe. This ancient air is still played by the
Irish harper and piper.

²¹ Ḋo'no eṗ. The word eṗ is of rare occurrence. We find it in
Fiacc's Hymn of St. Patrick: Ḟoṗṗuɩb a ċoɩṗ ṗoṗṗ ɩnb leɩcc; ma-
ṗaɩc a eṗ, nɩ bṗonna·: " He pressed his foot upon the stone ; its trace
remains, it wears not." In this passage eṗ is glossed ṗolⱡɩuċc, a mark.
In Zeuss., p. 473, *interlitus* is glossed ecaṗṗuɩⱡleċca ; and in " Scela
na Eṗeṗᵹe," p. 10, are read the words: Ḟuɩlⱡɩuċca na cneċ ṗoṗo-
baṁacáṗ aṗ Cṗɩṗc: " the marks of the wounds which they suffered
for Christ."

²² Cucann. This word is written cuca in MS., but with a hori-
zontal stroke over cuc, which I take to be intended for the final a. I
have, therefore, resolved as in text.

²³ coṅᵹu. This coṅᵹu = bo-ṗonᵹu. Ḟonᵹu is Lat. *pango*, another example of a primitive initial p becoming ṗ in Irish. This
formula, occasionally slightly changed, is very common in the more
ancient manuscripts. It is always, so far as I know, put into the
mouth of the Gentile Irish ; never into that of a Christian. The more
usual form is—conᵹu bo bɩa coɩnᵹeṗ mo ċuaċ: " I swear for an
oath the oath of my territories." In this form bo bɩa has hitherto

been rendered " to God." Now the words ꝺo ꝺɪᴀ in the sense of " to God," besides being absurd in the mouth of a Pagan, are frequently omitted. I therefore render " for an oath," " as an oath." In O'Davoren's Glossary, ꝺee is glossed mɪnnᴀ, an oath, (Skrt. *divya* (?), id.), and this I take to be the word here. In the next paragraph Findabair adopts the usual formula. Other forms are " conᵹu ꝺo ꝺɪᴀ," " I swear for an oath," (Lugaid in the Tain); conᵹu ᴀ coɪnᵹeꝉ mo cuᴀc: " I swear the oath of my territories," the words ꝺo ꝺɪᴀ not used (Fer. Rogain, Brudin da Derga). Cu Chulaind in the Tain has another form: conᵹu ᴀ coɪnᵹce Ulᴀꝺ: " I swear the swearings of the Ulaid." Even Cu Chulaind's charioteer swears in the same way. From this it will be seen that " my territories" does not mean *those in my possession*, but the territories in which I live; and it is in this sense that Find-abair swears in the same manner. It would appear that in ancient Eriu every tribe had a certain form of oath, and consequently a certain object to attest that oath, distinct from those of every other tribe.

²⁴ Ꝺo ben. This was Trebland, daughter of Froech, son of Aengus from the *Sid* of the *Brug*, as we learn from the " Courtship of Trebland," Book of Fermoy. She was then, like himself, a semi-deity. The writer of the story says: ꝺᴀ ꝺᴀlcᴀ ꝺo Coɪꝑꝑꝉe Mᴀc Ꝛoꝉᴀ ᴀn Cꝛeꝺlᴀnn ꝛɪn, uᴀɪꝛ ꝺoꝇleᴀꝼcᴀꝺᴀɪꝛ mᴀɪꝼɪ mᴀc Mɪlɪꝺ meɪc ⁊ ɪnᵹɪnᴀ ꝺo ᴀlcꝛom ꝺo ꝛɪᵹɪꝺ nᴀ ꝛɪᵹ ꝛoluꝛ-ᵹlᴀn, ꝺᴀ cóɪṁneꝛᴀ ꝺóɪꝺ, ᴀꝛ ꝺᴀɪᵹ nᴀꝼ clᴀeꝼloᵹꝺᴀɪꝛ ɪc nᴀ ꝺlɪꝼc nᴀ ꝺlᴀꝼ ɪn Eꝛɪnꝺ ꝛꝛɪ ᴀ lɪnꝺ: " This Trebland was a foster-child to Coirpre Mac Rosa, for the magnates of the sons of Miled were wont to foster the sons and daughters of the bright-pure *Sid's*, which were next to them, for the sake that neither corn, nor milk, nor bloom should decay in Eriu during their time."

²⁵ Conᴀll Ceꝑnᴀch. The second of the three great champions of the Ulaid; the first being Cu Chulaind, and the third Loegaire Buadach. See " Battle of Magh Rath," ed. O'Donovan, p. 83.

²⁶ Ɪnꝺ nᴀchɪꝛ. This serpent is found everywhere in our old Irish tales, as defending *duns*, native and foreign. The usual name is ꝺɪᴀꝛc, or ꝑéɪꝛc, Lat. *bestia*, but frequently nᴀꝼɪꝛ, as here, and its usual abode the sea, lake, or other water, adjoining or within the dun. In the case of the serpent of Cruachu we find that Froech, though probably looked on with jealousy by the demon, swam unharmed about the river until he touched the mystic rowan-tree. This

tree was guarded by the serpent, and accordingly in the Book of Fermoy it is said to have come from the root of the tree. Ailill knew this, but Froech was a demi-god, and consequently more than a match for the demon; and hence the result. Is not this the ancient serpent and the fruit-tree? The demon naturally took charge of that tree through which he brought death into the world, and cherished it with affection. But a Divine Being crushed the head of the serpent; and it is to be remarked that Froech did not completely cut off its head, but merely so as to have it hang on its side.

In the case of Conall Cernach the serpent entered into no contest with him, for he was a mere mortal; but not so on a certain occasion in the case of Cu Chulaind, a demigod, and a being whom I have already examined mythologically in my " Religious Beliefs of the Pagan Irish" (Journal of the Historical and Archæological Association of Ireland, April, 1869, p. 321). In the "Spirit-chariot of Cu Chulaind," Leb. na hUidre, it is related that St. Patric brought up Cu from the lower regions to speak to Loegaire, for the latter declared he would not otherwise believe. Cu addresses Loegaire in dark and mysterious language, but the king has a doubt if the stranger is really Cu. "If it is Cu that is in it," he says, "he should tell us about his great exploits." "That is true," says Cu. And then he recites for Loegaire some of his principal achievements. In the course of his narrative he says that he went once to Dun Scaith, a fort in the south of Skye, and there encountered and crushed a host of serpents and other venomous reptiles, who had their abode in a pit in the dun :—

> ba cuiçe ir in Dún,
>   Lar in pig, aopec;—
> Deió naçpaig bopoembaçan
>   Dan a óp—ba beç!

> Iap rin acapeçur-[r]a,
>   Cia p' abbol in bpong,
> Con bepnur an opbneóa
>   Eçip mo bá bopnb.

> Ceó lán bo lorcannaib—
>   Dopaplaicçe bún ;
> Míla gépa, gulbenóa,
>   Rolelçap i m' rnub, ⁊c.

There was a pit in the dun,
   Belonging to the king, it is related ;—
Ten serpents burst
   Over its border—it was a deed !

After that I attacked them,
   Though vast the throng,
Until I made bits of them
   Between my two fists.

A house full of toads,
   They were let fly at us ;
Sharp, beaked monsters,
   They stuck in my snout, &c.

This extract will illustrate the meaning of our phrase, " several tribes are let loose from her ;" that is, tribes of serpents.

[27] Dún Ollaic. Now Dunolly, near Oban. See Dr. Reeves' edition of Adamnan's Life of St. Columba, p. 180.

V.—TOCHMARC BEC-FOLA.

TRANSLATED AND EDITED BY

B. O'LOONEY.

THE text of the following tale of Bec Fola and king Diarmait, son of
Aedh Slane, is taken from a vellum MS. in the Library of Trinity College,
Dublin, Class H. 2, 16, compiled about the year 1390 by Donogh Mac
Firbis, of Lecan Mic Firbisighe in the county of Sligo. The tale commences on column 765, ninth line from bottom, and has been collated
with another copy in a vellum MS. of the year 1509, Class H. 3, 18, in
the same Library, p. 757.

'According to the Annals of the Four Masters, king Diarmait, son
of Aedh Slane, and his brother, Blathmac, assumed the sovereignty
of Ireland A. D. 657, and ruled conjointly for eight years, till they were
both cut off by the mortality called the Buidhe Connaill, A. D. 664.

This tale is of the class the knowledge of which constituted one of the
literary and legal qualifications of an ollamh, or poet; and though
not in the incomplete list of historical tales in the "Book of Leinster," printed by O'Curry, in his "Lectures on the Manuscript Materials of Irish History," p. 584, *et seq.*, it contains internal evidence
of antiquity. The language is old and well preserved, and the story is
told in an ancient style of diction. It contains some minute descriptions
of personal appearance, dress, and ornaments of gold and silver.

Of the lady Bec Fola I have found no mention elsewhere. The
name means literally "small dowry." *Fola* is used here in the sense of
Coibche, a price, reward, gift, or dowry; but in its technical legal
sense it was the name for the first gift which a husband gave to his
wife on marriage. The amount of the *Coibche* was defined by law
in accordance with the grade of the parties, but, the coibche, whether great or small, secured the woman in her marriage rights, and saved
her from personal dishonour. Professor O'Curry translated Bec Fola,
"Woman of the small dowry," in his work on "The MS. Materials
of Irish History," p. 283, where he has inadvertently printed Diarmait
Mac Cerbeoil, for Diarmait Mac Aedh Slane. Diarmait Mac Cerbeoil
was father of Aedh Slane, and grandfather of the hero of this tale,

as mentioned in the following passages from the story of the birth of Aedh Slane, preserved in Leabhar na Huidri, in the Library of the Royal Irish Academy, pp. 52, 53 :—

bɑe τρɑ́ mόρ ɑınɑ̀ mόρ pèc ɑnɒ h-í τɑllcın lɑ Ɗíɑρmɑıc mıc Ƒeρɜuρɑ Ceρbόoıl. "There was a great fair held one time at Taill-ten, by Diarmait son of Fergus Cerbeoil."   *   *   *   *

> " Compenτ Inuɜɑın mό cɑὸ clɑınɒ,
>   Ɗo mɑc cόıρ ὸubɑıɒ ὸeρbɑıll;
>   Iɑρom oρ ρόen ρ́ɑmɑὸ ρ́e,
>   In n-Ɑέɒ ρ́ɑeρ ρ́ύ̀ɑɜɑὸ Slɑ́nέ.

> Mugan bore, the greatest of all children,
>   To the right worthy son of Cerball;
>   After this over the heroic field he reigned awhile,
>   The noble Aedh Slane of hosts."

" Diarmait Mac Fergus Cerbeoil" died A. D. 592.

In illustration of some of the passages in the text, three Addenda are given :—

I. Dindsenchas of Dubthar, which identifies the places called Dubthar, Inis Fedach, and Inis Mic in Doill; and indicates the people called ua Feadach.

The contest of the ua Fedach referred to in the text may, perhaps, be identified with that of the sons of Dall Deas, of Inis Mic in Doill, given in the Dindsenchas as the origin of Fedach and Dubthar.

II. Dindsenchas of Loch n-Erne, illustrating the allusion to the " bearded heroes," and representing that Loch n-Erne afforded, in ancient times, a sanctuary for women.

III. A poem on the prohibitions of the beard, from the " Yellow Book of Lecan," in further illustration of the allusion to bearded heroes in the text, p. 180.

O'Curry considered this poem " to be a simple condensation of the law which regulated the wearing and responsibilities of the beard, and that it belonged to a period anterior to the year 900." He observed that " any person acquainted with the language of the earlier Irish MSS. will find no difficulty in ascribing the language and composition of this poem to a period at least five hundred years earlier than the MS. in which it is preserved," which belongs to the year 1390.

cochmorc bec fola.

ꞃaꞁ Ꝺiapmaic mac Aeꝺa Slane ippiʒi Cempach, Cpimchanꝺ
mac Aeꝺa i n-ꝺalcup ꝺo, ocup i n-ʒiallaiʒecc ꝼpi laim o
Laiʒniꝺ. Luiꝺpeom laa n-anꝺ ocup a ꝺalca, .i. Cpimchanꝺ, ꝺa Ach
Cpuim h-i Loeʒaipe, ocup oen ʒilla leo. Conaoacap in mnai ꝺap
pin n-ach aniap h-i cappac; ꝺa mael appa ꝼinꝺpuine impe, ꝺa
ʒem ꝺo lic loʒmaip eipciꝺ, lene ꝼo ꝺepʒ inꝺlaic oip impe, ꝺpac
copcpa, ꝺealʒ óip kánecaip co mbpeaccpaꝺ n-ʒem n-ilꝺachach ipin
ꝺpuc [op a ꝺpuinne⁴], munci ꝺi óp ꝼoplopce ima ꝺpaʒaic, minꝺ
n-óip ꝼop a cinꝺ, ꝺa each ꝺub ʒlapa ꝼo na cappac, ꝺa n-all óip
ꝼpiu, cunʒi co cuaʒmilaiꝺ aipʒꝺiꝺiꝺ ꝼopaiꝺ.

"Can ꝺo ꝺeachaiꝺ abean ?" op Ꝺiapmaic. " Ni ꝺo nach cein."
op pi; " Ciꝺ ꝺo ceiʒ ?" op Ꝺiapmaic, "Ꝺo cuinꝺchiꝺ pil cpuich-
neachca, [op pi]. Aca ꝺaʒ ichip lim ocup nimea pil a comaꝺaip."
"Maꝺ pil in cipipea ꝺap, ail ꝺuic," op Ꝺiapmaic, "ni ꝼuil ꝺo ꝺul
peachampa." " Ni opup ꝺin," ap pi "achc pombia a loʒ," "Roc-
ꝺia an ꝺealʒ m-ꝺeaʒ pa," op Ꝺiapmaic. "Ʒebcap ꝺin," op pipi.

Nombep lep ꝺo chum na Cempach. "Can ꝺon mnai a Ꝺiapmaic?" op cach, " Ni ꝼo ploinꝺi ꝺam ꝺin," ap Ꝺiapmaic, "Ciꝺ ꝺo
pacaip ina cinꝺpcpa?" [op cach], " mo ꝺealʒ ꝺec," op Ꝺiapmaic.
Ip ꝺec inꝺ fola op cach." " ꝺiꝺ eaꝺ a h-ainm ꝺin," op in ꝺpai,
"[.i.] ꝺec fola."

---

[1] " *Ath Truim ui Laeghaire*," Trim, in
the territory of *ui Laeghaire* in Meath.

[2] "*Findruine*," white bronze—a bronze
generally considered to contain a large
proportion of tin, or perhaps some alloy
of silver, sometimes used for ornamentation.

[3] " *Lene* and *Lened*," a kilt, a kind of
short petticoat worn outside.

[4] Words inserted in [ ] are supplied
from MS. H. 3, 18.

[5] " *Muince*," a generic name for any
kind of collar, ring, or necklace for men,
women, horses, dogs, and for the hafts

COURTSHIP OF BEC FOLA.

DIARMAIT, son of Aedh Slane, was in the sovereignty of Teamair, Crimthand, son of Aedh, was in pupilage with him, and in hostage-ship as pledge from the Lagenians. He and his pupil, i. e., Crimthand, went one day to Ath Truim, of ui Laeghaire,[1] and one servant with them. They saw a woman coming eastward over the ford in a chariot; she wore two pointless shoes of findruine,[2] two gems of precious stones in them, a lene[3] interwoven with red gold upon her, a crimson robe, a brooch of gold fully chased and set with gems of various colours in the robe [over her bosom[4]], a muince[5] of burnished gold around her neck, a mind[6] of gold upon her head, two black-grey steeds to her chariot, two n-all of gold[7] to them, a yoke with trappings of silver upon them.

"Whence have you come, O woman?" said Diarmait. "Not very far," said she. "Whither do you go?" said Diarmait. "To seek seed-wheat" [said she]. "I have good soil and I require suitable seed." "If it be the seed of this country you desire," said Diarmait, "you shall not pass me." "I do not object indeed," said she, "if I get a log."[8] "I will give you this little brooch," said Diarmait. "I will accept it," said she.

He brought her with him to Teamair. "Who is this woman, O Diarmait?" said they. "She has not given me her name indeed," said Diarmait. "What did you give as her tindscra?"[9] [said they]. "My little brooch," said Diarmait. "That is a Bec Fola," said they. "Let that be her name then" said the druid, "i. e., Bec Fola."

---

of spears where the head was inserted.

[6] "*Mind n-óir*," a diadem or coronet of gold.

[7] "*n-All* of gold," *All*, a double-reined chariot bridle, as distinguished from the *sruth ean, srian* or single reined riding bridle.

[8] "*A Log*," a price, wages, or reward; but here it means a *log lanamnais*, "bride price," or *coibche*, a marriage gift.

[9] "*Tindscra.*" See Additional Note, A, p. 194, for an explanation of this word in the sense in which it is here used.

Rola ṗ δın, [a] menmaın ꝑoꝑ a δalεaꝑom, .ı. ꝑoꝑ Cꝑımċhanδ mac n-Aeδa, baı ocá ʒuıδı ocuꝑ ocá εochluʒaδ cen máıꝑ.

Aεchoεaꝑ δın on ʒılla, .ı. εuδechε aꝑ a cenδꝑı co Cluaın δa Chaıleach εꝑaε εeıꝑεı δıa δomnaıċ δa δꝑeıch ꝑoꝑ aıċheaδ. Ro ınδıꝑ ꝑıδe δıa muınεıꝑ. Ruꝑεaıꝑmeꝑcaεaꝑ ıaꝑum a munεıꝑ; naċa δeꝑnaδ ben aꝑδ-ꝑıʒ h-Eꝑınδ δo εaδaıꝑε aꝑ aıċeaδ.

Aεꝑaıʒ ꝑı δın maıεın moch δıa δomnaıʒ o Dıaꝑmaıε, "Cıδ ꝑo a ben?" oꝑ ꝑe [Dıaꝑmaıε]. "Nı cıδ maıċ," oꝑ ꝑı, "Inδıle ꝑıl δamꝑa[11] oc Cluaın Da Chaıleach, ꝑoꝑꝑacaıδꝑeε na bachlaıch [ıaεε], ocuꝑ δo chuaδaꝑ ꝑoꝑ εecheδ." "Cıꝑꝑı ınδılı?" oꝑ Dıaꝑmaıε. "Sechε lenεı cona n-ımδenmaıb, ocuꝑ ꝑeċε n-δelʒı óıꝑ, ocuꝑ εꝑı mınδa óıꝑ. Iꝑ lıach a εeċε amuδa." "Na εeıʒ, oꝑ Dıaꝑmaıε, ıꝑ ın δomnach, nı maıċ ımaδall ın δomnaıch," "Neach lımꝑa aꝑ," oꝑ ꝑı [ꝑıu] "Nı ba h-uaımꝑea on," oꝑ Dıaꝑmaıε.

Luıδ ꝑı on δın ocuꝑ a h-ınaılε a εemꝑaıʒ ꝑoδeꝑ coꝑꝑanʒaδaꝑ Duδchoꝑ laıʒen; δoꝑ ꝑala ꝑoꝑ meꝑuʒaδ ann co εꝑaε δ'aıδchı conεaꝑεaεaꝑ coın alεaı co ꝑo maꝑbꝑaδ an ınılε, ocuꝑ luıδ ꝑı h-ı cꝑanδ ꝑoꝑ εecheδ.

Am baı ıꝑın ċꝑunδ conꝑacaı ın εenı ꝑoꝑ laꝑ na caıllı luıδ δochum ın εeneδ, conꝑacaı ın oclach ımon εenı oc uꝑʒnam na mucı. Inaꝑ ꝑıꝑecδaı ıme co n-ʒlan-ċoꝑcaıꝑ, ocuꝑ co cıꝑclaıb óıꝑ acaꝑ, aꝑcaıε, cennbaꝑꝑ δı óꝑ ocuꝑ aꝑʒuε ocuꝑ ʒlaıne ım a ċenn; mocoıl ocuꝑ ꝑıċhıꝑı óıꝑ ım cach n-δual δıa ꝑulε conıcı claꝑ a δá ımδaı, δá uδall óıꝑ ꝑoꝑ δı ʒabal a muınʒı, meδ ꝑeaꝑ δoꝑnn ceaċ εaꝑnaı; a ċlaıδeδ óꝑ-δuıꝑnn aꝑ a ċꝑıꝑ, ocuꝑ a δá ꝑleʒ coıcꝑınδı ıεıꝑ leaεaꝑ a ꝑoeıε, co coδꝑuıδ ꝑınδꝑuıne ꝑoꝑa;[18] δꝑuε ılδaεach [leıꝑ]. A δá laım lana δı ꝑaılʒıb óıꝑ ocuꝑ aꝑcaıε co a δı uıllınn.

Τeıε ꝑı ocuꝑ ꝑuıδıδ ocaı ocon εenı. Ruꝑδechaꝑεaꝑ, ocuꝑ nı

10 "*Cluain da Chaileach,*" near Baltinglas, in the county of Wicklow.

11 Ṗıl lımꝑa ꝑeꝑın, which belong to myself. MS. H. 3, 18.

12 "*Sunday journey.*" See Note B., p. 195.

13 "*Dubthor Laighen,*" now Duffry, a district in the barony of Scarawalsh, Co. of Wexford. Duffry Hall, in ruins, retains the name, in the parish of Templeshanbo: *vide* O'D. Suppl. ad O'R. Dict. She probably went by *Bealach-Dubthair* (road of *Dubthar*), now called *Bealach Conglais* or Baltinglas. See Four Masters, A. D. 594, p. 218, n. h.; and Addendum No. 1, p. 184.

She, however, fixed her mind on his pupil, i. e., on Crimtband, son of Aedh, whom she continued to seduce and solicit for a long time.

She, at length, prevailed upon the youth to come to meet her at Cluain Da Chaileach[10] at sunrise on Sunday in order to abduct her. He told this to his people; they then forbade him to abduct the wife of the high king of Eriu.

She rose early on Sunday morning from Diarmait. "What is the matter, O woman?" said he [Diarmait.] "Not a good thing," said she; "some things of mine that are at Cluain da Chaileach, the servants have left them, and have fled away." "What are the things?" said Diarmait. "Seven lenes with their garniture, and seven brooches of gold, and three minds of gold, and it is a pity to let them be lost." "Do not go," said Diarmait, "on Sunday, the Sunday journey is not good."[13] "A person will be with me from the place," said she. "Not from me indeed," said Diarmait.

She and her handmaid went then from Teamair southward till they reached Dubthor Laigen;[13] she wandered about there for part of the night till wild hounds came[14] and killed the handmaid, and she fled into a tree to avoid them.

When she was in the tree she saw a fire in the middle of the wood. She went to the fire, and saw a young warrior at the fire cooking a pig. He wore an inar[15] of silk of bright purple, and with circlets of gold and silver, a ceann barr[16] of gold and silver and crystal upon his head, bunches and weavings of gold around every lock of his hair reaching down to the tips of his two shoulders, two balls of gold upon the two prongs of his hair, each of them as large as a man's fist; his gold-hilted sword upon his girdle, and his two fleshmangling spears in the leather of his shield, with bosses of findruine[17] upon it;[18] he wore a many-coloured cloak. His two arms were covered with failgib[19] of gold and silver up to his two elbows.

She went and sat with him at the fire. He looked at her, but

---

[14] "*Wild hounds,*" *Coin alita,* wolves, foxes, any kind of beasts of prey, &c.

[15] "*Inar,*" a tunic, a frock.

[16] "*Ceann barr,*" a diadem, an ornament or cover for the head.

[17] "*Findruine.*" See *ante,* note 2, p. 174.

[18] ᚠᚬᚱᚹ, upon it. MS. H. 3, 18.

[19] "*Failgib*" (Nom. Sing. *Fail*) of gold. See Note C., p. 196.

concapb a mob coᴄaipnic[20] bo puine na muice. Do ᵹni ιapum bpobmuc bιa muιc, ιnbmaιb a ⅼama, ⅼuιb on ᴄenι; ⅼuιb pἰbιn ιna .bιaιb co pιᵹι ιn ⅼoch.

Lonᵹ cpebumae ι mebon ιn ⅼacha.　Ronb cpebumu ι mebon ιp ιn ⅼuιnᵹ ιᴄíp, ocup ponb aιⅼe ιpιn n-ιnbpι baι í mebon ιnb ⅼacha. Do ppenᵹa ιn ⅼoech ιn ⅼuιnᵹ, ᴄeιᴄ pι ιp ιn ⅼuιnᵹ pemιpeom, pacabaιp ιnb ⅼonᵹ ιⅼⅼonᵹ-ᴄιᵹ cpeba ap bopap na h-ιnbpι, ᴄeιᴄ pι pemι ιpa ᴄeᵹ; ampa ιn ᴄeᵹ h-ι pιn ιᴄíp ιppoapᴄab ocup bepᵹuba. Depιb- peom, bepιb pí bιn ιnna pappabpom; pιᵹιb a ⅼaιm peachu [ιna puιbι] co ᴄuc meιp co m-bιub boιb. Lonᵹaιᴄpom bιbⅼιnaιb ocup ebaιᴄ; co nap ba meapᴄaι[23] neaċ bιb. Nι boι buιne ιpιn ᴄιᵹ, nι manapⅼapᴄap boιb. Luιbpeom ιna ⅼιᵹι, bopⅼeιc pι po bpaᴄ- pom, eᴄuppu ocup ppaιᵹh ; nochop ιmpo bιn ppιapι co maιᴄιn, cocuaⅼaᴄap maιᴄιn moch an n-ᵹaιpm pop popᴄ na h-ιnbpι, .ι. "ᴄaιpp ιmach a Flaιnb bo pιⅼ na Fιpu." Aᴄpaιᵹ puap ⅼapobaιn ocup ᵹebιb a ᴄpeⅼam paιp, ocup ⅼuιb ιmach; ⅼuιb pι bιa bepcιn co bopup ιn ᴄιᵹι, conaoaι ιn ᴄpιap popp ιn pupᴄ. Comchpoᴄa, comaepa, combeⅼba ppιpιum a ᴄpιup.　Conacaι bιn oechpop ap puᴄ na h-ιnbpι ocup a poeιch a paenᵹabaιⅼ ιna ⅼamaιb; aᴄpaιᵹ- peom bιn a cechpop [a n-boċum ιn ceaᴄpap eⅼe]; ιma ᴄuapcaᴄ boιb[24] oom bo bepc cach bιb bιa paιⅼιu.　Co n-beachaιb cach bιb ppι ᴄopᵹa a ⅼechι ; ⅼuιb [Flann a óenap] ιna ιnbpι apιbιpι.

"buaιb ᴄhenιᵹ buιᴄ," op pι, "ιp ⅼoechba ιn ᵹⅼeo pιn."　"ba maιᴄ checup mab ppι naιmbιu," op pe.　" Can bona hocaιb ?" op pιpι.　"Mac bpaᴄhap bampa[25]," op pe ; "ᴄpι bpaᴄhaιp bam bιn na h-ι aιⅼι." "Cιb po ᴄopnaιb ?" op ιn ben. "Inb ιnιp[26]," op pe. "Cιa h-aιnm na h-ιnbpι ?" op pι.　"Inιp Febaιᵹ Mιc ιn Daιⅼⅼ," op pe.　"Ocup cιa h-aιnmpιu ?" op pιpι.　"Flann ua Feabaιch," op pe ; "h-uι pebaιb bιn pιⅼ ιcconb ιmchopnum."

IS maιᴄ ιapam ιn n-ιnbpι, .ι. ppaιnb ceιᴄ ιᴄíp bιab ooup ⅼιnn

---

[20] Conᴄaιpnιc. H. 3, 18.

[21] " *Brodmuc*," a spitted pig, a cooked pig roasted or browned on the *brod* or spit; a side or slice of roast bacon is also called *brodmuc*. See MS. T. C. D. H. 3, 18, p. 368.

[22] " *Creduma.* " The usual meaning of this word is bronze, but it is also used for the ore of copper, gold, or silver.

[23] Copbab mepcaι, till they were drunk. H. 3, 18.

[24] A ceaᴄpap a n-boċum ιn cea-

bestowed no further attention on her until he had finished the cooking of the pig. He then made a brodmuc[21] of his pig, washed his hands, and went away from the fire; she followed him till they reached the lake.

A ship of creduma[22] was in the middle of the lake. A cable of creduma from the middle of the ship to the land, and another cable from it into the island which was in the middle of the lake. The warrior hauled in the ship, she went into the ship before him, they left the ship in a ship-house of bronze at the port of the island, she went before him into the house; the house was admirable both in carvings and beds. He sat down, she sat near him; he reached his hand across [her in her seat], and drew forth a dish with food for them. They both ate and drank, but so that neither of them got drunk.[23] There was no other person in the house, nor were they interrupted. He went into his bed, she lay under his garment, between him and the wall; he did not turn towards her till morning, when they heard the call at early morning on the port of the island, i. e., "come out, Fland, the men are here." He rose up instantly, put on his armour, and went out; she went to look after him to the door of the house, and saw the three men on the port. In features, age, and form, the three were like him. She then saw four men moving along the island holding their shields down in their hands; the four men then advanced [against the other four men];[24] they struck each other till each party was red from the other. Then each party of them went off to his own side; he [Flann alone] went into the island again.

"The triumph of your valour to you," said she, "that was a heroic fight." "It would be good, truly, if it were against enemies," said he. "Who are the warriors?" said she. "One of them is my brother's son,"[25] said he; "the other three are my three brothers." "What do ye contend for?" said the woman. "This island," said he. "What is the name of the island?" said she. "Inis Fedach Mic in Daill,"[27] said he. "And what is your name?" said she. "Flann ua Fedach," said he; "it is the ui Fedach who are contending for it."

The island is good, indeed, i. e., the dinner of one hundred men[28]

cnan (ele), ᵹabaıb aᵹ comcuanᵹaın a ôele, &c., the four men advanced towards the other four, and each commenced to strike another, &c. H. 3, 18.

[25] Mac bnacan acan bamna, the son of my father's brother. H. 3, 18.

[26] Inb ınnın, this island. H. 3, 18.
[27] "Inis Fedach Mic in Daill." See Addendum I., p. 184.
[28] "Dinner for one hundred men." See Note D, p. 197.

iρe a h-imτaiρec cecha nona, cen pπichȝnam[30] o buniu oca; [aρeiρ]
ni paib achτ biaρ inci, niρ caiρic achτ a ρoiρċu.

"Ceρc," oρ ρi, " Cib na h-animρea laτρu?" " Iρ bρoch banaiρ
buicρiu cecuρ," oρ ρeρem. "anab limρa ocuρ ρi h-Eρenb bo
ρacbail, ocuρ beiτ buiτ poρamρa, ocuρ a ċeρoρ im biaibρi."

"Cib na compaicim?" oρ ρi, " Na τo bon chuρρa," aρ ρeρem,
mab limρa imoρρo inb iniρ, ocuρ bia maiρem ρeȝacρa aρ bo
chennρo, ocuρ iρ cuρu bich ben biaρ im ρaρρab, ocuρ aiρcρeo
bon chuρρa."

" Saeτ bam mo inailτ bo ρacbail," oρ ρi. " Aτa i m-beaċ-
aib i m-bun in chρoinn cheτnai," oρ ρeρem; "laiȝ na h-inbρi ρo-
ȝabρeb immρi ocuρ ρeȝċaiρ biaρ n-iolocon." ba ρiρ ρon.

Ric ρi a τeȝ, co ρaρnic inni Diaρmaiτ oc eiρȝiu iρin bom-
naċ ceτnu. "Amρa ρin aben," oρ Diaρmaiτ, " na beaρnaiρ
imaball in bomnaiċ baρ aρ n-uρȝaiρi," " Ni ρolamaρ ρon[32]," oρ ρi,
"imchim bo bρeichρiρiu," amail na τeiρeb ρi eτeρ: ba h-e a h-aen
[ρ]ocal ón uaiρ ρin na bec ρolab.

"baρa abaiȝ iρin choill
Iciȝ inbρi mic in baill[33]
Ciaρ bo la ρeρ niρ bo chol,
In τan ρcaρρom niρ ba ρom[34]

Iniρ Peabaib Mic in Doill[33]
Iċiρ laiȝin i n-Dubċaiρ
Ciaρo ρocuρ bo ρooc
Ni ρaȝbaib oiȝ ulchaiȝ."[34]

ba h-inȝnab la cach n-oen in n-aċeρc ρin. Alla ρin bin,
cinb bliabna boi, Diaρmaiτ ρoρ a beρȝab, ocuρ a ben, .i. beo Pola,
conacaban in ρeρ ρeach boρuρ in τiȝi, ocuρ ρe achȝoici, .i. Plann,
iρ anb aρbeρτ bec Pola.[37]

"Poρȝalo ρeρ biρu amiρiρ
Don bebaib i n-Dam Iniρ
Inab in cechρuρ ρo bρiρ
Poρ ceaċhρuρ i n-Dam Iniρ."

29 " Linn." See Note D., p. 197.
30 " Frithgnam." See Note D., p. 197.
31 " Calves of this island." See Note E.,
p. 197.
32 Ni ρolamaρρium. I should not

have dared. H. 3, 18.
33 "Inis Mic in Daill," i.e. Damh Inis.
See Addendum, No. 1, p. 184.
34 In τan ρcaρρomne ba ρomh

both of food and linn[29] is its supply every evening, without any frith-gnam[30] from the people; there were only two persons in it [last night], there came but their supply.

"I ask," said she, "why should I not remain with you?" "It would be a bad espousal for you, indeed," said he, "to remain with me and to abandon the King of Eriu, and you [i. e. your blame] to be upon me, and its vengeance to follow me."

"Why should we not dwell together?" said she. "Let us not this time," said he, "but if the island be mine, and that I live, I will go for you, and you shall be my constant wife residing with me, but depart now for the present."

"I am grieved to leave my handmaid," said she. "She is alive at the foot of the same tree," said he; "the calves[31] of the island surrounded her and detained her to screen us." This was true.

She reached her house, and found Diarmait there rising on the same Sunday. "It is well, O woman," said Diarmait, "that you have not journeyed on the Sunday against our prohibition." "I should not have dared to do that,"[32] said she, "to disobey your order," just as if she had not gone at all: her only word from that time forth was, the Bec Folad.

> "I was a night in the wood
> In the house of Inis Mic in Daill:[33]
> Though it was with a man, there was no sin,
> When we parted it was not early.[34]
>
> Inis Feadaid Mic in Daill,[35]
> In the land of Laigen in Dubthar,
> Though it is near unto the road,.
> Bearded heroes do not find it." [36]

Every person wondered at these words. At the end of a year from that day, however, Diarmait was upon his bed, with his wife, i. e. Bec Fola, they saw a wounded man passing the door of the house, i. e. Fland, it was then Bec Fola said :[37]—

> "Superior in valour of fierce men, I ween,
> In the battle of Damh Inis,
> The four men who conquered
> The [other] four men in Damh Inis."

---

when we parted it was early. H. 3, 18.

[35] "*Inis Feadaid Mic in Daill*," now Damh Inis. See Addendum, No. I., p. 184.

[36] "*Bearded heroes.*" See Addendum, No. III., p. 190.

[37] Aᵹbeⱴcɼᵻⱴe .ɪ. beo Fola, said she, i. e., Bec Fola.

Inbe bixic Ƒlanb:

"Ꝺ bean na bean in n-achꞇen[38]
Ƒon na h-obu bia n-aꞇliᵹ;
Ni bac ᵹala pen no cloi,
Ꝺóc pin con upbaiᵹ pon ᵹai."[39]

" Ni po ꝼaᵹbaim," on ꞃiꞃi " an ᵹáil buni b-ꝼulaꞇcain, cꞃaꞇ iꞃ pon Ƒlanb bo bencab,[40] a comlunn in ꞇomóꞇaiꞃ laꞃobain noꞃ," leici uaibib an in ciᵹ ina biaib cona h-aꞃꞃuꞃ. "Noꞃ leiciö, uaib," on Diaꞃmaic, " a n-uꞃꞇob, an ni ꝼeaꞃ cia cheic, no cia chubchaib."

Ꝺm bacaꞃ pon a n-imꞃaicib conacacan cechꞃuꞃ mac cleiꞃech iꞃan cech. "Ciö ane?" on Diaꞃmaic, " in meic cleiꞃiᵹ oc im- ꞇeaꞇc iꞃin bomnuch !"[41] La cobaiꞃc a bꞃuic baꞃ a cenb conach an paca iꞃiꞃ.

"Iꞃ comaꞃlecub ꞃꞃuicí bonꞃuc," on na meic cleꞃich, " nim- ꞇholca, .i. Molaꞃi Dam-Inöꞃi[42] bonꞃaib bo c'acallaim, .i. columun bo muincꞃ Dam-Inöꞃi po bui oc aiꞃeꞃᵹi abo iꞃin macin, ꞃe, inbiu, conꞃaca in cechꞃaꞃ po naꞃmaib cona ꞃciachaib poinᵹabala iaꞃ ꝼuc na h-inöꞃe; conꞃaca bin in ceachꞃoꞃ aile aꞃa cinb: Im- moꞃꞇuaiꞃcec co cloꞃ pon möꞃe n-uile ᵹaiꞃ na ꞃciac ocon n- imꞇuaꞃᵹain, comma coꞃchaiꞃ boib aꞇc aen ꝼeꞃ achᵹoici acꞃulai aꞃ namma."

" Ro abnachca la Molaꞃi in moꞃꝼeꞃiuꞃ ele; pon pacaib reab, imoꞃꞃo, bi óꞃ ocuꞃ aꞃᵹuc aiꞃi beꞃi uanni, .i. bo neoch po bui po m-bꞃocaib, ocuꞃ im a m-bꞃaiᵹbib, acaꞃ im a ꞃciachaib, acaꞃ a n-ᵹóo, acaꞃ a claibiu, acaꞃ im a lama, acaꞃ im a n-inaꞃa. Co ꝼeꞃaꞃaꞃu bo chuic binb n-óꞃ acaꞃ binb n-aꞃᵹab ꞃin."

" Na có," on Diaꞃmaic, " an bo ꞃab Dia boꞃom noꞇo ꞇuiciöꞃa ꝼꞃiꞃ. Denaiꞇheꞃ a ꝼechla[44] laiꞃeom be." ba ꝼiꞃ ꞃoin.

Iꞃ binb n-aꞃᵹub ꞃin, imoꞃꞃo, acaꞃ bon óꞃ ꞃocumbaiᵹeb minna Molaiꞃi,[45] .i. a ꞃeꞃiꞃi,[47] acaꞃ a miniꞃciꞃ[48] acaꞃ a baꞇall. Do choiö, imoꞃꞃo, bec Ƒola la Ƒlann ua Ƒebaich, acaꞃ ni chainic beoꞃ. Cochmoꞃc bec pola ꞃin. Ƒinic.

[38] Ꝺ bean na beiꞃ aꞃ n-aichꞼeꞃ ꞃoꞃꞃ na h-ócu biaꞃ n-aꞇliᵹ. H. 3, 18.

[39] " *Men with charms on their spears.*" See Additional Note, F., p. 198.

[40] Inac Ƒlann, ꞃoꞃ no benᵹab aꞃ

ꞇaö, in revenge of Fland I shall wound them. H. 3, 18.

[41] " *Clerics travelling on Sunday.*" See Note B., p. 195.

[42] " *Molasa of Dam Inis,* who sent us," &c. See Note G., p. 199.

Then Fland said :

> "O woman, cast not thy reproach[38]
> Upon the heroes to disparage them ;
> It was not manly valour that vanquished them,
> But men with charms on their spears."[39]

"I cannot help," said she, "from going to oppose the valour of the men, because it was Fland that was wounded[40] in the conflict of the eight," and so she went from them out of the house after him to his own abode. "Let her depart from ye," said Diarmait, "the evil, for we know not whither she goes or whence she comes."

While thus conversing, they saw four ecclesiastical students coming into the house. "What is this?" said Diarmait, "the clerics travelling on Sunday!"[41] Thus saying, he drew his cloak over his head so that he might not see them at all.

"It is by order of our superior we travel," said the ecclesiastical students, "not for our pleasure, i. e. Molasa of Damh Inis[43] who sent us to parley with you, i. e., a farmer of the people of Dam Inis[43] while herding his cows this morning—to-day, saw four armed men with their shields slung down traversing the island; he then saw four men more coming against them: they struck each other so that the clangour of the shields was heard all over the island during the conflict, till they all fell but one wounded man who alone escaped."

"Molaisa buried the other seven; they left, moreover, the load of two of us of gold and silver, i. e. of that which was upon their garments, and upon their necks, and upon their shields, and upon their spears, and upon their swords, and upon their hands, and upon their tunics. To ascertain thy share of that gold," [we have come, said they.]

"Not so," said Diarmait; "what God has sent to him, I will not participate in. Let him make his fethla[44] of it." This was true.

It was with this silver now, and with this gold, Molaisa's minda[45] were ornamented, namely, his shrine[46] and his ministir[47] and his crozier. Bec Fola, however, went off with Flann ua Fedach, and she has not since returned. That is the courtship of Bec Fola.   FINIS.

[43] "Dam-Inis," now Devinish Island in Loch Erne. See Addendum, No. I. p. 184.

[44] Fethal, pl. Fethla, an ornamental facing or covering, as of shrines, cases, and sacred reliquaries.

[45] "Minda," here sacred reliquaries, &c.

[46] "Shrine of Saint Molasa." See Additional Note, G., p. 199.

[47] "Ministir," a portable box or case, a safe in which the sacred vessels and Gospels or Lectionary for the service of the altar were preserved and carried.

Dinosenchas Duibthir.

———•———

Duibthir canar ro h-ainmniʒeb? nin. ba mac roppacaib
ʒuaιpι Mιc ιn boιll, .ι. ʒuaιpι ʒann acar Oaιpι Ouιbchear-
cach. Co po mapb ʒuaιpι ιn Oaιpι oc Oaιm Inιr conιb be roleach
Fιb acor mochap⁴⁸ bar Cpιch n-ʒuaιpι bon rinʒaιl rιn bo poιmbe
ʒuaιpι ror ιn Oaιpι n-Oubchearbach⁴⁹ ror a bpachaιp,—ror a
chιneab oιrobaιn, unbe bιcιcur Ouιbchιp Oaιpι bιa n-ebpab.

Duibchιp ʒuaιpι ʒnιm ba⁵⁰ ruιl,
Ir roel rιr, co rearabaιr,
baι rel nar bo buchor bor
In cpιch oruchach comrolaιr.

Da mac roppacaιb Oall Oear
ʒuaιpe Oall Oaιpι Oιlear
Imon cpιch can buιlʒe
Oenιbbar cuιbbe comroιnbe.

Fιllιr ʒuaιpι ʒnιm n-earbach
For an Oaιpι n-Ouιbbearcab,
Co ropchaιr leιr Oaιpe ιn baιʒ
Can ʒne n-aιlιb n-ιmcoroιch

On lo ro ʒaeb ʒuaιpι bron
A n-Inιr Oaιm can bιchor,
Ir rιch, co m-buaιne mochaιr,
Cpιch ʒuaιpι bon chomochaιn.⁵¹

---

⁴⁸ "*Mothar*," an enclosure, a place
studded with bushes or brushwood.

⁴⁹ For an Oaιpe n-bιan n-buιbbear-

cab. Upon the vehement Daire Duib-
cheastach. Book of Ballymote, referred
to hereafter by the letter B.

DINDSENCHAS OF DUBTHAR.

Book of Lecan (fol. 251 *a.b.*)

Duibthir, why so called? Answer. Two sons that were left by Guaire Mac in Doill, i. e. Guaire Gann and Daire Duibhcheastach. Guaire killed Daire in Dam Inis. A wood and a mothar[50] overspread the land of Guaire on account of that fratricide which Guaire committed upon Daire Dubcheasdach[49] i. e. upon his brother,—upon his race also, unde dicitur Duibthir Dairi, of which was said :—

> Duibthir Guari, the deed whence it is,
> It is a true story, be it known to you,
> There was a time when it was not a bushy Duthor,
> The broad delightful region.

> Two sons were left by Dall Deas,
> Guaire Dall and Daire Dileas,
> Of that region, without contention,
> They made an appropriate equal division.

> Guaire wrought a wicked deed
> Upon Dairi Dubcheastach,
> And he killed Daire the good,
> Without shade of blemish or disgrace.

> Since the day that powerful Guaire slew
> In Inis Daim, without provocation,
> It is a heath, a perpetual mothar,
> The land of Guaire of the foul treachery.

[50] ᵹnɩm-ᵭɩa ꝼuɩl. H. 2, 18, and B.   [51] Comꝓoohaɩn. B.

Maiṅ ḃa ʒṅ piṅʒal oo h-om
Ʒṅim ḃo na ṫimʒaṅ ṫoṅaḃ
Cṅioh Ʒuaiṅi óaṅ ohoṅnum ḃe
Fil na ḃoṅ-maʒ Duiḃṫhiṅe. ḃ.

Nomṅaeṅa aṅ ḟill iṡ aṅ olc
A cṅiṡṫ ṅoohiḃ[62] mo óaem óoṅṡ
Aṅi ṡuḃaoh na ṡiṅe[63]
Niṡ ḃum ḃuḃaoh ḃuiḃṫhiṅe. D.

[ADDENDUM, No. II.]

DINDSENCHAS LOCHA N-EIRNE.

Loċ n-Eiṅne canaṡ ṡo h-aiṅmṅiʒeḃ? Niṅ. Fiacha Laḃṅaiṅḋi
ḃo ṡaḃ caṫ[64] anḃ ḃo Eṅnaiḃ conaḃ anḃ ṡo meḃaiḃ in loch ṡo chíṡ,
unḃe Loch n-Eṅne ḃiciṫuṡ no ṡoṡ Eṅnaiḃ.

Aileceṡ Eṅni, inʒen ḃuiṡc ḃuiṡeaḃaich mac Maċin mic
Machon[66] ban-ṫaiṡech inʒenṡaiḃ na Cṅuachnai, acaṡ ban-choime-
ḃaich ḃo chiṡaiḃ acaṡ ḃo chioiṡiḃ[67] Meiḃḃi Cṅuachan.

Fecht anḃ ḃo luiḃ Olcai[68] a h-uaim Chṅuachan ḃo comṡoḃ[69] ṡṅi
h-Aimiṡʒin Maṡʒiuḃaoh[60] ḃia ṡo ṡai le Finḃchaim inʒin Maʒach,
conaḃ anḃ ṡochṡoich Olcai a ulcha acaṡ ṡo ḃean a ḃeḃa,[61]
co n-ḃeachaiḃ Eṅne cona h-inʒenaiḃ ṡoṡ ṡualanʒ aṡ a imomon
co ṡiachṫ loch n-Eṅne co ṡo ḃaiḃeaḃ anḃ ḃiḃlinaiḃ, unḃe loch
n-Eṅne ḃiciṫuṡ.

Eiṅne chaiḃ can chuaiṡḃ chneḃaiʒ
Inʒen ḃuiṡc ḃain ḃuiṡeaḃaiʒ
ḃa ṡaṡaʒaḃ ṡaeṡ cṡin ṡon ḃan
Mac Maiṅchin mic Machon.[62]

[62] "Roohinḃ." Who rules. B.

[63] Aṅi na ṡuḃaiḃ, n a ṡiṅe, O king
of the joys [of the] elements. B.

[64] "*Fiacha Labrainde.*" See Note H.,
p. 202.

[65] Do ḃṅeṫa caṫ, gave battle. B.

[66] Mac mamóṁn, son of Mainchin. B.

[67] Cleṅaiḃ. B.

[68] Olccai. B.

[69] Comṡuʒ, to contend. B.

[60] h-aimiṡʒin maiṡʒiunnaḋ. B. See
Additional Note, I., p. 202.

Woe to him who commits a cold fratricide,
A deed of which no profit comes;
The land of Guaire is through it unprotected,
A bushy plain of Duibtihr. D.

Save me from treachery and from evil,
O Christ, who seest[62] my comely body,
O benign king of the elements[63]
That I be not a sorrowful Dubthor. D.

[ADDENDUM, No. II.]

DINDSENCHAS OF LOCH ERNE.

Book of Lecan R. I. A. (fol. 250 *b. b.*)

Loch n-Eirne, why so called? Answer. Fiacha Labrainde[64] that gave battle there to the Ernans and it was then the lake burst forth over the land, unde Loch n-Erne dicitur, or it was over the Ernans [it came].

Or Erni, daughter of Burc Buireadach, son of Machin,[65] son of Machon, mistress of the maidens of Cruachan, and mistress in charge of the combs and caskets of Medb of Cruachan.

At one time Ulchai came out of the cave of Cruachan to contend with Aimirgin Mairgiudach who had espoused Findchaom, daughter of Magach, and it was then Ulchai shook his beard and he gnashed his teeth, so that Erne and her maidens fled precipitately through fear of him till they reached Loch n-Erne and they were all drowned in it, unde Loch n-Eirne dicitur.*

Eirne chaste without shade of stain,
Daughter of Burc Buireadach the fair,
It was an insult to the honour of her noble father;
He was the son of Maichin, son of Mochon.[62]

[61] Deta, teeth. B.

[* Eleven stanzas follow here on the first derivation, which do not, however, bear on our subject.]

[62] ba saragad saer trian in son ban
Mac mainchin mac mochon. B.,

The following is the text of H 2. 18, which is followed in the translation with the correction indicated in brackets:

ba saragad saer [a] thir in son
ba Mac Maichin mic mochon.
H. 2, 18, fol. 154, a. a.

Eipne noipeoh oen eamain[63]
   Fa toipeoh fop inᵹenaib
Ipaich Cpuachan na peb peib,[64]
   Nip uachab ben oa bich-péip.

Aici po bibip pe meap[65]
   Min peoib meabba na mop tpeap,
Aoip pa ohoip oan ohlob
   Iap na tmol bo bepᵹ óp.[66]

Co tanaio a opuaioh cheapa
   Oloai oo n-uach n-imchana,[67]
Cop ohpoich a uloha ap in ploᵹ,
   In ᵹapb pep, baiᵹep baich mop.[68]

Ro poappab pa Chpuaioh Cheapa
   Na h-anpi na h-inᵹena
Caibpin a ohpocha, pochóip.
   Ᵹlan pin[69] aᵹotha ᵹlopaioh.

Ro cheioh Eppe ilap m-ban
   Co Loch n-Eppe nach inᵹlan
Cop bail tappri in cuile chuaib,
   Co pup baib uili a n-aen uaip.

Ᵹiamab uabib ip bpeach cheapc,[70]
   Fiab na pluaᵹaib ni paeb peaóc,
Ip caipm cap cpooha po chaipᵹ
   Ainm Locha Eppi imaipb. L.

A aipb pi peibil, pip bám
   Failci bemin bom bibnab;
Fop nim oo m-buabaib pombae,
   A pip cuapcaib Loó Eppe. L.

---

[63] oen n-eamain. H. 2, 18, fo. 154, a. a.

[64] Reb peib, Lecan, is peb peb. In B. Book of Leinster has—

   I paió cpuaóhan na cneab bo oein
   Nip b'uatab ban oa Compeip.
   In Rath Cruachan of wounds of old.
   Not few the women in her charge.
H. 2, 18, fol. 154, a. a.

[65] bibip pia meap; had them in charge to care. B.

[66] A oip, a cpioll oan ohlob.
   Cona n-biol bo beapᵹ óp.
   Her combs and caskets without stain.
   With their adornments of red gold.
H. 2, 18, fol. 154, a. a. and B.

Eirne noble without guile
　Was mistress of the maidens
　In Rath Cruachan of heroic feats,
　Not few the women in her constant charge.

Hers was the task to care
　The polished jewels of Medb of great battles,
　Her combs and caskets without stain
　When embellished with red gold.

Till from Cruach Ceara came
　Olcai of flight-causing visage,[67]
　And shook his beard at the host,
　The fierce man, terrific, hideous-coloured.[68]

Over Cruach Ceara in fright they fled,
　The timid youths and the maidens,
　On beholding his form, though comely.
　Clear was the sound[69] of their resounding voices.

Erne with her many maidens fled
　To Loch n-Erne which is not impure
　Till the rude wave rolled over them,
　And drowned them all at the one time.

Though it be from these, it is a right judgment,[70]
　Before the hosts 'tis not a trifling cause,
　The overwhelming sudden deaths proclaimed
　The name of Loch Erne aloud. L.

O high King of Mercy, give to me
　A true welcome to protect me;
　In heaven in joys may I be,
　O man, who caused the eruption of Loch Erne. L.

[67] Co canaio i Cruachan caiṗ.
Olcoai con ḃ bláḃ amnaiṗ.
Till to Cruachan of valour came.
Olccai of beautiful bold countenance.

[68] In ʒanḃ ꝼeꝛ baiṫ baiʒeꝛ moꝛ.

[69] Ꙃlan ꝛin, Lecan, is ʒanḃ ꝛin, rough sound. H. 2, 18, 154 a. a.

[70] Ciambaḃ uaḃiḃ ꝛi ꝼaeḃ ꝛeóc though it were from them it is no trifling cause. B.

ᵹeıѕı uᴌcaı.

Coneıᵹıuɼ ᴅuıᴅ ᵹeıɼı uᴌċaı
    ın caċ ınᴅaıᴅ.
Feᴅıᴌ paᴅᴌaıċ, oᴌc ᴅo anmaın ;
    Cɼom ᴅo mıᴅᴌaıᵹ.
ᴀca ceıċıɼn ᴅıan coıċ uᴌċaı
    Nı baɼ baeᴌı—
ᴀɼᴅɼuım cuaċ ocuɼ muıɼe
    Ocuɼ ᴌac ᵹaeᴌı.
Saeɼ ċᴌanna ɼıᵹ ɼeᴅᵹa aᴌᴌuᴅ
    ᴀ huıċċ buıᴅean ;
ᴀn cınᵹıᴅ ᴌoeċ ɼɼıɼ na ᵹeᴅċeɼ
    comᴌonn ᵹuıneaċ,
Maᴅ aɼ chena ceᴅoɼ ᴌeceaᴅ,
    Nıɼ o ᴅeɼıᴌ [ᴅıɼıᴌ .ı. ᴅeıɼeoıᴌe]
Moo a meᴅaᴌ ᴅı, cıᴅ a ɼoıɼeaɼ
    Maᴅ ɼo ᵹeɼıᴅ.
ᵹeɼ ᴅı nomaıᴅe na ᴅeaɼᵹɼaıᴅeaɼ ᴌé ɼınᴅı,
    Ceaᴅ maᴅ uıᴌᴌı ;
ᵹeıɼ ᴅı ᵹɼıan ᴅo cuɼcbaıᴌ ɼuıɼɼı
    ına ᴌıᵹı.
ᵹeıɼ ᴅı eıᵹem can a ċobaıɼ
    Maᴅ ᴅo ᵹneceɼ,
ᵹeɼ ᴅı ᵹen ᵹaıɼı ᴅıa cɼoċaᴅ ;
    ᵹeıɼ ᴅı cecheᴅ ;
Comɼuᴅ ɼɼı ᴌoech, ıɼ ɼeıᴅm ınᵹneaċ,
    ᵹeıɼ ᴅı oɼaᴅ,

PROHIBITIONS OF BEARD.

———◆———

H. 2. 16. T. C. D. col. 919.

I shall relate to you the prohibitions of a beard
    At all times.
Curled and hedgy, 'tis bad for the timid;
    'Tis too heavy for the coward.
There are warriors who are entitled to a beard
    Who are not cowardly—
Noble chiefs by land and sea
    And battle champions.
Noble sons of kings who inflict wounds
    In the front of battalions;
The kingly champion over whom is not gained
    The woundful battle,
If then he should suffer reproach
    It shall not be from pusillanimity.
Its disgrace will be the greater, should it come
    Under the prohibitions.
A prohibition of it, a nomaid[71] unreddened with spears,
    If oftener it is allowable;
A prohibition of it, the sun to rise on it
    In its bed.
A prohibition of it, to hear a moan without relieving it
    If made to him;
A prohibition of it, to laugh when shaken;
    A prohibition of it, to retreat;
To battle with a champion, to fight with the nails
    A prohibition of it, to refuse.

maid," a space of time: some- Laws it is generally put for nine d
means one day, but in the Irish   or the ninth day.

Cıb beaϭ, no beϲ, ıϲır ıϲır,
   Ꝛer bı obar;
Ꝛer bı ꝛualach ocur mıanach;
   Ir orb rnımaϲ;
Ꝛer bı alϲrom ꝛer bı carϲaϭ,
   Ꝛer bı ϲıraϭ.
Ꝛer bı rloıbı mna no ꝛılla,
   Ir orb melı.
Aϲϲ a roıach ar rcaϲ a rıꝛı,
   Ꝛer bı erı;
Ꝛer bı ꝛlun ralaϭ a h-ımbaıb—
   Nı baıl bulbϲaı;
Na nı on leanub co raılϭı
   Inra n-ulϲaı.
Ceϲ mac aϲaıch, aϲ rop raıϲech,
   Sernab rupu,
Poemaı cormaılır ır baϲu
   Prır na buccu.
Ro rela bam, conba ϭolaϭ
   raırrı ar chulpaı.
Pear ecna moır amaıl ır coır
   Prı ceϲ n-ulϲaı.
Cerba, ꝛobaınb, raır luınb,
   Leꝛa le ıceab labaır,
Bıa beıϲ bıa rcır berrab ceϲ mır
   Ar a naıꝛıb.

However small, ever so small, at all, at all,
      A prohibition of it to labour ;
A prohibition of it to mine for coals or mineral,
      And to wield the sledge ;
A prohibition of it to nurse ; a prohibition of it to shovel ;
      A prohibition of it to kiln-dry.
A prohibition of it to abuse women or boys,
      And the habit of a sluggard.
Save his shield sheltering his arm,
      A prohibition of it to carry a burthen ;
A prohibition of it, to bring an unclean knee into a bed,—
      Not an unreasonable condition ;
Nor anything filthy from the child
      In the beard.
Every son of an Athach, if rich,
      Grows the wisps [beard],
They desire to be like in appearance and colour
      To the bucks [he-goats].
It has been revealed to me, therefore I know
      The privileges of the collars [whiskers].
I am a man of great knowledge of what is lawful
      For every kind of beard.
Artificers, smiths, house-builders,
      Physicians who cure the infirm,'
Because of their fatigue they shave every month
      [The beard] on their faces.

ADDITIONAL NOTES.

(A.) " *Tindsora.*" *Tinsora*, a gift, price, reward or dowry: here it is used in a general sense to represent the " Bride Price," the " marriage gift," and the " morning gift." *Bec Fola* having consented to receive King Diarmait's brooch as her *Folad*, which is also called Tinsora in this passage, (p. 174), and this being the only pledge or price given her, it represents the three; and, with the adjective *Bec*, little or small, affixed to it, it forms the name *Bec Fola*, or little dowry, as O'Curry has rendered it in his work on " The MS. Materials of Irish History," p. 283. The following passages show that the word meant " Bride Price" and " morning gift."

Cabpaιὸ ὸαmρa, ρορ Oenɜuρ, ὸo mnaι Eιέnι, .ι. ρuρ n-ὸalca, acaρ ὸo bϵρρa ρϵρanὸ ὸuιb na cιnρcρa .ι. ρϵρanὸ ριl ὸαmρa la oρραιɜe ρριnὸ a n-ὸeρ, acaρ ιρ cec ὸuιbριu aρaρριnɜuὸ ροραιb.

" Give me, said Oengus, Eithne as wife, namely, your foster child, and I will give you land as her *Tinsora*, namely, land which I have near to Ossory by us on the south, and it shall be permitted to you to make it more extensive for yourselves."—*Leabhar na h-Uidhri*, p. 54, col. 2, top.

Ὀo ɜnίceρ ιmacallaιm oc Ulcaιb ιmon caιnɜιn ριn : ιρρeὸ ιαροm comaιρle αρίcc léo, Emeρ ὸo ρeιρ la Concobaρ an aιὸέι ριn, acaρ Feρɜuρ acaρ Catbaὸ a n-oen leραιὸ ρριu ὸo coιmeὸ enιɜ Conculaιnὸ ; acaρ bennacc Ulaὸ ὸon lanamaιn aρ a ραemaὸ. Faemaιὸ an nι ριn, acaρ ὸo ɜnιec ραṁlaιὸ. Icuὸ Concobaρ cιnρcρa Emιρe ιαρ na maρuὸ, acaρ ὸo bρecaι eneclanὸ ὸo Conculaιnὸ, acaρ ραιὸeρ ιαρ ριn lιa bιn ćela, acaρ nι ρo ρcaρρac ιαρρuὸιu co ρuαραcαρ bαρ ὸιblιnαιb.

" The Ultonians held a consultation on this difficult question: the counsel on which they determined was to have Emer to sleep with Conchobar that night, and Fergus and Cathbadh in the same bed with them to protect the honour of Cuchulaind ; and the thanks of the Ultonians were offered to the pair for agreeing to this. They consented to this, and it was so done. Conchobar paid Emer's *Tinsora* on the morrow, and he gave *eneoland* (honour price) to Cuchulaind; and he embraced his wife after that, and they did not separate afterwards till they both died."—" *Leabhar na h-Uidhri*," p. 127, col. 1.

(B.) "Clerics travelling on Sunday." This is an allusion to the *Cain Domnaig*, a rule for the observance of Sunday as a day free from every kind of labour; the copy of the tract preserved in the " Yellow Book of Lecan," T. C. D., Class H. 2, 16, col. 217 opens thus :—" Ireḋ inṛo poṛuṛ chana in ḃomnaiᵹ ḃoṛṗuc Conall mac Ceolmaine ḃi chuaḋ ḃia ailiceṛi ḃo Róm acaṛ ṛo ṛcṛiḃ a láim ṗéin aṛ in eiṗiṛciḷ ṛo ṛcṛiḃ láim ḃé ṗoṛ nim a ṗiaḃnaiṛi, ṗeṛ nime acaṛ ṛolaḃ ṗoṛ alcoiṛ pecaiṛ aṗṛcaiḷ iṛin Róm.   " This is the knowledge of the *Cain Domnaig*, which was brought by Conall, son of Ceolman, who went on his pilgrimage to Rome, and was written by his own hand out of the epistle which was written by the hand of God in heaven, in presence of the men of heaven, and which he placed upon the altar of Peter the Apostle in Rome." This account is repeated in the version of the rule incorporated with the ancient laws preserved in Cod. Clarend. Brit. Mus., vol. 15, fol. 7, p. 1 a. b., and in the following stanzas from the metrical version of the Cain Domnaig which follows it in the same MS. :—

> Leaḃaṛ ḃo ṛaḃ lám ḃé móiṛ
>   Ṗoṛ alcoiṛ pecaiṛ iṛ póiḷ;
> Iṛ ṗṛié iṛa leḃuṛ ceaṛc
>   Ᵹan ḃomnaḋ ḃo caiṛmceaḋc.

> Comaṛḃa peḃaiṛ iṛ póiḷ,
>   Ṗuaiṛ an leaḃaṛ ṗa oécóiṛ,
> Oouṛ ṛo leiᵹ an leḃaṛ
>   Maṛ ḃuḃ leiṛ bu lan meḃaiṛ.

> A book placed by the hand of the great God
>   Upon the altar of Peter and Paul;
> It has been found in the appropriate book
>   That the Sunday should not be transgressed.

> It was the Comarb of Peter and Paul,
>   Who found the book first,
>   And he promulgated the book
>   As he had it well in memory.
>
>   Cod. Clarend. Brit. Mus., vol. 15, fol. 7, p. 1, col. a. b.

Saint Conall, son of Ceolman, who is said to have brought the Cain Domnaig from Rome, was founder of a church on Inis Cail, now the Island of Iniskeele, near the mouth of the Gweebara bay, in the barony of Boylagh, and county of Donegal. His name is commemorated in the Festology of Aengus Céle Dé in the Leabhar Breac, fol. 34, a., at 11th May.

The Cain Domnaig enjoins under severe penalties that every class shall abstain from all kinds of work on Sunday, and that none shall travel on that day ; but wherever one happens to be on Saturday evening, there he should remain till Monday morning. To this there were some exceptions, such as bringing a physician to a sick person, relieving a woman in labour, saving a house from fire, &c. A priest was forbidden to travel on Sunday or Sunday night, or from vesper time on Saturday night till Monday morning, unless to attend a sick person supposed to be likely to die before the following morning, in which case the Cain says :—

> Ƒeaɲ ᵹɲdıꝺ ꝺıa ꝺomnaıᵹ ꝼoɲ ɲéꝺ
> ꝺo coɲɲuma neıch bíɲ ɲe n-éᵹ,
> ꝺo ᴄaꝺaıɲᴄ ꝺo cuıɲɲ Cɲıɲᴄ cáın,
> ma ꝺoıᵹ a éᵹ ɲe maꝺaın.

> A priest may journey on a Sunday
> To attend a person about to die,
> To give him the body of Christ the chaste,
> If he be expected to expire before morning.

Thus to see a priest travelling on Sunday was considered an omen of disaster, or of immediate death to some member of the *Fine* or tribe into whose house or territory he came; and hence King Diarmait's astonishment at perceiving the young priests approaching him on Sunday morning.

(C.) " *Failgib óir,*" rings, or bracelets of gold; the *Failge* was a kind of open ring or bracelet for the wrist, arm, ankle, or finger, worn by men and women : by men in token of deeds of valour, as in the case of Lugadh Lagadh, who is said to have killed seven kings in successive battles, and who wore seven *Failgib* upon his hand in token of these deeds, of whom Cormac Mac Airt, monarch of Eriu (whose father was one of the seven) is recorded to have said, " ní ᴄeıl a ꝺoıꝺ ꝼoɲ laᵹa ɲo bıᴄ ɲıᵹa ꝺoɲıᵹaı, .ı. a ɲeaᴄᴄ ꝼaılᵹı óıɲ ıma laım ;" i. e. " His hand does not conceal of Laga the number of kings he has slain, i. e. he has seven *Failgib* of gold upon his hand." Book of Lecan, R. I. A., folio 137 b. a. top; and the same occurs again in the same MS. fol. 124 a., margin col. mid. where the *Fail* is called a *Buindi* (i. e. a twisted ring) "ιр τe aгbeрτ сoрmaс ррıр, nı oeıl a boıb foр laʒa роbı рıʒa .ı. a рeċτ m-buınbı óıр ıma boıb no ma meoıр." "His hand does not conceal of Laga that he has slain kings, i. e. he has seven *Buinnes* (twisted rings) of gold upon his hand or on his fingers." The *Fail* was used by women for the double purpose of personal ornament and munificence, as in the present instance, and in the case of King Nuada's wife, who is said to have had her arms covered with *failgib* of gold for the purpose of bestowing them on the poets and other professors of arts who visited her court.

(D.) "*Dinner for one hundred men each night of food and Lin*" (p. 179). This allusion shows that Bec Fola's sojourn was in the house of a king, and that *Inis Fedach Mic in Doill* (now Devinish Island), was the residence of a *Righ Buiden* (king of companies). According to an ancient law tract on the constitution and legal rights and duties of the different ranks of kings, preserved in vellum MS. T. C. D., Class H. 3. 18. p. 1 *et seq.*, four score men was the lawful retinue of a king, in addition to which he had his *Foleith* or leet of twelve men, his five tribemen, his wife, and his judge, making in all one hundred men, which constituted the legal *Dam* (company) of a *Righ Buiden* (king of companies), and he was entitled as *Frithgnam* (supplies) to their free maintenance from his people. This tract will appear with a translation and notes, by W. K. Sullivan, in the Appendix to O'Curry's Lectures on the Manners and Customs of the People of ancient Eriu, Vol. II., p. 532.

"*Lin*," often used for ale or other malt drinks; but in the laws it means the full amount of any thing, and here it appears to mean the full amount of food accompaniments that constituted the lawful dinner of the *Dam*, or company of the king.

(E.) "*Calves of this island.*" *Laegh*, a calf. But here, as in many other instances, it is applied to the young of the deer, e. g. "aр ann рın bo ċonсabaр na cleıрe eılıτ allτa uaτa aр an рlıab aсaр laeʒ рe na h·aıр. And then the clerics saw a wild deer from them on the mountain, and a calf (fawn) near her." Life of St. Findbar, O'C. MS. C. U. I., p. 4; and Ordnance Survey of Cork, R. I. A., vol. ii., p. 622.

(F.) "*Men with charms on their spears.*"—There are many references to charmed swords and spears to be met with in our ancient
writings. In the tale of the battle of the second or northern Magh
Tuireadh, we find the following:—

Iſ an caṫ ſin biń ꝼuaiſ Oʒmai cſen-ꝼeſ Oſnai, claiḋem
Ceċſa, ſí Ꝼomoiſe. Coſoſlaic Oʒma in claiḋem ocuſ ʒlanaiſ ó
Iſ anḋ inḋiſ in claiḋem naċ a n-ḃeſnaḋ ḃe, aſ ba ḃéſ ḋo cloiḋmiḃ.
in can ſin ḋo coſſilciciſ ḋo aḃḃaḋiſ na ʒnima ḋo ʒniċea ḋiḃ.
Coniḃ ḋe ſin ḃleʒaiḋ cloiḃme cíſ a n-ʒlancai iaſ na coſlucaḋ. Iſ
ḃe ḋno ꝼoſcomecaſ ḃſeċca h-i claiḃme ó ſin amaḋ. Iſ aiſe ſin
no laḃſaiḃiſ ḃemna ḃ'aſmaiḃ iſ in aimſiſ ſin, aſ no aḃſaiḃiſ
aiſm o ḃainiḃ iſ in ſe ſin; acaſ ba ḋo comaiſciḃ na h-aimſiſe na
h-aiſm.

"It was in this battle that Ogma the champion obtained Ornai, the
sword of Tethra, king of the Fomorians. Ogma opened the sword, and
cleaned it. Then the sword related all the deeds that had been performed by it; for it was the custom of swords at this time to recount
the deeds that had been performed with them. And it is therefore that
swords are entitled to the tribute of cleaning them whenever they are
opened. It is on this account, too, that charms are preserved in swords,
from that time down. Now the reason why demons were accustomed
to speak from weapons at that time was, because arms were worshipped
by people in those times, and arms were among the protections (or
sanctuaries) of those times."—*MS. Brit. Museum, Egerton,* 5280, *and
see O'Curry,* vol. ii. p. 254, *et seq.*

On those charms and their venomous effect, the same tale has
the following:—

Imma comaiſnic ḃe Luc acaſ ḋo ḃoluſ ḃiſuſḃeſʒ eſ in caṫ.
Suil millḃaʒaḋ leſeom. Ni h-oſſcailcie in ſoul aċc iſſoi Caċae
namma. Ceċſaſ cuſcḃanḋ amalaiʒ ḃie ꝼol Conu ḃſoluim omliċhi,
cſie na malaḋ. Sluoac ḋo n-eceuḋ ḃeſ ſan ſól nin ʒeſciſ ꝼſi h-
occo cie ſiḃiſ liſ ilmili. Eſ ḃe ḃoi innem ſin ꝼuiſſiſ: .i. ḃſuiċ a
aċaſ ḃocaſ oc ꝼuluċc ḃſaiʒeċcae, canacſeum acaſ ſo ḃeaſc caſ
ſan ꝼunḃeoic, con ḃeḋaiḋ ḃe en ꝼoulaċcae ꝼuiċi ʒoniḃ ꝼoſ ſan
ſuil ḋo ḃeḋoiḋ nem an ꝼoulaċca ieſ ſin.

"Lug and Balor Birurderg met in the battle. He (Balor) had a
destructive eye. This eye was never opened but in the field of battle.
Four men were required to raise the lid off the eye with a hook
which was passed through its lid. A whole army that he looked upon

out of this eye could not prevail against [a few] warriors, even though
they were many thousands in number. The cause why this poison was
on it was this, namely : his father's druids had been boiling a druidical
spell, and he came and looked in through the window, so that the fume
of the boiling passed under it, and it was upon the eye that the poison
of the brewing passed afterwards."—See "*Battle of the Second or
Northern Magh Tuireadh*," *MS. Brit. Mus. Egerton*, 5280 *O'Curry,
MSS., Catholic University*.

(G.) "*Molasa of Damh Inis, who sent us,*" &c. (p. 183). This was Saint
Molaisa or *Laisren*, patron of the island of *Damh-Inis*, i. e. Ox Island,
now Devenish, an island in Lough Erne near the town of Fermanagh.
He was Molaisa or Laisren, son of Nadfraech, whose day is 12th
September, to be distinguished from *Molaisa* or *Laisren*, son of
Declan, Saint of Inis Murry (12th August), and from *Molaisa* or
Laisren, son of Cairell of Leighlin (18th April).

See Annals of the Four Masters, A. D. 563, n. t. See also *Felire
Aenguis*, and O'Clery's Calendar, &c.

The Shrine of Saint *Molaisa* of *Damh Inis*, alluded to in the text
(p. 183), and referred to in note 46, is now preserved in the Museum
of the Royal Irish Academy, and popularly known as *Soisceal Molaisa*,
or Molaisa's Gospel. For some account of it see Proceedings of R. I. A.
Vol. VII., p. 331, and Academy Registry. The allusion in the text to
the battle spoils of the fallen warriors may be illustrated by the following extracts from the Laws of Waifs and Strays, preserved in Brehon
Law MS. Rawlinson, 487, Brit. Mus. fol. 62, p. 2, col. a. *et seq.*

In this law, the Waifs and Strays of a *Fine* (tribe) are divided into
seven classes, and special laws are laid down for the recovery and ap-
propriation of every class of waif found within the *Fine* as follows :—

Táic recc rrichʹé la ṗéine, .ı. a cáıc recc rriche bo ʒabur ba
n-aırneıbenn ın ṗéınecur : Ḟrıche cṙeıbe, .ı. bo ʒabur ır ın cṙeıb.
Ḟrıche cachrach, .ı. bo ʒabur ırın cachraıʒ call. Ḟrıche ṗaıche,
.ı. bo ʒabur ırın ṗaıcche, .ı. ır na ceıcrı ʒorcaıb ır nerum bon
baıle. Ḟrıche raıce, .ı. ıcır raıċċe acar bırraınn. Ḟrıche
ṙoṗıba, .ı. bo ʒabur ırın ṗorḟó. Ḟrıche rléıbe, .ı. bo ʒabur
ırın c-rʹlıab. Ḟrıche cṙaċca, .ı. bo ʒabur ırın cṙaċc. Ḟrıche
raırʒe, .ı. bo ʒabur ar ın raırrʒe amuıʒ.

" There are seven waifs in the *Fine* (tribe), i. e. there are seven waifs which are found, of which the *Fenechus* takes cognizance :—*Frithe Treibe*, i. e. the waif which is found in the *Treb* (family home). *Frithe Cathrach*, i. e. the waif which is found in the distant *Cathair* (city). *Frithe Faithche*, i.e. the waif which is found in the *Faithche*, i.e. in the four fields which are nearest to the *Baile*. *Frithe Raite*, i. e. the waif which is found on the road between the *Faithche* and the *Dirrainn* (mountain). *Frithe Rofida*, i. e. the waif which is found in woody places. *Frithe Sleibhe*, i. e. the waif which is found on the mountain. *Frithe Trachta*, i. e. the waif which is found on the strand. *Frithe Fairrge*, i.e., the waif which is found abroad on the sea."—Rawlinson, 487, folio 62-63.

Ḟṗíche ṗaiche, .i. ṗṗiche ᴅo ᵹaḃuṗ iṗin ṗaiċce, a ċṗian aṗa h-eccoimoiᵹ, acaṗ aleċ aṗ a coimoiᵹ. Iṗṗeᴅ coimoiᵹ ṗaicce ano a culċain acaṗ a inaᴅa aiṗeċcaiṗ, no iṗṗeᴅ iṗ coimoiᵹ ṗaiche ano, aṗliᵹċi acaṗ a inaᴅa ṗéiᴅe aṗᴅa, acaṗ na h-inaᴅa a m-bí aċiᵹi cafċh. Iṗṗeᴅ iṗ ᵹcoimoiᵹ inci a imli acaṗ a cúla, no iṗṗeᴅ iṗ eccoimoiᵹ ṗaiċce ano a cabana, acaṗ a h-inaᴅa ᴅiamṗa, acaṗ in baile nach aiċiᵹino caċ aiṗe. Iṗṗeᴅ iṗ ṗaiche ano na ceiċṗi ᵹuiṗc iṗ neaṗa ᴅon baili, .i. ᵹoṗc caċa aiṗᴅi, ime, acaṗ cro hé in ṗliab buᴅ neṗa ᴅon baili, ṗo ba aṁail ṗaiche. Iṗṗeᴅ iṗ ṗeċcaṗ ṗaiche ann in aiṗec acaṗ ṗo ṗoich cuaiṗᴅ inᵹelca on ṗaiche amach, na iṗṗeᴅ iṗ ṗaiche ano an ṗo ṗaiᵹ ᵹuch an cluiᵹ.

"*Frithe Faithche*, i. e. the waif which is found in the *Faithche*, one-third of it [goes to the finder] out of the *Ecoimdig*, and one-half out of the *Coimdig*. The *Coimdig* of a *Faithche* are its hills and its places of assembly, or the *Coimdig Faithche*, in it are its roads and its clear high places, and the places resorted to by the people. The *Ecoimdig*, in it are its border lands and its obscure places, or, the *Ecoimdig*, of a *Faithche* are its secluded places, and its obscure places, and the places not frequented by every *Aire*. A *Faithche*, in it are the four *guirt* (fields, Nom. Sing. *Gort*,) which are nearest to the *Baile*, i. e. a field on each side, around it, and even though the mountain happens to be nearest to the *Baile*, it is considered equal to a *Faithche*. A *Sechter Faithche*, in it is the distance which the grazing land extends out from the *Faithche*, or the *Faithche* is the distance at which the sound of the bell is heard from it."— Rawlinson, 487, fol. 62, p. 2, col. b. fol. 63, p. 1.

After having thus particularized the places and the circumstances of the different kinds of waifs, this law goes on to say :—

In buine puaip no pozebuiḃ ppíti, ir na h-inata rin ireḃ bleʒap be. Mára ppíche círe, a ercaire areċċ n-inata a beir bliʒe, co pí, co h-aircinbech, co ppimʒabainb cuaiche, co bpiuʒaḃ, co bpeichemain, co muilinḃ cuaiċe, pia luċc aen lip, acap oen baile.

Mára ppíċe pairʒi, bleʒap a ercaire bo buine maiċ in cach orich bo na crí críchaib ir nepa bo, no coma reċċ n-inata in cach críċ bib, acap muir in cetrama críċh; acap ba m-becair baíne ar in muir, ir a n-ercaire bóib.

Ma ro ercaire pia báine, acap bo rinbe bliʒe ppíche acap ro mair oo iar n-bechma, ir lan cuiċ a ppíche bo.

Muna bepna a bliʒeḃ ppíche, acap poċaiċ pia n-bechmaiḃ, ir lán piach ʒaici uaḃ. Mana bepna a bliʒeḃ ppíċe, acap romair aioe oo iar n-bechmaiḃ, no má bo roine a blíbe ppíche, acap ro ċaiċ pia n-bechmaiḃ, cin caiċe ppíche bo aoar cin piach ʒaici uaiḃ aċċ aichʒin in ppíche.

"The person who has found, or who shall find a waif in those places, this is what he is bound to do. If it be a land waif, to proclaim it in the seven places specified by law [i. e.] to the king, to the *Airchindech*, to the chief smith of the *Tuath* (territory), to the *Brughadh*, to the judge, at the mill [miller] of the *Tuath* (territory), to the people of the same *Lios*, and the same *Baile*.

"If it be a sea waif, he is bound to proclaim it to a good man in every *orich* of the three *oricha* which are nearest to him, or he might proclaim it in seven places in every *crich* of them, and the sea makes the fourth *crich;* and if there be people upon the sea, it is right that it be proclaimed to them.

"If he have proclaimed it before people, and have fulfilled the waif law and it [the waif] remained [unclaimed] till after the tenth day, he is entitled to the full amount of his proportion of his waif.

"If he have fulfilled the waif law, and have consumed (appropriated) it before the tenth day, he is liable for the full amount of a theft liability. If he have not fulfilled the waif law, and that the waif remain with him till after the expiration of the tenth day, or if he have fulfilled the waif law, and if he have consumed (appropriated) it before the expiration of the tenth day, he is entitled to the consideration of a waif wasting, and he is bound to forfeit the debts of a charge of theft all but the restitution of the waif."—Rawlinson, 487, fol. 63, p. 1, col. b.

(H.) "*Fiacha Labrainde*" was monarch of Ireland from A. M. 3728 to A. M. 3751, when he was slain by Eochaidh Mumho of Munster, in the battle of Bealgadan, now Bulgadan, a townland in the parish of Kilbreedy Major, near Kilmallock, in the county of Limerick. The Four Masters record this battle, fought by him against the Ernans, and the eruption of Loch n-Erne, under the year A. M. 3751. There is a curious poem of sixteen verses on the reign of Fiacha Labrainde preserved in the Book of Leacan, in the R. I. A., folio 30, a. a.

(I.) Ɑimiɼʒin Mɑiɼʒiubɑch bia ɼo ɼɑi le Ⅎinbchɑim inʒin Mɑʒɑch. "Aimergin Mairgiudach, who had espoused Findchaem, daughter of Magach." These names frequently occur in our oldest tales and best MSS.; but Amergin is more generally styled Ɑmɑɼʒin lɑɼnʒiunɑiʒ than mɑiɼʒiubɑch, as in the text, and Findchaem is more generally made daughter of Cobthad than of Magach. Their names occur in the story of Bricriu's feast in Leabhar na h-Uidhri, p. 103, col. 2, where she is mentioned as one of the eleven princesses who accompanied Queen Mugan, wife of Conchobar Mac Nessa, King of Ulster, at the feast: " Ⅎinbcɑem inʒen Cɑtbɑb ben Ɑmɑɼʒin lɑɼnʒiunɑiʒ—Find-chaem, daughter of Cathbad, wife of Amargin Iarngiunach." They are also mentioned in the beɑn ɼeɑncɑɼ eɼenb or history of the noteworthy women of Eriu in the Book of Leacan, as father and mother of the hero Conall Cearnach of Emania. The passage is as follows:—" Ⅎinb-chaem inʒen Chɑthbɑib beɑn Ɑmiɼʒin lɑɼnʒiunɑiʒ mɑthɑiɼ Ċonɑill Cheɑɼnɑiʒ. Findchaem, daughter of Cathbad, wife of Aimirgin Iarngiunach, mother of Conall Cearnach." See Leabhar na h-Uidhri, R. I. A., p. 103, col. 2, line 22, and Book of Leacan, folio 204, a. a. &c.

Lightning Source UK Ltd.
Milton Keynes UK
UKOW06n2030210715

255600UK00007B/62/P